The Disrupted Workplace

THE DISRUPTED
WORKPLACE

Time and the Moral Order
of Flexible Capitalism

Benjamin H. Snyder

OXFORD
UNIVERSITY PRESS

OXFORD
UNIVERSITY PRESS

Oxford University Press is a department of the University of Oxford. It furthers
the University's objective of excellence in research, scholarship, and education
by publishing worldwide. Oxford is a registered trade mark of Oxford University
Press in the UK and certain other countries.

Published in the United States of America by Oxford University Press
198 Madison Avenue, New York, NY 10016, United States of America.

Library of Congress Cataloging-in-Publication Data
Names: Snyder, Benjamin H., author.
Title: The disrupted workplace : time and the moral order of flexible capitalism /
Benjamin H. Snyder.
Description: Oxford ; New York: Oxford University Press, [2016] | Includes
bibliographical references and index.
Identifiers: LCCN 2015047847 | ISBN 978-0-19-020350-4 (pbk.: alk. paper) |
ISBN 978-0-19-020349-8 (hardcover: alk. paper) Subjects: LCSH: Flexible work
arrangements. | Capitalism--Moral and ethical aspects. | Industrial sociology.
Classification: LCC HD5109 .S595 2016 | DDC 331.25/7—dc23 LC record available
at http://lccn.loc.gov/2015047847

9 8 7 6 5 4 3 2 1
Printed by Webcom, Inc., Canada

All becoming irregular [*dereglement*] . . . of rhythms produces antagonistic effects. It *throws out of order* and disrupts; it is symptomatic of a disruption that is generally profound, lesional, and no longer functional. It can also produce a lacuna, a hole in time, to be filled in by an invention, a creation. That only happens, individually or socially, by passing through a *crisis*. Disruptions and crises always have origins in and effects on rhythms: those of institutions, of growth, of population, of exchanges, of work . . . (Lefebvre 2013:52–53).

CONTENTS

CONTENTS

ACKNOWLEDGMENTS

The great irony of writing a book about time is that you have to ask people with so little of it to give so much of it. I am deeply grateful to the respondents in this study for giving so much of their energy and attention when they were already stretched so thin, especially those who invited me into their personal workspaces, gave an interview while running to the airport, or were kind enough to share their hopes and dreams with a total stranger.

I received so much support in writing this book, which began as a dissertation, from so many sources. I am deeply indebted to the Sociology Department at the University of Virginia, most importantly Jeff Olick, who was the kind of advisor every graduate student dreams of and who showed so much patience and unwavering confidence in me, even when I began to doubt myself. Allison Pugh taught me everything I know about ethnography and was a model for how to be both objective and compassionate as a qualitative researcher. Simone Polillo and Shige Oishi gave me constructive comments at several critical stages. Christina Simko, Tara Tober, Haiming Yan, and the other members of our dissertation writing group were unendingly supportive and read dozens of drafts over the years. I received essential financial support from The Institute for Advanced Studies in Culture. A special thank you to James Hunter and Joe Davis for creating such a fantastic intellectual community with a passion for asking big questions, and to the Culture of Capitalism work group, especially Stephen Macekura, Julia Ticona, and Claire Maiers, for pushing me to keep asking big questions in new ways.

I am also deeply grateful to Eviatar Zerubavel, without whom the sociology of time would not exist and who was a continual source of encouragement. And to the National Science Foundation, whose Doctoral Dissertation Improvement Grant made it financially possible to collect the data for this project. To my colleagues at Victoria University of Wellington, thank you for creating such a welcoming and warm place to think and write.

And to the Work/Culture group, especially Joe Klett and Alison Gerber, where I met so many creative thinkers. The Junior Theorists Symposium, especially Ann Swidler, encouraged me to be creative with social theory. Andy Abbott, Mary Blair-Loy, Nina Eliasoph, Gary Alan Fine, John Hall, Anne Mische, and Isaac Reed helped me think through specific problems. And finally to Carrie Lane, Ofer Sharone, Iddo Tavory, Bob Zussman, and one anonymous reviewer, I appreciate the lengthy comments that shaped the final draft.

Above all, I could not have done this project without the love and support of my family, especially my partner Greta Snyder, who has one of the best theoretical minds I have ever come across, who read *countless* drafts, and whose influence can be felt throughout these pages. Thank you for taking this journey with me.

The Disrupted Workplace

CHAPTER 1

The Disruption of Work Time

Kevin and I have finally emerged from under a lingering drizzle that has hampered our travel for the last several days. I am riding high above traffic in the passenger seat of his tractor-trailer as the sun begins to warm the inside of the cab. Glad to be on the last leg of our 1400-mile, two-day delivery of fifty tons of Gatorade, we strike up a conversation again for the hundredth time to make the miles pass a little faster. We travel down Interstate 44 just south of St. Louis talking about long-haul truck driving in ways that are both romantic and tragic. Kevin loves the challenge, constancy, and speed of these long-haul runs—so different, he tells me, from the kind of hectic stop-start-stop-start runs he has in the more densely populated areas of the country. He says, "You have more time to shape your time the way you want it. You can decide when and where to stop, how fast to run." He pauses, and then qualifies, "But then again you also have no time to slow down. It is totally constant. You are just going all the time until your hours run out. On breaks, even, you feel rushed." Pausing again, he again tacks back, "But, you know what? I kinda like that—running my ass off. You feel like you're getting stuff done." I ask him if he would feel that way even if the load did not pay well—if he had to run all those miles at that kind of pace but without a big reward at the end. He thinks about my question for a second. "If I were offered to run this truck for the same money but half the miles, it would be great financially, but I'd get bored out of my mind. Because you feel like you're not accomplishing anything. It's not satisfying. I take pride in running this truck hard."

I believe what Kevin has told me because the evidence is written on his body. Though he has only been working consistently in the trucking industry for two years, he tells me that he has already gained a lot of weight due to the sedentary lifestyle and tendency to eat heavy meals—typically the only kind of food conveniently available out here on the road. I see some worrying health signs that speak to the many physical risks of working as a truck driver. He complains of an intense thirst he cannot seem to satisfy— a classic sign of diabetes. At his last visit to the doctor, he got some flack over high blood pressure and was encouraged to start taking medication. At just 27 years old, Kevin is resistant. "I'd rather do it the natural way," he says, "through diet and exercise." But during the weeks I have spent on the road, traveling across the eastern, southern, and central United States, I have seen precisely one truck driver exercising. The vast majority is just like Kevin—too pressed for time.

If I could tell Kevin's story as a Greek tragedy, he would be the protagonist in a duel between the two Greek gods of time: Chronos and Kairos. Chronos is the god of pure duration, of quantitative time, the time we mark and measure with devices. In the modern era, Chronos has long overseen the predictable, machine-like workings of industrial capitalism. He has ruled over the factory floor with precise timetables and ruled over the executive boardroom with elaborate long-term business plans. In the context of truck driving, he takes the form of a rigid, federally mandated schedule of clock hours to which drivers must orient their every move. Chronos is Kevin's constant companion. He marks each passing minute and provides Kevin with reminders of the measure of his time through the portal of Kevin's digital logbook—a handheld electronic device that communicates a driver's movements to the company's dispatch headquarters via GPS technology.

Kevin's other constant companion is Kairos. Kairos is the god of good timing, improvisation, and strategic advantage. He symbolizes a more qualitative conception of time—the time of ripeness, rhythm, and nimbleness. Kairos is the form of temporality we recognize when we entrain our attention with the rhythmic flow of phenomena within our immediate environment, see a window of opportunity open up before us, and have the instinct to immediately act upon it. Kairos rules over newer post-industrial forms of "flexible production"—the capitalism of service providers, knowledge producers, lean businesses, and global flows of financial capital. Rather than seeking to mass-produce objects with a machine-like consistency and regularity, the forms of capitalism in the post-industrial era value flexibility and fluidity in their quest to capitalize on brief moments of profit that emerge in a quickly changing and highly competitive global space. As a driver in the flexible logistics system, which prides itself on serving this economic model by delivering products "just in time," drivers like Kevin have become increasingly responsible to Kairos. When customers' tastes change, the companies that scramble to meet that new demand hire people like Kevin to get their products to market with extreme temporal precision—neither too early, nor too late.

Between Chronos and Kairos sits Kevin's body. Chronos tells him to work in a regularized, clock-like pattern of shifts, but Kairos requires him to be much more nimble. This tension causes him to do all kinds of strange things to his body, like wake up at a different time each day, which requires him to set nine alarm clocks. His body is unwilling to synchronize its internal rhythm to such an erratic pattern, so it needs extra encouragement. Like a lot of younger drivers I met, Kevin finds that the toll taken on his body as it is stretched between Chronos and Kairos is easy to ignore at first. Some drivers even embrace it. As Kevin continually reminds me during our week of travel together, a rugged, hard working driver, much like a soldier in battle, must be willing to sacrifice his body for the sake of the job. As I learned from dozens of conversations with older drivers, however, eventually one must come to terms with the fact that doing well in the job is actually unsustainable for the body. As they get older, drivers become increasingly aware of the risks to their health of simultaneously serving both gods of time. It thus becomes increasingly difficult to imagine what a sustainable, rather than just profitable, future in the industry will look like. The future becomes a mysterious domain to which present experience and past habits provide little help in deciphering a path forward.

I am being dramatic, of course. Kevin's life is not a tragedy. He does not live in a stark moral universe of villains and heroes, nor do Chronos and Kairos fully capture his experience of work. Nevertheless, these rough impressions bring into deeper relief the subtle tensions between labor, temporal experience, and moral imagination that characterize the conditions of work in the contemporary post-industrial economy.

This book is about time. More specifically, it is about the human costs of the radical restructuring of work time in America over the last four decades or so under an economic regime known as flexible capitalism. As I describe below, flexible capitalism is a catchall term that imperfectly captures a variety of changes to production processes, employment arrangements, management strategies, and the like that are reshaping the conditions of work. I argue that these changes amount to a significant transformation in how workers experience "social time"—the sense of pace, rhythm, and trajectory given to people by social institutions. This restructuring of social time has important implications for workers' moral lives—the cultural narratives they use to link experiences of the past and present to a set of expectations about the future that provide a sense of goodness, rightness, direction, and ethical coherence.

The book describes three years of research I conducted with three groups of people working in the flexible economy: financial professionals, truck drivers, and unemployed job seekers. These workers experience flexible capitalism in dramatically different ways, but everyone I talked to told me that the way time is structured by their employment experiences creates perplexing moral dilemmas. They described a frustratingly staccato experience of the flow of their lives that disrupted their sleep patterns, unsettled their nerves, disordered their careers, and generally made it difficult to anticipate the future. In almost the same breath, however, they also described experiences that gave them energy, autonomy, discipline, and even occasional moments of transcendence because of the very same sources of disruption. What I ultimately took away from these observations is that the flexible economy asks these workers to make a kind of Faustian bargain with the working self. If they agree to sacrifice things like security, standardization, and predictability they are offered new "opportunities" to be more personally responsible for carving out a unique path in life. These opportunities may offer convenience, relief from boredom, gratification, individuality, or even a sense of freedom, but they often come attached to new risks and responsibilities that are extremely difficult to assess. The flexible economy affords workers a moral order full of dilemma, contradiction, and disorder.

FLEXIBLE CAPITALISM

Since the end of World War II, but especially within a crucial period of transformation between the 1970s and 1990s, economies like that of the United States have introduced new forms of production, exchange, and human resource management that have changed the structure of the workplace and the flow of employment over the life course. Many scholars refer to this set of transformations with the imperfect catchall term flexible capitalism (Boltanski and Chiapello 2005; Kalleberg 2011; Sennett 2006; Standing 2011).[1] As I discuss below, one of its central features is an

1. I chose to use the term "flexible capitalism" only toward the end of writing this book. There are myriad terms for referring to the current economic regime (a sign of just how unclear scholars are about how to describe it). It has been referred to as "post-industrial" and even "post-Fordist." These terms point to the turn away from mass production models in developed economies, which championed the hyper-efficient labor systems pioneered at Ford, to a focus on something new. They are slightly misleading in a number of ways, however, not least of which is the fact that, if anything, efficiency and the streamlining of processes through technical control is more important to businesses now than ever before (Hirst and Zeitlin 1991; Lomba 2005; Vidal

emphasis on disruption—uprooting, dismantling, or repurposing anything in the chain of production, exchange, and consumption that is fixed, predictable, and resistant to change. Flexible capitalism is largely a product of economic elites (business owners, policymakers, management experts, economists, etc.) who have restructured production and employment practices based on certain preferences, such as improvisation over planning, fluidity over fixity, and abstraction over concreteness. As Peter Cappelli (1995, 1999) observes, in America these preferences have some roots in earlier forms of late 19th and early 20th century work organization, but were enacted on a massive scale most recently in the 1970s, filtering into the majority of large companies throughout the 1980s and 90s.

One of the central dynamics of flexible capitalism is a preference for improvisation over planning. Where older bureaucratic forms of organizing favored more centrally directed business plans that could churn out consistent products on a mass scale evenly over a long period of time, flexible capitalism favors arrangements that can respond to rapid and unpredictable change (Boltanski and Chiapello 2005; Cappelli 1995). The emphasis on nimbleness is a response by economic elites to what they perceive as rising domestic and global competition and a shift in consumer preferences toward customization and personalization. As one business strategist notes in *Forbes*, "I've talked to many CEOs who say that they are no longer doing Strategic Planning as such . . . with a number of them adding that they are trying to be more nimble. [. . .] Strategic planning is dead. The new king is execution and flexibility" (Conerly 2014). A concrete outcome of this emphasis has been a preference to dispense with "bloated" workforces in exchange for a "leaner" workforce, composed of a small core of permanent employees and a larger periphery of part-time, temporary, and contract workers (Cappelli 1999). Too many secure and long-term employment contracts, the argument goes, simply cannot respond quickly enough

2011). Have we actually moved beyond industrialism and Fordism in any meaningful sense? Other scholars refer to the new economic regime as "the new capitalism" and often point to the rise of financial capital as the major source of transformation (Foster 2007; Krippner 2005; Sennett 2006). But labor historians are quick to point out that many of the workplace practices associated with this "new" financialized regime—such as core/periphery models, independent contracting, and outsourcing—were actually quite common in the late 19th century in America, before the rise of Fordism and the large bureaucratic firm (Cappelli 1995, 1999). In what sense is the new capitalism really new? Perhaps it is actually a return to the status quo that reigned before the historical blip that was the mid-20th century. In the end, I settled on the imperfect term "flexible," because it best highlights the temporal dimension of the current regime. Flexibility summons images of movement, change, and unsettledness, thereby centering the conversation on the issues that arose from my interviews and observations.

to the kinds of rapid change and targeted, short-term execution that will keep a company competitive. Organizational lifecycles are now punctuated with many more periods of restructuring and thus many more opportunities to hire and fire workers (Ho 2009). The frequent and repeated use of outsourcing, downsizing, and temporary contracting—what scholars call "external numerical flexibility"—has become a routine strategy for hedging an organization's exposure to the risk of rapid change (Cappelli 1999; Kalleberg 2003).

This has resulted in a remarkably bifurcated landscape of employment arrangements (Kalleberg 2011). "Core" employees, made up of mostly skilled professionals, receive a lot of investment from their employers, including a great deal of decision-making power, so that they will align themselves with the goals of the company and work passionately. Putting in long hours is often seen as a sign of commitment and dedication to the job. As a result, core employees are often both overemployed and overworked. They tend to work more hours than they would like and feel rushed (Clarkberg and Moen 2001). And since many of these workers are married to another skilled professional, they are often in an overworked household (Jacobs and Gerson 2001, 2004). With the burden of "time scarcity" concentrated heavily among the most economically secure households, for the first time in history some of the most powerful individuals in American society are not part of a "leisure class" (Veblen 1994) but a "harried class" (Linder 1970). Some of these privileged workers are even given a great deal of control by their employers over when and where they work. They have "flexible workplaces" that provide high autonomy, at least on the surface. But constant deadlines, constantly changing work teams, and high performance expectations can fill these environments with stressful time pressures all the same (Blair-Loy 2003; Crowley 2012; Fraser 2001).

In contrast to core employees, more "peripheral" employees—those with less specialized skills who often work for lower wages—tend to experience a strange combination of both underemployment and overwork. As has long been the case, low-wage workers are finding it difficult to get enough hours with high enough wages to make ends meet, but they are also finding it increasingly difficult to get *regular* and *predictable* hours (Greenhouse 2008; Lambert 2012). As Harriet Presser (2003) has documented, nearly two fifths of American workers now work a non-standard schedule (something other than 9-to-5, Monday-to-Friday), and the majority of them do not do so by choice; it is a requirement of their jobs. In industries as diverse as retail, food service, and transportation, low-wage workers are asked to be constantly available—to be "on call" in case employers decide to ramp up or push down hours in order to match changes in demand (Halpin 2015).

As a result, low-wage workers are often run ragged from part-time job to part-time job and from unpredictable shift to unpredictable shift. They are economically insecure because of a lack of good paying full time jobs, but also frazzled from trying to coordinate a chaotic assemblage of irregular schedules (Golden 2015).

Flexible capitalism goes beyond an emphasis on the flexibility of schedules and contracts. It also involves flexibility in the actual stuff of work. Facilitating the goals of nimbleness and adaptability, for example, are digital technologies that have made work more abstract, quantifiable, fluid, and portable. This has made work more flexible in the sense that the actual objects and process of work—the stuff that engages workers' mental and physical energy—are less beholden to a physical time-space. In professional workplaces, for example, workers spend most of their time sitting in front of a screen that gives them access to a virtual workspace—a non-physical space of communication and exchange that lives within but transcends the physical boundaries of the office (Bechky 2006). Communication in these spaces can happen in real time via digital representations, which may symbolize things taking place in the same room or, just as easily, on the other side of the planet. The objects of work—emails, spreadsheets, codes, reports, and so forth—flow through a slick, non-physical medium of virtual time-space. Unlike the fixed, heavy, analog labor of industrial workplaces, this labor is highly portable and "task" or "project" oriented, which means workers can more easily take work with them wherever they go, further exacerbating the impetus to overwork (Bauman 2000; Dubinskas 1988; Lee and Liebenau 2002). Despite the fact that this kind of portable digital labor is an almost taken-for-granted part of the American workplace now, it is remarkable just how little we know about what digital work requires of the mind, body, and emotions (Bechky 2006).

Among low-wage workers, digital fluidity and abstraction have also influenced how work gets done, but in different ways. Some manual labor jobs have been automated, which means they can now be conducted from behind a computer screen (Zuboff 1989), but even those manual laborers who use their physicality to work with real objects and machines are often overseen by managers using digital surveillance systems that track their productivity and remotely tweak their efficiency. Even though manual labor can still be physical, then, it is often managed from behind a computer screen and is therefore thought about (at least among managers) in the language of digital abstractions. This virtual vision is partly what allows physical work to be flexibilized. Managers can measure work rhythms in minute detail through digital surveillance and manipulate those rhythms so that workers' effort more precisely matches demands for output. Aside from studies that mainly focus on shop floor politics (Jamieson 2015; Levy 2015; Sewell 1998; Sewell and Wilkinson 1992; Zuboff 1989), we still know very little about how this kind of "arm's length" control through remote micromanagement shapes moral life.

Flexible capitalism is also cultural. It is a moral order characterized by a hegemonic, legitimating discourse that tells workers how they ought to conduct themselves in order to be of value to the economy (Boltanski and Chiapello 2005). The buzzword of this discourse is "disruption." The main sentiment of disruption culture is that those who stick to a plan based on knowledge from the past will be blindsided by the inevitable changes coming over the horizon of the future from more nimble and creative competitors. Rather than wait for that inevitable crisis, the narrative goes, one should proactively dismantle what is fixed and constantly reinvent. Never get comfortable, because in comfort lies blindness to the next opportunity. As Joseph Schumpeter (1954:32), one of the foundational figures of disruption culture, presciently described it, "Every situation is being upset before it has time to work itself out. Economic progress, in capitalist society, means turmoil." Disruption culture enjoins people to have an almost paranoid aversion to the missed opportunity and engage in an almost obsessive pursuit of good timing. Embodied in a long line of neo-liberal theorizing, from Schumpeter's (1954) "creative destruction" theory of the business cycle to Clayton Christensen's (1997) *The Innovator's Dilemma*, disruption culture has produced a powerful set of narratives that have filtered out of the boardrooms of the economic elite into the language of management texts, self-help literature, and career development advice that is meant for the average worker, such as bite sized articles on the popular networking site *LinkedIn* (Chiapello and Fairclough 2002; Vallas and Prener 2012). As the historian Jill Lepore (2014) observes, "The eighteenth century embraced the idea of progress . . . Our era has disruption."

Taken together, flexibility (with all its many meanings), digital abstraction, and the legitimating culture of disruption have opened the way for a deeply problematic downward shift of risk from employers to workers. The kinds of risks that were once born by employers in the form of regular, secure, and long-term employment, such as the problem of maintaining steady wages and appropriate levels of output during market downturns, are increasingly passed down to workers (Cappelli 1999; Kalleberg 2009; Standing 2011). But, in an era of deregulated markets and deunionized industries, and with one of the thinnest social safety nets in the developed world, American workers must typically manage these new risks without collective representation and a strong welfare system. This is having troubling consequences for workers' health, psychology, and relationships.

People feel more work-to-family conflict and have trouble coordinating multiple temporary jobs into a steady stream of income when they cannot predict their work schedules (Golden 2015). Hyper-efficient digital labor systems have intensified work, even in many white-collar settings, leading to more complaints about overwork and stress (Crowley et al. 2010). Independent contracting, while promising more control over work, in reality often results in being at the beck and call of multiple clients and an inability to switch off (Barley and Kunda 2004). But while we now know a great deal about the sources and outcomes of this downward shift of risk, there has been remarkably little effort to examine the subjective meaning and lived experience of working in flexible times and how that experience shapes moral life (though see Ehrenreich 2001; Lane 2011; Pugh 2015; Sennett 2000, 2006, 2009; Sharone 2014; Smith 2001). What do people actually do in flexible workplaces? How do the rhythms and trajectories of engaging in flexible labor shape workers' understandings of good work and the good life?

RETHINKING WORK TIME

This book is about time and work, but not in the typical sense that those terms are discussed. Sociologists, economists, management scholars, and other labor experts typically discuss the issue of time in flexible capitalism in much the same way that scholars have long discussed work time—in the language of the clock. They focus on how workers attempt to "balance" different amounts of time, as measured by a mechanical clock. Actors' strategies for "allocating" time are typically observed with a structured interview or time-use survey that divides the flow of activities into predetermined types: paid work, non-paid work, care, leisure, and so forth. This clock time perspective has helped us understand the broad landscape of work time patterns and has revealed crucial insights into a specific range of dilemmas within modern workplaces, such as the conflicts between work and family among people in "time-hungry" professions (Blair-Loy 2003), the persistent mismatch between employees' preferred and actual work schedules (Clarkberg and Moen 2001; Reynolds and Aletraris 2006), or the pernicious "time squeeze" and decline of leisure time within duel-earner households (Jacobs and Gerson 2004; Robinson and Godbey 1997; Schor 1993).

The clock time perspective, however, has several limitations. Time diaries and some forms of structured interviewing tend to treat work time as the same *type* of thing as any other kind of time—a quantity of clock hours allocated to categories of tasks. But work time also has distinct and historically variable qualities. The *type* of thing work time is changes through history. Why? Because clock time, indeed the entire concept of the hour, is itself an historical construct that, over the course of several hundred years, became associated with a particular form of economic production, which we call capitalist (Dohrn-van Rossum 1996; Landes 1983). If capitalism has changed so dramatically, has the nature of work time also changed? There are so many things other than the clock hour that shape the temporality of work time today—project cycles with their own clock-independent deadlines, an overwhelming stream of emails, the sense that there are no more secure and long-term organizational trajectories— yet these temporalities tend to go unnoticed by observing work time only with the clock. Seen from this perspective, then, clock time is not an objective tool with which to analyze work, but one of the objects of analysis.

One of the major theoretical tasks in this book, then, is to step back from the traditional clock time approach in order to examine work *temporality*: the subjective experience of work time. This task requires that I develop a richer palette of terms beyond the traditional language of hours, minutes, weeks, and so forth to describe work time. If clock time becomes just one object among others within a wider analysis of work temporalities, then we need some other way of talking about work time that incorporates but also goes beyond the language of hours, minutes, weeks, and so forth. As I describe in the next section, I develop a "temporality" approach to the study of work time, which theorizes not how time is objectively "spent" at work, but how it is subjectively experienced. I draw on two related theoretical traditions—processual social theory and the sociology of time—to construct this approach, using a number of concepts coined or inspired by theorists like Barbara Adam, Norbert Elias, Gary Alan Fine, Michael Flaherty, Alfred Gell, Anthony Giddens, Henri Lefebvre, George Herbert Mead, and Eviatar Zerubavel.

In addition to analyzing the problem of work time in the language of the clock, researchers have also tended to focus on the fraught boundaries between work and non-work spheres as the main source of problems— what I call a "work and" orientation to the problem of work time (Sabelis et al. 2008; Whipp, Adam, and Sabelis 2002). Researchers focus on how work time can overflow its social boundaries and begin to degrade the quality of non-work time, and vice versa. This research has been invaluable for understanding how contemporary work practices strain relationship dynamics, particularly for women, parents with young children, and married couples (e.g., Becker and Moen 1999; Bianchi, Robinson, and Milkie 2006; Blair-Loy 2003, 2009; Jacobs and Gerson 2004). Considering all the attention scholars have given to work boundaries, however, there has been surprisingly little interest in work itself—that is, what people actually do when they engage in flexible labor (Barley and Kunda 2001; Bechky 2006). What requirements are made of workers' bodies, minds, and emotions when they engage in, for example, irregular shift work, when they craft a detailed spreadsheet for a globally-distributed team project, or when they learn that their thirty-years of experience in a job is being traded for an online application that can do things cheaper and faster? More concerted attention to work itself is needed because without opening up the black box of flexible labor to see how people's physical and mental energies are spent in workplaces we miss what kind of thing workers are trying to balance with their family lives in the first place, what kinds of time pressures workers experience other than shortages and excesses of clock hours, or what a preferred schedule means to workers in the context of their wider notions of a good life.[2]

The next section is dedicated to developing this temporality approach to work time. I first provide a very precise definition of social time, of which work time is a subtype, and then build outward to a conception of work time. I introduce an array of both borrowed and new concepts—including rhythm, timescape, and time map—in order to assemble an analytical vocabulary that is up to the task of examining work time from a new angle.

WHAT IS WORK TIME?

Work time is a specific form of social time. By social time I mean the system of rhythms and trajectories that humans create as they engage in interaction within social institutions. Social time is not the same as "natural time"—seasonal cycles, the phases of the celestial bodies, and the like—though these processes certainly affect social life in fundamental ways. Nor is social time synonymous with clock time—the abstract quantitative language of hours, minutes, and seconds—though clock time is certainly a product of modern social institutions and therefore a constitutive part of social time today (Elias 1994; Sorokin and Merton 1937). Social time is made up of three elements: rhythms, timescapes, and time maps.

2. This is not to say that focusing on the meeting points between work time and other domains of temporal experience is not important. Indeed, I hope other scholars will spend equal effort opening up the black box of, say, "family time" to see what sorts of unique temporalities are arising within new 21st century family formations. In this way, scholars can gain purchase on some of the new tensions both between work and non-work domains, as well as *within* those domains themselves, that may go undetected by a "work and" perspective.

Rhythm

Rhythm has received surprisingly little attention from social theorists, even though action (and thus movement) is a primary domain of analysis in sociology (See Abbott 2001; Collins 2004, 2012; Dewey 1934; Emirbayer and Mische 1998; Goffman 1977; Summers-Effler 2010 for important exceptions).[3] Following Henri Lefebvre (2004), one of the only theorists to have deeply considered rhythm sociologically, I think of rhythm as the meeting place of change and energy. As Lefebvre (2004:15) puts it, "Everywhere there is a place, a time, and an expenditure of energy, there is rhythm." Place means the meaningful spaces where people interact, time means change—the passage of events—and energy means the effort people muster to negotiate the changes they encounter in space. Whenever individuals engage with a social space, they must anticipate what goes on there, choose from a number of possible trajectories of action that open up before them, and project themselves into the future as they pass out of that space, thereby anticipating the next "beat" in the flow of action (Emirbayer and Mische 1998).[4] Anticipating, choosing, and projecting all require the expenditure of mental and physical energy. The rhythm of anticipating, choosing, and projecting amid perceptions of change in our environment is the most basic building block of our experience of time.

Rhythm is fundamentally communicative (Dewey 1934; Langer 1953). Watch a group of children playing double-dutch jump rope. By moving rhythmically, they signal to others what they are about to do, and use this information to create a meaningful social encounter together. Within the context of social groups, rhythm means the expenditure of mental and physical energy in anticipation, evaluation, and projection *with others* (Young 1988; Young and Schuller 1988). As social beings, we anticipate, evaluate, and project in *coordination* with others, which requires mundane but taxing mental activities like paying attention to others' actions, moving one's body to coordinate with other bodies, or shifting the definition

---

3. As Randall Collins (2008:53) notes, "Sociological theory does not pay enough attention to the dynamics of processes over time. [...] But processes have shapes in time, patterns of intensity, rapid shifts, and gradual declines, which sweep people up at one moment and bring them down at another."

4. In her philosophy of aesthetics, Susan Langer (1953:126–127) writes, the "essence of rhythm" is not repetition but "the preparation of a new event by the ending of a previous one." "A person who moves rhythmically need not repeat a single motion exactly. His movements, however, must be complete gestures, so that one can sense a beginning, intent, and consummation, and see in the last stage of one the condition and indeed the rise of another. Rhythm is the setting-up of new tensions by the resolution of former ones."

of the situation to be in line with others' assumptions (Goffman 1977). This rhythmic coordination of energies with other people within the same space of interaction makes up our most primitive experience of *social* time (Abbott 2001:238; Durkheim 1995). With the rise of complex societies in the modern era, much of this activity became governed by widely shared and standardized temporal practices like clocks and schedule, but even without these formal tools of coordination, all societies have some form of social time (Elias 1994; Evans-Pritchard 1939; Sorokin and Merton 1937; Zerubavel 1980).

From this perspective on time, then, to work does not mean to "allocate hours" to work tasks, though that is one useful way of looking at it, but to engage in the rhythmic coordination of energy with other people in a work*place*. People in both paid and unpaid work expend mental and physical energy by anticipating, choosing, and projecting in coordination with others in a (real or virtual) space of work. What matters most in a temporal perspective, then, is not the type of task to which time is being allocated by individual actors, but the institutional and situational contexts in which groups experience time *together*. This basic shift in language—from the clock hour to the rhythm, from the individual allocator of time to the group as collective maker of temporality—turns our attention away from how much time workers have to spend on tasks to the *configuration of rhythms* that groups of workers negotiate in order to coordinate action.[5]

Timescapes

Timescapes, a term I borrow from Barbara Adam (1990, 1998), are the configurations of rhythms actors create within a space of interaction. They are the unique synchronizations and desynchronizations, pauses and progressions, harmonies and dissonances created when multiple rhythmic processes intersect. Think of the concentric waves created by a steady drip of water into a still pond. If I throw a small pebble into that pond, new patterns

---

5. I see the temporality approach to work time as highly complimentary to the clock time approach. Where the clock time approach is better suited to comparing trends in time allocation across a broad spectrum of cases, the temporality approach is better suited to examining the complex ways time is practiced and performed within specific domains of action. Where the clock time approach helps us see trends in familiar and well-established categories of temporal practice, such as the hour, the temporality approach helps us discover hidden categories of temporal practice, see how familiar forms of time interact, or how seemingly familiar categories are being used in new and unfamiliar ways.

of waves emerge as the two forces interact. This complex interplay of waves is like a timescape. Now, take a more social example. If a parent promises to read to his child every morning before he goes to work, this "beat" in the domestic rhythm of everyday life becomes a normal and expected part of his home's timescape, which must now be coordinated with other domestic rhythms, such as the micro-sequences of making breakfast or getting dressed, and other non-domestic rhythms, such as work schedules and deadlines. These multiple rhythmic processes can come together well, creating a satisfying experience of being "on time," or they can fall apart into a chaotic "rush" (see, e.g., Chenu and Robinson 2002; Lesnard 2009). As this example suggests, timescapes can certainly be made up of clock based rhythms, such as a nine-to-five schedule, but they are also likely made up of other non-clock based rhythms, such as the body's sleep/wake cycles, the ineffable give-and-take of attention required to show care for a child, or the patterns of concentration required to meet a cycle of deadlines.

Many of the timescapes that people encounter on a daily basis are a function of their working lives (Zerubavel 1979). Work timescapes constrain when we are free or occupied, with whom we are able to interact at a given moment, and how much energy we have to give to different activities. They involve schedules, deadlines, and sequences of tasks, as well as spaces and machines to which we tailor our bodies, cognitive processes, and emotional expressions. They are therefore some of the most important spaces that shape the "texture" of social time (Flaherty 2010)—whether the day feels fast or slow, staccato or legato, empty and boring, or full and busy. Each work timescape features the braiding of multiple rhythms of mental and physical energy expenditure, giving the individual worker different experiences of pace, sequence, tempo, and articulation (Fine 1996).

Work timescapes, however, are not always variable and random. Following Lefebvre (2004:67–68), I suggest that there are a few ideal typical timescapes that workers regularly encounter, which give workplaces different recognizable textures. Understanding these common timescapes can give us a much richer palette of terms for describing and explaining the ways social time, and thus work time, shapes experience.[6]

Unification characterizes timescapes of perfect synchronization and total immersion. It describes that lovely experience, so rare unfortunately, when

6. Lefebvre calls these common timescapes *isorhythmia, eurythmia, arrhythmia*, and "fatal desynchronization." I find these terms to be rather exotic and precious. This is unfortunate because they are meant to reflect common forms of experience to which most people can probably relate. For the sake of simplicity, readability, and to reflect the fact that they are not as exotic as Lefebvre's makes them sound, I have replaced his terms with unification, synchronization, desynchronization, and crisis.

processes come together perfectly in one surging moment of sublime coordination, essentially creating a single unified rhythm. The experience of unification is characteristic of awakenings, epiphanies, and love (DeGloma 2010; Tavory and Winchester 2012). In more mundane contexts, such as the workplace, unification might appear in those precious moments when everything seems to fall into place at work. A brief opportunity for profit presents itself, and one is perfectly poised to capitalize. A group of individuals comes together in a cohesive group mind that generates a breakthrough idea in a vibrant collaborative exchange. Dozens of failed attempts at a new strategy finally result in just the right outcome.

Synchronization, by contrast, describes multiple rhythms working together in functional coordination but without perfect identification, much like the rhythms of a healthy body. In a well functioning workplace, synchronization occurs all the time. It is nothing particularly remarkable. Schedules are made. People keep to them, more or less. Projects are planned for and completed, not perfectly, but without major hiccups. Synchronization is the experience of normalcy commonly given by things like regularized schedules and predictable trajectories of employment. It can, in fact, be quite boring if it goes on too long (Barbalet 1999; Roy 1959).

Desynchronization describes the clashing of rhythms, "a pathological situation . . . depending on the case" (Lefebvre 2004:67), thus invoking the rhythmic structure of an unhealthy body (i.e., arrhythmia). Desynchronization is quite common in workplaces, especially those that require extensive multitasking (Chisholm et al. 2001). Oftentimes things simply do not function smoothly. A sequence of tasks is interrupted by some other sequence of tasks that demands attention. Plans to deliver on a promise meet unexpected delays. The steps one usually takes to solve a problem no longer work because the nature of the problem has changed. Goals are often met and projects are completed in desynchronized timescapes, but it is sometimes difficult to see exactly how it happened. Somehow, through creativity, quick thinking, or gut instinct, we muddle through them.

Finally, there is *crisis*. The opposite of unification, crisis describes the complete breaking apart and alienation of rhythms, or what Lefebvre (2004:68) calls "fatal desynchronization." It refers to the halting and abrupt temporality of cataclysm, emergency, revolution, and sudden death (Gibson 2011; Kurzman 2004; Wagner-Pacifici 1994). Sometimes everything falls apart and one is left with the sense that forward movement is no longer possible, at least not under the current design of things. At work, crisis signals a deep failure of the system, what structural engineers call a "cascading failure." The processes and procedures that brought workers to the present moment suddenly break down and are no longer capable of producing further meaningful activity. A new product is launched and immediately shows signs of design failure. A whole sequence of processes goes awry resulting in the injury or death of employees. A sudden shock to the economic system makes it financially impossible to continue employing people. In these situations, unlike desynchronization, employers and employees must come to terms with the fact that only a new way forward will suffice—new plans, new sequences of action, and perhaps even an entirely new vision for the future.

Time Maps

"Everything that prepares a future creates rhythm," notes Susanne Langer (1953:129). Rhythms make up timescapes, but timescapes are themselves embedded in larger temporal structures that mark out the general shape of the remembered past and the expected future. These larger "time maps," to borrow Eviatar Zerubavel's (2003) phrase, set the stage for the rhythmic experiences of everyday life (see also Gell 2001). Time maps are schemas of movement within institutions that structure people's lives into standardized trajectories (Koselleck 2002; Olick 2007; Zerubavel 2003).[7] When we look forward or backward in time, what we see coming over the horizon of the future and what we remember as having already slipped over the horizon of the past is shaped by shared narratives that hint at what kinds of lives have been available in the past, how those life trajectories will proceed through the present moment, and where they will take us into the future (Tavory and Eliasoph 2013). These narratives, then, give us some meaningful access to relatively objective systems of ordered succession that organize our lives into broad trajectories. They are like maps of the possible and most likely trajectories of social time. A time map, like the arc of a plot line, can take many shapes—straight or winding, linear or circular, upward or downward, continuous or with sharp breaks and hops (Zerubavel 2003). The time map of a series of work promotions, for example, takes the form of an upward, step-wise trajectory, with slices of horizontal movement followed by sharp upward rises in status, followed again

7. From the perspective of the philosophy of time, timescape and time map roughly (though not perfectly) parallel the A-series and B-series of time respectively (McTaggart 1993). Where timescapes refer to the subjective "tensed" experience of time "passing," time maps refer to the more objective "tenseless" system of ordered succession in which all tensed experiences of time occur (see Gell 2001 for a thorough discussion of this relationship).

by a slice of smooth horizontal movement (Pearson 1966). This time map became popular in American workplaces after the first World War (Cappelli 1999:60–61), but, even prior to this, its general shape can be seen in other social groups that feature well defined hierarchies of positions, for example, military organizations (Zerubavel 2003:35).

As is the case with timescapes, workplaces are a major carrier of some of the most important time maps in contemporary societies. Careers, promotions, pensions, pay grades, hirings, firings, and the like inform our capacity for retrospection and prospection, shaping the possible ways we can talk about our lives moving on the grand scale of the life course. If clearly articulated and intact, time maps can help us evaluate whether or not the mental and physical energy we put in to work is going to be "worth it" in the long run or simply a "waste of time." They give us larger patterns of movement that can link each day's activities to the next. Work time maps, therefore, inform whether we see our lives as progressing, regressing, or stagnating, moving up or down in power and status, and so on.

To summarize, in the temporality approach, work time is not (only) clock time but *an assemblage of timescapes and time maps in a workplace.* Work timescapes and time maps contribute to (though do not, of course, totally determine) workers' experience of both the texture and direction of social time. In this light, analyzing work time in the flexible economy is not about looking at how people have changed the way they "spend" time. It is a matter of looking at the new timescapes and time maps that have been introduced into different kinds of workplaces to see how they shape people's subjective experience.

WORK TIME AND MORAL ORDER

This book is not only about work time but also about moral life. I am interested in what visions of good work and what conceptions of a good life contemporary workplaces invite workers to create. By moral, I do not have in mind a particular idea of what is good and worthy. As a sociologist, I assume that "morality is whatever a person or group takes it to be" (Hitlin and Vaisey 2013:55).

I also assume that morality is "thick." It is not only something that guides decision-making in the moment (thin), but also extends to encompass identity and long-term vision. In this way, I do not see the moral only as a "resource that can be put to strategic use" (Dimaggio 1997:265), though that is certainly one of its uses. Moral order can be an end in itself, and thus actually drive action (Strand and Lizardo 2015). This may sound rather obvious, but in the context of cultural sociology it is still a somewhat radical claim. I am saying that when people make meaning, they often do so in order to discern the contours of the good, navigate competing conceptions of the good, avoid conceptions of the bad, or balance goods and bads that pull in opposite directions. In my view, people do not only desire to make meaning or sense of their worlds, but also desire to know whether or not their lives are moving in a good or bad direction. They create meaning in order to create moral order (Smith 2003; Wolfe 1989).

Adults spend a great deal of their waking hours thinking about work or in their actual workplaces, making them major sites of moral formation (Kunda 1992; Lamont 2000; Sennett 2000).[8] Workplaces shape moral world making in two significant ways. The first is through the sense of positive significance and satisfaction (or lack thereof) that workers find in the tasks of their work and in relationships with coworkers (Hodson 2001). Workers interact with each other as well as with the shared objects of work, such as a spreadsheet or a trailer-load of grapes, to imbue a job with meanings that place it on a spectrum between artistry and drudgery—from a job that is good, valuable, and worthwhile to a job that is bad, degrading, and a "waste of time." Workers are often interested in this moral construction of work because it helps them find the motivation and resolve to keep coming back day after day. This is what we might call the "thin" moral ordering of work.

A "thicker" way that workplaces influence moral order is by the shape and direction they give to a worker's sense of selfhood (Hodson 2001). In going to work day after day (or choosing not to) one is also in some sense becoming a certain kind of person. If the meaning of the self is a shared meaning that emerges in the context of the social and cultural structures that surround us (Stets and Burke 2005), then workplaces, by sheer volume of time spent in them, must be important sites of moral formation in this thicker sense. How does one know one is leading a good life or, at

---

8. Moral action overlaps with other types of cultural action that scholars have observed in organizations, but differs in one important way. It shares, for example, many of the same characteristics of "sense-making," (Weick 1995) or efforts to construct a "coherent self" out of intersecting work and non-work identities (Thatcher and Zhu 2006). Like these forms of cultural action, moral action is about infusing work tasks and roles with meaning for the self. Unlike these forms, however, it is specifically about engaging in meaningful action in order to construct and clarify a moral universe (Lamont 2000). This is a crucial difference. A clearly degrading work task could seem perfectly meaningful or a conception of the self as wretched could feel perfectly coherent, but that tells us nothing about whether or not an individual gains emotional energy from that task or seeks to further cultivate that conception of the self. Only a moral conception of meaning-making will tells us that (Smith 2003).

the very least, doing well with the cards one has been dealt? Workplaces and work identities give us clues to answering these larger existential questions. This does not mean that all workers seek a deep and meaningful connection between work and their sense of self. As Michele Lamont (2000) notes in her comparative study of working class men's moral worlds, some people may very well draw moral boundaries by specifically rejecting a close and obsessive connection to work. Sometimes a job is "just a job." Workers may seek to place a thick wall between their "work self" and "real self." Nevertheless, even in these cases, workplaces influence moral order by challenging workers to maintain such a boundary and discover which performance of identity is the "real me" (Hochschild 2003).

What I hope to demonstrate in this book, then, is that workplaces influence moral world making in large part because of the forms of social time they produce. Timescapes and time maps organize our economic activity, but they also act as a kind of "cultural scaffolding" (Lizardo and Strand 2010; Swidler 2001) for meaning-making more generally and thus influence moral order. The timescapes we encounter in the workplace often dictate to what degree we evaluate our jobs as good or bad, artistry or drudgery—the "thin" sense of moral order. A workplace that is chaotically desynchronized, for example, may be experienced as invigoratingly complex for some or exhaustingly distracting for others. Similarly, the time maps we encounter in the workplace often dictate how we view the past and project ourselves into the future, allowing us to weave stories of our lives as proceeding in a good or bad direction—the "thick" sense of moral order. An organization that promises a steady sequence of promotions, for example, might produce a satisfactory sense of forward movement for some or a feeling of suffocating predictability for others.

In short, how work institutions pattern our lives in time shapes our moral imaginations. In studying flexible timescapes and time maps, then, I want to understand not only how these structures are shaping things like people's sense of economic security or stress levels, but also their conceptions of themselves *as people* with hopes and dreams to become good, honorable, and dignified.

STUDYING FLEXIBLE TIME

Flexible capitalism is a deeply unequal economic regime (Kalleberg 2011; Standing 2011). Many of its most pernicious consequences are shouldered more directly by women, racial minorities, and the lower and middle classes than among privileged workers who have resources and special arrangements that buffer them. When I set out to study the temporalities of flexible capitalism, I wanted to capture the ways this economic regime is inflected specifically by social class, though the other dimensions of inequality are certainly also important. I selected three groups of workers whose experiences could capture important class variations in the types of timescapes and time maps on offer to workers: financial professionals, truck drivers, and job seekers.[9] Financial professionals tend to work long and erratic hours, in cutthroat organizational cultures, and in workplaces that are infused with digital technology—a clear window onto many of the wider changes happening among elite knowledge workers (Blair-Loy 2003). Truck drivers' work exemplifies some of the forces under flexible capitalism that are reshaping low-wage labor, such as deregulation, casualization, and digital surveillance. Their workplaces also mirror the new forms of erratic scheduling that are increasingly used in shift work (Halpin 2015). Job seekers provide a window onto the changing nature of employment agreements and the rise of new types of "precarious" work practices, such as temporary contracting, outsourcing, and downsizing (Kalleberg 2009; Standing 2012). These practices affect a wide range of workers, but I focus specifically on middle class white-collar job seekers because, following the Great Recession of 2008, they have become the symbol of the expansion of insecurity to sectors that once enjoyed the most security (Lane 2011; Sharone 2014; Smith 2001). Many of the workers I examine in this book have been studied before, then, but never have they been examined side by side and rarely with such a specific focus on temporal experience and moral life.

I studied these workers using a combination of in-depth interviews and participant-observation, which I discuss in greater length in the methodological appendix. I made every attempt not just to talk to them about their jobs, but also to experience first hand the temporalities of their workplaces. In addition to interviewing dozens of financial professionals from a variety of areas in finance, for example, I also observed bond traders in one of the world's most powerful asset management firms in New York

9. I modeled my research design on Arlie Hochschild's (2003) groundbreaking book on emotion management, *The Managed Heart*. I see my research as doing to time what Hochschild's did to emotion—showing how time is socially constructed in workplaces in ways that shape workers' conceptions of self and moral order. I consciously adopted her logic in thinking about connections between cases. She selected cases that, on the surface, appear to be unrelated but are in fact connected by a wider cultural logic. By studying both flight attendants and bill collectors she attempted to capture extreme ends of variation, what she calls the "toe" and "heel" of service work, in an emotional regime that is deeply gendered. In a similar way, I selected cases that show variation in a temporal regime that is deeply class stratified.

City. Much like an intern, I shadowed traders as they interacted with the global debt markets through their computer screens. I sat in truck stops and interviewed dozens of different kinds of truck drivers, but I also rode with independent owner-operators who contract with a large, corporately owned motor carrier firm headquartered in Missouri. Because long-haul tractor-trailers are equipped for two people, including bunk beds located behind the cab, I was able to ride with drivers for multiple consecutive days and mirror their sleep/wake rhythms so that I could better understand the physical demands of delivering freight. To study unemployed job seekers, I conducted paid interviews using an online classified service, but I also became a regular participant in a job search support group located in Richmond, Virginia. I sat with job seekers as they listened to impassioned speeches at workshops, participated in inspiring conversations with them about building a new life, and listened to advice from change management experts about navigating the job market after the 2008 financial collapse.

These cases certainly do not represent all types of workers in the global flexible economy. They are, most importantly, *American* workers. They live in one of the most economically productive societies in the world, which also has a unique combination of weak social supports for struggling workers, such as affordable healthcare and strong unions, as well as some of the strongest economic incentives to work continuously without rest. Unlike its peer nations, America provides no guaranteed paid leave for things like births, deaths, and illnesses nor guaranteed vacation time—these are considered perquisites of a "good job" rather than basic standards (Gornick and Heron 2006). America also has a notoriously "industrious" national culture, which values hard work—even overwork—as a badge of honor (Blair-Loy 2004). This context certainly shapes the data. As with any research based on case studies, then, this book is not meant to capture statistical representativeness, but to generate new theoretical insights that can be challenged and refined in other national and organizational contexts (Luker 2008; Small 2009).

OVERVIEW

Chapter 2 provides some important historical background for understanding flexible capitalism as a regime of work time. We can learn a lot about what is going on today by looking at how earlier forms of work time have influence moral order in American culture. In this spirit, I give a brief history of the temporal regime that came to dominate American work culture: Chronos or chronological social time. I analyze the rise of Chronos in terms of his two "faces." On one side, Chronos has been associated with some of the most important disciplinary tools of capitalist labor systems, which elites have long used to exploit workers for economic gain. On the other side, Chronos has appeared as a benevolent guide for moral development, allowing the disciplined individual to cultivate virtues like vigilance, constancy, and inner drive. I show how the two faces of Chronos have influenced the organization and meaning of work over hundreds of years of Western history. Chronos introduced contradictory tensions into the American workplace, which produced a set of perplexing moral dilemmas whose solutions have deeply influenced American work culture. I conclude by examining what earlier transformations in work time can teach us about the relationship between work time and moral order during periods of economic change.

Against this historical backdrop, I then present three ethnographic case studies. In Chapter 3, I discuss the world of financial professionals and the financialization of time-space. I consider financialization in two senses: first, in terms of a shift in the center of gravity of capitalism toward financial channels; second, in terms of the rise of two practices that are transforming both the temporal and spatial dimensions of knowledge workplaces. I call these, following Anthony Giddens (1986, 1991, 1995), disembedding and abstraction. I show how two generic types of workers in the financial services industry—dealmakers and market workers—manipulate their minds and bodies to become entrained with the intense and erratic rhythms of financial timescapes. They must develop new temporal languages and new cognitive strategies to cope with the simultaneously engrossing and overwhelming nature of their work.

Chapter 4 examines the truck driving industry and the deregulation of time-space. Deregulation requires a specific kind of workforce that is not only much cheaper to employ, but also able to continually adjust its movements according to sudden shifts in market demand. While I examine different types of truck drivers, I focus specifically on new kinds of owner-operators because they exemplify attempts within the industry to pass risk down to drivers as a response to the extreme competition spawned by deregulation. Drivers reveal how seemingly traditional blue-collar workplaces are being reshaped by these new work arrangements, yet workers continue to be subjected to remarkably traditional forms of "Taylorist" time management. Drivers are faced with, on the one hand, the demand to deliver products "just-in-time" to consumers and, on the other hand, a rigid shift work schedule designed by the federal government. They must find ways to transmute two antagonistic temporal systems—clock time and freight time—in order to deliver goods both quickly and safely.

In Chapter 5, I shift registers of analysis, from the level of daily tasks and workflows to the level of the life course. I examine the lives of unemployed white-collar workers who are looking for work in the aftermath of the 2008 financial collapse, which extended new forms of insecurity to a once relatively stable sector of the labor market. Drawing on theories of projectivity and future making, I examine how white-collar workers become aware of and construct a response to the implosion of the career model for the life course, one of the most influential time maps of the last half-century. They must move from one construction of their life's future to another while coming to terms with the cataclysmic experience of job loss. To build a new future, they often employ the help of job search support groups, which encourage them to not only develop new expectations of themselves and their future employers but to develop new emotional habits that can help them embrace a future of permanent insecurity.

I turn to the implications of flexible time for questions of moral life in Chapter 6. What possible selves, what visions of the good life, and what conceptions of good work do flexible temporalities invite workers to create? Drawing on Michael Burawoy's (1979) theory of the labor process, I show how respondents construct working lives that feel meaningful and dignified by engaging in risky "work-games." These games offer energizing and absorbing experiences that allow them to build moral worlds around virtues of personal resiliency. But in the process, they find that the meanings available to them by gaming their work ultimately lead to pernicious long-term consequences that are difficult to grapple with. Workers ultimately struggle with the contradiction, so characteristic of flexible capitalism, of being given the "freedom" to work themselves harder and harder.

In the final chapter, I step back and draw out the wider cultural and political implications of these findings. I argue that flexible capitalism fragments social time producing perplexing experiences of labor that often feel unsustainable. Yet many workers also find fragmentation to be energizing and meaningful. This tension makes for a tricky moral dilemma that exacerbates the risks of working flexibly, especially for the most vulnerable workers. The workers I met construct moral worlds of heroic resiliency that are deeply accommodating to an economic system based on the willingness to lead a "disruptable" life *for one's whole life*. Heroic disruption can become a kind of cultural straightjacket that gives even the most well-off workers few other ways to conceive of the future than a life of constant change, and tends to blind low-status workers to the fact that they are being asked to take on many of the risks that were once borne by their employer. I argue that we need a new politics of time that is neither naïve nor nostalgic— that can properly critique disruption while still doing justice to the fact that workers find some forms of flexibility to be convenient, energizing, and meaningful.

This book touches on many different issues concerning the problem of work time in flexible capitalism. For those interested in inequality and management policy, the empirical chapters provide a rare detailed comparison of how classed work temporalities are received by different kinds of workers who have different perceptions of both the joys and miseries of work. The conclusion brings those observations to bear on how we might think more creatively about time research and labor policy. For those interested in capitalism as a cultural institution, the combination of historical and contemporary evidence gives a suggestive, though by no means definitive, picture of the longer trajectories of transformation in the culture of capitalist "time discipline." The book also addresses the political implications of flexible capitalism by providing a rich ethnographic portrait of how some American workers endure and sometimes even embrace workplace practices that can be deeply exploitative. Above all, this book speaks to those who want to make sense of the moral dilemmas of being a worker today—who are looking for a richer language in which to articulate their anger and disappointment with the current system but also honor the meaningful edifices they have built in their work identities. What does it mean to become an excellent worker today? Are the kinds of bargains that flexible capitalism asks workers to strike in their lives worth it? And if not, how might we critique these arrangements without falling into naïve ideas about how working life could be or nostalgic tropes about how it used to be?

CHAPTER 2
A Brief History of Work Time

It was about this time I conceived the bold and arduous project of arriving at *moral perfection*; I wished to live without committing any fault at any time . . . As I knew, or thought I knew what was right and wrong, I did not see why I might not *always* do the one and avoid the other.

—Benjamin Franklin (*1910:79*)

The American works harder than does any other man or woman on earth. His business is always with him, he has no rest, no cessation, no relief from the strain. Were he to reduce the effort, his competitors would pass him at once. [. . .] He has been aptly likened to a steam engine running constantly under a forced draught. He must have a stimulus even in his recreations.

—Dr. Cyrus Edson (*1892:282*)

L ike many of his Puritan ancestors, Benjamin Franklin was enamored with scheduling. The ordering of his life in time was an important part of his quest to achieve moral perfection. In his early adulthood, he constructed a weekly schedule centered on the practice of thirteen essential virtues: Temperance, Silence, Order, Resolution, Frugality, Industry, Sincerity, Justice, Moderation, Cleanliness, Tranquility, Chastity, and Humility. Franklin created a "little book," as he called it, which he carried with him for much of his adult life. Each page was dedicated to one of these virtues (figure 2.1). For some period of time he might focus on, for

Portions of this chapter appear in Snyder, Benjamin H. 2013. "From Vigilance to Busyness: A Neo-Weberian Approach to Clock Time." *Sociological Theory* 31(3):243–266.

FORM OF THE PAGES.

TEMPERANCE.

Eat not to dullness; drink not to elevation.

	Sun.	M.	T.	W.	Th.	F.	S.
Tem.							
Sil.	*	*		*		*	
Ord.	*	*			*	*	*
Res.		*				*	
Fru.		*				*	
Ind.			*				
Sinc.							
Jus.							
Mod.							
Clea.							
Tran.							
Chas.							
Hum.							

Figure 2.1 Benjamin Franklin's weekly schedule.
Reprinted from Benjamin Franklin. 1910. *The Autobiography of Benjamin Franklin*. New York: Macmillan.

SCHEME.

Hours.

MORNING. The *Question.* What good shall I do this day?	5 6 7	Rise, wash, and address *Powerful Goodness!* Contrive day's business and take the resolution of the day; prosecute the present study and breakfast.
	8 9 10 11	Work.
NOON.	12 1 2	Read or look over my accounts and dine.
AFTERNOON.	3 4 5	Work.
EVENING. The *Question.* What good have I done to-day?	6 7 8 9	Put things in their places. Supper. Music or diversion or conversation. Examination of the day.
NIGHT.	10 11 12 1 2 3 4	Sleep

Figure 2.2 Benjamin Franklin's daily schedule.
Reprinted from Benjamin Franklin. 1910. *The Autobiography of Benjamin Franklin*. New York: Macmillan.

example, perfecting temperance. At the end of each day he would reflect on his successes or failures at keeping this virtue. If he had failed, he would place a black dot in the box under that day. Franklin notes that the virtue of Order, for example, which he defines as "Let all your things have their places; let each part of your business have its time," was particularly difficult to achieve (Franklin 1910:80). "I made so little progress in amendment, and had such frequent relapses," Franklin (1910:86) recalls, "I was almost ready to give up the attempt, and content myself with a faulty character in that respect."

Rather than give up, however, Franklin redoubled his efforts to achieve Order by creating a daily, rather than just weekly, schedule (figure 2.2). This allowed him not only to take account of his virtuous and non-virtuous actions on a weekly basis but also to order his life by the hour, giving a precise time for sleep, work, and leisure. In this way, daily Order allowed him to practice another of his thirteen virtues: "Industry—Lose no time; be always employed in something useful; cut off all unnecessary actions" (Franklin 1910:80). Thus, by using the temporal practices of clocks and schedules to systematically fix his attention "on *one* [virtue] at a time," Franklin could "be master of that [virtue], then to proceed to another; and so on till I should have gone through the thirteen." In this way, Franklin (1910:81) aimed to "acquire the *habitude* of all these virtues" slowly and methodically over many years. Through vigilant attention in every minute, he could string together hours, days, weeks, and years into an entire life that was filled with moral living and nothing else.

Over one hundred years later, in an essay entitled "Do We Live too Fast?" Cyrus Edson, Chief Inspector of the New York Board of Health, addressed the readership of the *North American Review*, a literary magazine, with views about time that are wholly different from Franklin's. For Edson, time is not a tool for achieving moral order but a symptom of the corrosive habits of living that characterize American workers. He remarks, "In the main ... the American strives for wealth as the great reward in life. But the free competition and the social environment that make it possible have between them driven the pace up to a fearful speed" (Edson 1892:282). The pace of work in America, Edson fears, while primarily responsible for the nation's incredible material wealth, is unsustainable—particularly when it comes to workers' bodies. "To supply his rapidly exhausted system," Edson (1892:282) notes, "[the American] is compelled to consume large quantities of rich food and to stimulate himself with alcoholic beverages." As a result, "his system does not receive its proper nourishment and he soon literally burns out." Edson sees the intense and unyielding relationship to time, which Franklin held up as a model of good living, as a barrier to the good life.

Franklin and Edson give voice to a fundamental tension within American temporal culture, which can be traced back to the very roots of the chronological temporal regime within pre- and early modern Europe. This regime is best known by its practices: the mechanical clock, the schedule, and the career. These have been the most influential social structures on the temporality of American workplaces. As techniques for organizing the day, week, month, year, and even one's entire life, they have created a taken-for-granted background texture to the flow of social time against which people narrate their lives. But how this regime became dominant in the American workplace is a surprisingly rich story, taking us in directions that may seem rather far afield, such as the inside of a medieval Benedictine monastery. Understanding this history, however, is an important first step because it allows us to see how earlier forms of work time have shaped moral order in the past, especially during periods of economic transformation. What does the history of the chronological temporal order tell us about how work time can influence moral life in general?

As I explain in this chapter, chronological time has followed two parallel stories throughout its history. On the one hand, as Franklin so clearly understood, it has long been an institution of self-discipline. Clocks, schedules, timetables, and the like became popular because they helped the individual cultivate disciplined conduct toward virtuous goals (Snyder 2013; Weber 2011). On the other hand, as Edson notes, these practices also became popular because they were a means of disciplining others, of effectively ratcheting up the intensity of labor, sometimes to worrying levels (Lukacs 1971; Marx 2011; Postone 1996). Punch clocks, piece-rates, shiftwork, and eventually the career model of employment became the quintessential tools for employers to create the kind of reliable, dedicated, driven, and busy workers needed for industrial mass production (Thompson 1967). Chronos has two faces: on one side, a stern but caring moral guide, and on the other, an impatient taskmaster. The contradictions, tensions, and dilemmas created by these two faces generated influential narratives about the good life that have deeply shaped American work culture.

CHRONOLOGICAL TIME: MARX VS. WEBER

Chronological time, which includes the mechanical clock as well as the schedule, timetable, and the career, is based on a highly abstract notion of time. Chronological techniques treat time as a kind of "container" in which events are placed along a unidirectional line. The spacing between these events is given a precise, typically numerical, measure (Adam 1990). A work schedule, for example, is a temporal container for energy expenditure in paid activity. It tells precisely when (by the clock), where (in a place of work), and in what order (by a sequence of tasks) the worker should expend his or her mental and physical energy. A career has a similar container function, though it operates on a much larger timescale and with perhaps less precision than a schedule. Career trajectories tell us when (by level of seniority, calendar year, etc.), where (in an organization or division), and in what order (by a sequence of roles) to expect movements within or between organizations. These techniques are useful in large, complex societies because the coordination of so many people and processes would be impossible without some standardized language for planning the "when" and "for how long" of social action (Elias 1994).[1]

The historical emergence of chronological time was of great interest to early sociologists (e.g., Durkheim 1995; Hubert 1999). Right from the beginning of the discipline, it caught the attention of two of its most esteemed theorists—Karl Marx and Max Weber. They differed significantly in how they saw things. For Marx, clocks, schedules, and timetables are tools of capitalist coercion and control. They facilitate the alienation of worker's labor power from the fruits of labor through their abstracting capacity. Commodified chronological time is what we refer to with the phrase "time is money." It divides the sensuous flow of everyday life into abstract zones of work time, home time, leisure time, and quality time, which, under the abstract measure of the hour, are then valued using the abstract measure of money (Marx 1993:37, 2011:45). Chronological time, for Marx, is therefore inseparable from

---

1. The opposite of chronological time is what Barbara Adam (1990) calls the "time in events," which describes the often overlooked fact that everything which moves or changes is in some sense a clock unto itself. The sleep rhythms of a human body, for example, are a kind of biological clock. The steps of getting everyone dressed, fed, and out the door before work or school are a kind of social clock. These rhythmic processes, though they lack the quantified precision of a stopwatch, do in fact figure in our experience of temporality more generally. When, for example, the rhythms of one's work schedule are desynchronized from the rhythms of one's biological clock—e.g., the morning alarm goes off "too early"—one feels fatigued. With bleary eyes, we might say to our colleague when we arrive at the office that morning, "I only got four hours sleep last night." What we really mean is that the time of the clock is reading a different hour than the time of the body. They are beating different, desynchronized rhythms. We may then use coffee or a power nap to work with the body so that it becomes better synchronized to the rhythms of the mechanical clock and work schedule.

the wider phenomenon of commodification, and is one of the primary mechanisms by which older pre-capitalist ways of life, typically based on the rhythms of agricultural production, were replaced by a world of factories based on wage labor (Thompson 1967). From this point of view, Chronos is a taskmaster, vigilantly surveilling the movements of his subjects, stopwatch in hand, in order to increase efficiency and productivity.

Though he never engaged in a systematic analysis of time, Weber had a wholly different view from Marx. He acknowledged the pre-capitalist origins of common chronological temporal practices, not least of which was the mechanical clock itself (Segre 2000; Snyder 2013). For Weber, chronological time is a pre-modern moral institution with its roots in medieval Christianity. Though it is often associated with industrial culture—particularly with factory life—Weber saw that Protestant religious communities had an almost obsessive relationship to chronological time long before there were such things as punch clocks and piece rates. By emphasizing what he calls "this-worldly asceticism"—a disciplined life that remains engaged with outer society, and by sacrilizing the idea of working in a "this-worldly calling"—a meaningful vocation in economically productive labor—Weber observed that Protestants encouraged an even, predictable order to one's life (Weber 1946:291). It makes sense, then, that Protestant ascetics would be attracted to clocks and schedules, not necessarily as tools to coerce labor, but because of their ability to assist the faithful in developing personal discipline. Protestant culture sacrilized forms of disciplined conduct that are reflected in the unwavering beat of the mechanical clock and the methodical routine of the daily schedule (Weber 2011:130–132). From this point of view, Chronos is a moral guide, assisting the diligent and ascetic laborer in his effort to achieve Virtue.

Marx and Weber are both right. They describe two important ways in which chronological time has been used in the West over the course of its long history.[2] These two views were compellingly combined by E. P. Thompson (1967) in his landmark paper "Time, Work Discipline, and Industrial Capitalism." Thompson showed that Marx and Weber provide different and complimentary views of the same thing: time discipline. Time discipline refers to the extent to which one's actions conform to the

2. Two additional arenas in which the mechanical clock developed, which I do not consider here, are science and transportation, used particularly in studies of the physical universe and for purposes of sea navigation (Needham, Ling, and Price 1960).

dominant rhythms of a social group (Glennie and Thrift 1996).[3] Where Marx details how modern chronological time disciplines have functioned as an external coercive force, Weber traces their older history as internal spurs for meaningful conduct. Thompson's challenge to future labor historians, then, was to show how these two ways of using chronological time have interacted over its long history and in different social contexts. How have the two faces of Chronos shaped the meaning and practice of work at different points in history? Why do so many contemporary workers take for granted the notion that methodical and disciplined conduct in paid work, which is marked and measured by clock hours, leads to existential security? How were these notions about the good life built, and who built them?

CHRONOS CLOISTERED

Any discussion of the history of chronological time disciplines must begin, perhaps unexpectedly, inside the ancient Christian monastic system. The precursors to the mechanical clock and some of the earliest and most influential ideas about work time were born there (Zerubavel 1980). Though these developments took place hundreds of years ago, they are nevertheless important for establishing the basic contours of the timescapes and time maps workers take for granted today.

The most fundamental aspects of the chronological temporal regime are the schedule and the mechanical clock. The invention of the schedule preceded the invention of the mechanical clock by over one thousand years (Zerubavel 1980). The first example of a kind of proto-schedule can be found in the many systems of rules recorded in the 3rd through 5th centuries by early Christian monks who practiced together in the Egyptian desert. These books of rules, such as that recorded by Pachomius, provided guidelines for how to run a monastery and included directions on how to use time signals to call monks together for group prayer (Jennings 2003). A standardized system of collective timing based on these earlier books of rules was further refined by Saint Benedict of Nursia, perhaps the most important western figure in the early history of chronological time. *The Rule of Saint Benedict*, written in the mid 6th century, became the paradigmatic system

3. In most modern societies, as Durkheim (1995) noted, dominant social rhythms are set to the abstract "beat" of clocks, schedules, and calendars, but we can observe many other examples of time discipline involving other means of timekeeping, such as ancient agricultural communities, which regulated social action more by the rhythms of the seasons and the movements of celestial objects (Adam 1990).

for organizing monastic life in western Christendom, spreading through-out western Europe during the medieval period. This system, which was based on the concept of the hour, was known as the *horarium*.[4]

The problems encountered in meeting the demands of the *horarium* spurred interest in the development of the first mechanical clock, which occurred sometime in the late 1200s (Dohrn-van Rossum 1996; Glennie and Thrift 2009; Landes 1983). More like what we would today call a timer, these early clocks were some of the first automated machines created in the West.[5] Their primary purpose was to help the monks wake up at the "proper time," according to the *horarium* schedule, in the middle of the night to perform a set of prayers known as Vigils (Landes 1983:67).[6]

The clock, however, was more than just a practical tool for group coor-dination. It was foremost a moral practice. Hence, activities like waking up for Vigils live on in moral language today, such as the word vigilance, the virtue of being watchful, and the sin of being lazy and distracted. The clock assisted the monks in achieving a central spiritual goal of the *horarium*: to prevent sinful distractions from God's work, known as *ace-dia* or "sinful sloth" (Wenzel 1967).[7] The schedule and clock allowed the

4. The *horarium* consisted of eight "divine offices"—discrete spans of time with pre-cise sequences of prayer to be carried out each day. The prayer offices were given names and were signaled to the community of monks using bells. Seven offices occurred during the day: Lauds, Prime, Tierce, Sext, None, Vespers, and Compline. One office occurred at night: Vigils (Cohen 2009:24). All other activities—chores, private medita-tion, reading, sleeping, and eating—were to be arranged with regularity in the "time remaining" around these offices (Zerubavel 1981:33–34). The system was called the *horarium*, the hours themselves "canonical hours," and the performance of the system "reciting the hours" (Landes 1983:61). The goal of the *horarium* was to chant all one hundred and fifty Psalms at least once within the span of the seven-day week (Dohrn-van Rossum 1996:35). Scholars have long argued, then, that Benedictine monks were the first officially scheduled people (Bendix 1962; Innis 1951; Knowles 1949; Le Goff 1980; Mumford 1963; Thrift 1988).

5. Not an uncommon trend in world history, automated timing devices appeared much earlier in China than in Europe, but were never put to the same sort of religious and dis-ciplinary uses we see in the Benedictine tradition (Landes 1983; Needham et al. 1960).

6. The office of Vigils presented particular difficulties. It was seen as the main daily pivot point that triggered the other liturgical activities beginning at dawn. Yet dawn would have shifted considerably over the course of the seasons (Dohrn-van Rossum 1996:38–39). How were the monks, fast asleep in their beds, to be made sensitive to this slowly shifting hour in such a way that the office could be performed at the proper time each night? In response to this problem, they engaged in several centuries of experimentation with different timing devices, the most successful of which was the mechanical clock (Dohrn-van Rossum 1996).

7. Rodulfus Glaber, for example, an 11th century French monk who lived at the height of Benedictine influence, gives us some idea of how clock time discipline may have been regarded in the monastery as an important sign of spiritual worth. "One night, when the bell sounded for [Vigils]," Glaber (1989:221) recalls, "I did not get up immediately as I ought to have done, because I felt wearied by my labours." Remaining

Benedictine monk to tether his body to a regular rhythm that protects the soul from distraction by the weaknesses of the body and, by proxy, from the fleshly temptations that drag the faithful to hell. By focusing the monk's restless energy, it was hoped that his day would be filled with the pursuit of God and nothing more. The surest road to salvation, according to the Benedictine system, is a regular routine consisting of a high volume of action—constant prayer and study—and low variety of action—spiritual work and nothing more.

The early history of the clock and schedule suggests that, right from the beginning, Chronos had two complimentary faces that functioned as a kind of cultural scaffolding for moral life. In the monastery, clocks and schedules were used both as tools of external control to put the less determined and more distractible monks in line and as techniques for developing inner excellence through regularity and constancy. Together, the two faces of Chronos urged the monks to cultivate vigilance—the ability to focus on spiritual work and nothing else—and thus ensure they make a place for themselves in heaven. Though mundane in their application, the schedule and clock were meant to transcend the mundane and orient the whole of one's life to God.

CHRONOS UNBOUND

The tradition of chronological time that grew up inside the Benedictine monastery had a profound influence on late medieval and early modern Europe, particularly in the context of economic life. The system of bell ringing used to mark the beginning and end of monastic offices could be heard throughout the landscape and quickly became a convenient way to coordinate non-religious activities outside the monastery. Markets, court proceedings, the changing of guards, schools, and, most importantly for our purposes, the marking of the workday began to rely on the ringing of bells to function smoothly, thus disseminating the beat of the clock and structure of the schedule throughout lay life (Dohrn-van Rossum 1996:197–209). By the 15th century, large public clock towers that were separate from the church could be found in all the major and many of the minor population centers in both western and eastern Europe (Dohrn-van Rossum 1996:125–160).

A constitutive part of the medieval aural environment, then, were dozens of temporal signals for day laborers—work bells. Before the dissemination of the mechanical clock, work time for wool shearers, weavers, fullers, and other sorts of guild laborers were determined in part by sunrise and sunset and partly by monastic office signals. Thus, the workday would have been longer in the summer and shorter in the winter, and workers' wages larger in the summer and smaller in winter. Conflicts over fair pay for fair work inevitably arose under this system because of the loose and flexible relationship between effort and reward. Employers claimed they were not receiving sufficient pay for work (Dohrn-van Rossum 1996:293–294).[8] At least at first, the mechanical clock proved a fair, transparent, and precise way to quell these disputes over the ratio of pay to effort in cases where more traditional forms of timing were unhelpful (Dohrn-van Rossum 1996:296, 304).

Out of this environment of increasingly precise and abstract time-keeping within an increasingly politically charged workplace emerged prototypical forms of the hourly wage. But routine payments gauged to a standardized, precise, and abstract unit of time—the hour—did not catch on immediately.[9] It was not until the arrival of industrial labor relations, and the portable and precise mechanical clocks that accompanied them, that the full abstraction of work time into commodified hours would occur.

In addition to monastic timing *technology*, monastic temporal *culture* had an equally important influence on work, especially among educated elites. An internalized chronological time discipline became a sign of moral worth even among the non-cloistered. Nowhere is this influence more apparent than among Renaissance Humanists and the burgeoning merchant class

---

in his bed with a few others who had been "seduced by this evil habit," Glaber was startled by the appearance of a "devil" in the monks' sleeping quarters. "Leaning against the wall with his hands behind his back," Glaber recalls, "he repeated two or three times: 'I am he, I am he who stays with those who hang behind.'" The devil appears to Glaber in this story in the form of a taskmaster who calls the monks to account for their lack of vigilance.

8. The usual answer to this problem had been to define the workday, in keeping with "tradition immemorial," as "the entire period of daylight" (Dohrn-van Rossum 1996:295). But determining the precise boundaries to demarcate that slice of time was remarkably difficult in practice given the variety of work tasks and workplaces that made up the late medieval economy. Some laborers, for example, worked more intensely during the warmer seasons. Should they receive the same wage during the longer, more intense workdays of summer as they did for the shorter, gentler days of winter? Some projects ran on a tighter deadline and would require extra labor to complete. How could workers and employers determine fair pay during these heightened periods (Dohrn-van Rossum 1996:300)?

9. The hourly wage emerged first in the 15th century on large construction sites, such as cathedrals, and strictly as a way to determine fairness in cases of exceptionally long labor, such as "overtime" on an urgent project, or exceptionally short labor, such as an unsanctioned work absence or suspension of work due to weather. These types of pay adjustments, unlike regular pay, would be the same during winter or summer and regardless of context. Importantly, however, "hour money," as the hourly wage was sometimes called, was not typically used to calculate pay during the main workday (Dohrn-van Rossum 1996:313–314).

of the 15th through 17th centuries (Quinones 1972). Chronological time discipline was important in this social context because it was seen to organize and direct one's scattered attention, thus enhancing ambition and the drive for worldly success.[10] As the humanist educator Leon Battista Alberti writes, "He who knows how not to waste time can do just about anything; and he who knows how to make use of time, he will be lord of whatever he wants" (quoted in Landes 1983:91–92). Unlike in the monastery, chronological time was seen among the Renaissance merchant class as a means to manage a "busy life"; a life that is both high volume—lots of activity—and high variety—many different types of activity.[11]

During the 14th through 17th centuries, then, clocks and schedules were unbound from the institution of the monastery. Chronological time became a common feature of a limited number of specific European timescapes, such as those inhabited by guild laborers and worldly merchants. What drew people to a more abstracted form of timing? In part, its political appeal. In the context of guild labor, for example, schedules and clocks were useful for coordinating complex spaces of action where disputes over the relationship of effort to reward were common.[12] Chronos held the promise of transparency and neutrality for employers and workers. But, at least among educated elites, the appeal was also moral. Chronological

10. A clear example is the humanist moral educator Leon Battista Alberti. In his widely read educational treatise *I Libri Della Famiglia*, written in the 15th century, he describes his morning routine: "In the morning when I get up, the first thing I do is think to myself: what am I going to do today? So many things: I count them, think about them, and to each I assign its time . . . I'd rather lose sleep than time, in the sense of the proper time for doing what has to be done. [The important thing is] to watch the time, and assign things by time, to devote oneself to business and never lose an hour of time" (quoted in Landes 1983:91–92). As an educator to young Italian merchants-to-be, Alberti is clearly attempting to model the type of internal conversation with which a good person, within the moral order of Alberti's world, should greet each morning. Like the Benedictines that preceded him, Alberti sees the value of clock time for spurring and channeling one's energy toward virtuous goals. Unlike a monk, however, he has in mind the non-cloistered life of the ambitious, worldly businessman. Alberti therefore arises each morning with a question on his lips that would likely never have been entertained by a cloistered monk: "What am I going to do today. So many things . . ." Watchfulness of time is an important virtue in itself for Alberti, but not because it cultivates a singular focus that guards against sinful distraction.

11. At this moment in history the words *busy* and *busyness* come into their modern usage. Older uses connote something closer to Benedictine vigilance, "concentrating on a particular activity." But, beginning in the late fourteenth and early fifteenth centuries, the meaning shifts toward the modern meaning: "constantly occupied with many things" (OED 2012).

12. As Glennie and Thrift (2009) note, work was not the only context that encouraged the widespread use of abstract timing techniques among laypeople. Clocks and schedules were useful for all sorts of activities, from marking the death of a loved one to gambling.

time, via its Benedictine roots, was associated with a particular vision of the good life as successful and ambitious. A good person leads a "busy" life that involves the careful management of time through precise measurement and allocation.

CHRONOS PRIVATIZED

The story of Chronos in the 17th through 19th centuries centers on the commodification of the hour within the early factory system and the increasing use of precise timing techniques by employers to wrest more control over the labor process from workers. Marx, in particular, focused on this moment in the history of chronological time for his analysis of alienated labor (Engels 1969; Marx 2011; Postone 1996). Crucial to this period was the increasing portability of mechanical clocks (Landes 1983). Smaller and more precise devices could now be made more cheaply and, in the context of workplaces, put into service alongside the already common sandglass. Rather than being owned by the city and housed in a public tower, then, clocks could now be owned by, say, a silk manufacturer and housed in the factory itself.[13] Factory clocks allowed owners to shift entirely to a pay-by-the hour system. As the precision and portability of these newer technologies improved, employers began to use ever more refined ways of accounting for work time, such as early forms of the punch clock (Dohrn-van Rossum 1996:317–319). By the end of the 18th century, the marriage between work, the hour, and pay became standard within the factory.

For workers, the tying of work to hours and hours to pay ended up being a Faustian bargain. The earlier struggle among guild laborers to gain some degree of fairness in the workplace by linking the effort-reward relationship to an abstract unit of time had the unintended effect, in the new context of the factory, of ceding control over the *pacing* of work to employers. What changed most dramatically about work timescapes in this new context, then, is an increasing *regularity* and *intensity* to the rhythm of labor (De Vries 2008:110–112). Pre-industrial weaving, for example, could generally be carried out at an irregular pace, featuring breaks that could be taken whenever the worker saw fit. In factories, however, people had to work a

13. These early factory clocks, while innovative, drew extensively on medieval temporal practices to gain legitimacy. Much like in Benedictine monasteries, they were often placed in the highest position in the factory and, by the middle of the 18th century, were often housed in majestic towers that harkened back to the architectural centrality and grandeur of the public clock tower within a medieval city (Rodgers 1979:156).

certain number of hours and take precisely timed breaks when and where they were told (Huggett 1973:19; Smith 1980:66).[14]

The new factory timescapes, then, were partly a product of the increasingly privatized nature of clock time. Work time was no longer a strictly public resource housed in a centralized civic tower. It could be controlled by whoever had the means. As a result, Chronos became not just a taskmaster but a *patronizing* taskmaster. Who owns the clock, and hence the duration and pacing of work, became a hot-button political issue that dominated early industrial workplaces, leading to massive reform movements in the latter half of the 19th century, including fights to establish a 10-hour and 8-hour day, and eventually a 40-hour week (Hunt 1981). As E. P. Thompson (1967) notes, however, the fight over work hours also firmly entrenched privatized chronological time as the only legitimate temporal language in which to carry out debates about work conditions—a legacy that lives on in contemporary debates about work time based on "time diaries." In fighting over work hours, early factory laborers normalized work time as chronological.

For their part, employers clearly favored the privatization of chronological time because of the disciplining capacity it lent them. In their efforts to harness Chronos the taskmaster, however, employers also relied heavily on Chronos' other face. They were able to legitimize their support for regularized and intensified labor by appealing directly to the now ancient tradition of chronological time as a stern moral guide. This elite discourse about time discipline, as Weber (2011) clearly understood, had been passed on from Benedictine Catholicism and Renaissance humanism to the "industrious" Protestant sects, such as Lutherans, Calvinists, and Methodists, and inspired figures like Richard Baxter and Benjamin Franklin (Snyder 2013).

In the secular context of the factory, the hyper-moralized discourse about "internalized" time discipline was often used simply as a means to justify the driving of labor (Thompson 1967). This invocation of Chronos was carried out with great fervor in the rapidly growing northern industrial regions of 19th century America.[15] In an 1878 report from the Ohio

14. It is difficult to assess everyday reactions to this rhythm of work because average workers left so few records behind, but there is certainly suggestive evidence that work became more exhausting and monotonous (Engels 1969). Resistance groups, many of which would form the first working class labor movements, symbolically resisted industrial work conditions by smashing factory clocks (Dohrn-van Rossum 1996:318).

15. There are numerous examples from the Southern United States as well. Perhaps the most extreme example of the privatization of chronological time and its exploitative uses comes from the southern slave plantations. After the 1830s, slaveholders adapted the clock and schedule systems they saw in northern factories, encountered through the transportation industry, and which they had long known from urban centers, as well as the rhetoric of time thrift they encountered among colonial merchants, to ratchet up the productivity of agricultural slave labor (Smith 1997).

Bureau of Labor Statistics, for example, the bureau asked for comments from American factory owners on the then hotly contested issue of the eight hour day. Their resistance reveals the continued influence of Chronos' moral face. A carriage manufacturer, for example, argued that "[An eight hour work day] would be ruinous to workmen, it would curtail their wages and increase their habits of idleness. Never reduce labor to less than ten hours per day, twelve would be better, for when they are at work they are out of mischief" (Ohio Bureau of Labor Statistics 1878:281). "The majority of men are like boys," complained a furniture manufacturer, "the less they have to do the more time they put it in deviltry. Give them plenty to do, and a long while to do it in, and you will then find them physically and morally better" (Ohio Bureau of Labor Statistics 1878:281). Appealing to the ancient discourse about chronological time as the best means to create sober and diligent people, manufacturers could justify their control over work time.[16]

CHRONOS TAYLORIZED

Up to this point, the story of Chronos has been limited to a few select groups living in what otherwise would have been a much less time disciplined—though not necessarily less time conscious (Glennie and Thrift 2009)—world. In the 20th century, as gainful employment moved increasingly from agricultural to industrial centers, chronological time discipline became a more widespread phenomenon. As the factory system grew in the booming 20th century war economy, for example, America began to surpass Europe as the world's innovators in new uses of chronological time at work. The most important of these innovations, scientific management, had some

16. In more extreme cases, Chronos was seen by factory owners as a means to prevent them from having to use external time discipline in the first place. Clearly understanding the religious sources of chronological time, some industrial experts preached the position that efficient workers must be made from the inside out. In his widely read 1835 treatise on the British factory system *The Philosophy of Manufactures*, the Scottish academic Andrew Ure noted that an important first step in creating an efficient factory is recruiting workers who already possess an internalized sense of time discipline and surround them in a protective environment that features, among other things, religious instruction. "It is, therefore, excessively the interest of every mill-owner," Ure (1835:417) writes, "to organize his moral machinery on equally sound principles with his mechanical, for otherwise he will never command the steady hands, watchful eyes, and prompt co-operation, essential to the excellence of product." While probably not representative of the typical techniques of early factory management, Ure demonstrates just how salient the moral face of Chronos continued to be in thinking about the creation of good industrial laborers.

precursors in Europe (Dohrn-van Rossum 1996:318; Rabinbach 1990), but was systematized and popularized by an American: Frederick Winslow Taylor. While in hindsight Taylor's methods proved to be revolutionary, at the time they were seen as just the next logical step in the tradition of Chronos the taskmaster, which had long sought to increase the regularity and intensity of labor for the sake of increased output (Cappelli 1999:58).

Scientific management is essentially the installation of a preplanned piece-rate production system based on the objective gathering of evidence about the labor process through time-and-motion research. Time-and-motion studies make use of an even more precise, portable, and privatized timekeeper: the stopwatch. Much like the original mechanical clocks used in the monastery, these devices were designed to measure a purely abstract duration within the context of a larger process. Unlike monastic timers, however, stopwatches can be started and stopped at will, allowing the user to break processes down into discrete micro movements and thus gain control over the time that lives "within" a work task or even the worker's body—what Michel Foucault (1995:152) describes as "a kind of anatomo-chronological schema of behavior." In the context of industrial labor, scientific managers used stopwatches to measure "each of the elements of various kinds of work . . . and then find the quickest time in which each job could be done by summing up the total times of its component parts" (Taylor 1911:148). Once a baseline total was established, managers could then experiment with accelerating the pace of each element, isolating and removing any "unnecessary" elements, and manipulating the work environment to lower the total time required, all while maintaining a relatively constant or even lower expenditure of effort by the worker compared to the baseline measurement.

Taylorism had a profound effect on the timescapes of industrial labor, which has been much remarked on by sociologists (e.g., Braverman 1974). But accounts of Taylorism often miss the reasons behind its invention. Taylorism emerged out of a desire to solve the problems of worker inefficiency that were a common feature of the 19th century contracting system (Cappelli 1999). Much like the contemporary era of "lean" and streamlined businesses that focus on their "core competencies" while outsourcing everything else, 19th century American companies generally divided their labor among a complex patchwork of independent contractors. These contractors would use the factory owner's facilities, but manage themselves. Over time, these contracting arrangements became a tangle of inefficiencies, especially because of resistance by skilled contractors to "productivity improvements that made them work harder or took some of their control away" (Cappelli 1999:55).

At the turn of the 20th century, the contracting system was rapidly replaced in many companies by the so-called "drive" system, which consisted of foremen and workers who were directly employed by the company, essentially moving the entire production process in house. Having gained direct control over both management and labor, owners could now better monitor the output and quality of products. What they found was that some workers were faster and some slower, leading to bottlenecks and moments of high inefficiency (Cappelli 1999:56). Taylorism, then, was just the most successful version of a widespread effort to improve output by standardizing the regularity and intensity of labor across a workforce with varying degrees of skill and motivation.

Seen in the context of the drive system, Taylor's biggest impact was not the invention of time-and-motion study per se, but the powerful political legacy he left behind by inserting the "objective" and "scientific" symbol of chronological time between the foreman and the worker, a relationship that had become notoriously tense. Rather than bicker over piece-rates, the rate could be scientifically determined in advance by a distant "time man" whose office would be located somewhere outside the workers' view. In this way, chronological time facilitated the separation of "brain" work from "hand" work, thus, it was hoped, neutralizing controversies over the pacing of output (Braverman 1974). Taylor (1939:143–144) is worth quoting at length here.

> As one of the elements incident to this great gain in output, each workman has been systematically trained to his highest state of efficiency, and has been taught to do a higher class of work than he was able to do under the old types of management; and at the same time he has acquired a friendly mental attitude toward his employers and his whole working conditions, whereas before a considerable part of his time was spent in criticism, suspicious watchfulness, and sometimes in open warfare.

While he is deservedly (in)famous for having pushed the agenda of Chronos the taskmaster to its extreme, Taylor also clearly had in mind an ambition to instill the moralizing face of Chronos into the industrial workplace. Not only did time study allow for the disciplining of an unevenly skilled and motivated workforce, but, at least in Taylor's mind, it also held out the promise of lifting those workers, and ultimately their entire workplaces, to a higher moral standard—one that is more democratic, transparent, and peaceable. Whether this aspect of Taylor's thought was mere instrumental justification for an exploitative system or a genuine belief in Chronos as a moral guide is unclear.[17] Regardless, Taylor clearly understood the two faces of Chronos and sought to create industrial timescapes that could capitalize on both.

Unlike in previous historical eras, there is ample evidence of how everyday workers experienced this new work temporality. As Harry Braverman (1974) shows, work under Taylorism went through a profound "deskilling" trend in which laborers became increasingly responsible for just one discrete part of the production process, which they were instructed to carry out with monotonous intensity under the preplanned direction of the "time man." Taylorist work was, not surprisingly, boring and repetitive compared to work under the contract system.

Contrary to Braverman's depiction, however, employees in Taylorist shops did not just passively submit to the "lash" of the clock. They sought ways to actively transform stopwatch-timed labor into something more meaningful. Taylorism's hyper-regularized style of work created new timescapes that offered new opportunities for moral world building. Donald Roy, in his classic 1945 ethnography of a piecework machine shop, gives us an unprecedented glimpse into Taylorist labor at the height of its influence at the end of World War II. Workers' main concern, Roy (1959:158) suggests, is "combating" the "beast of monotony." The main way they do this, he observes, is by turning work into a "game." Roy's (1953:510) reflections on his own physical and mental experiences while playing the game of piecework are telling.

> The writer found that fast rhythmic work seemed less fatiguing, although the reduction of fatigue may have been closely related to the reduction of boredom. He discovered further that the same job that had bored and wearied him as a "time study," or non-piecework operation, now interested him and gave him exhilaration on piecework.

Taylorist work is boring and monotonous by nature, Roy indicates, but in its very repetitiveness, it also affords the worker a certain temporal texture—"fast" and "rhythmic"—that can actually result in something like

17. Taylor was clearly aware of how morally charged meticulous timing of workers could become, having experimented with the technique himself at the Midvale Steel Company in Philadelphia. "The writer does not believe at all in the policy of spying upon the workman when taking time observations for the purposes of time study," Taylor (1911:153) notes. "If men . . . are to be *ultimately affected by the results* of these observations, it is generally best to come out openly, and let them know that they are being timed."

exhilaration. For Roy, the rhythm of work under these conditions becomes a kind of reward in itself because of the cognitive and emotional experiences it delivers—experiences of skill, smooth acceleration, cleverness, and triumph. Roy goes on to give examples from his coworkers that corroborate his own experience, leading him to a rather unforeseen conclusion.

> Making quota called for the exercise of skill and stamina, and it offered opportunity for self-expression. The element of uncertainty of outcome provided by ever-present possibilities of bad luck made quota attainment an exciting game played against the clock on the wall, a game in which the elements of control provided by the application of knowledge, ingenuity, and speed, heightened interest and lent to exhilarating feelings of accomplishment (Roy 1953:511).

Roy was no apologist for Taylorism. He would no doubt agree with later observers that Taylorist piecework is alienating (Roy 1959), and, indeed, he was active in the labor movement throughout his life. But in experiencing Taylorism firsthand, Roy was also made privy to the hidden meanings of working under the gaze of Chronos the taskmaster. In his very struggle to keep up with the clock, he finds the other face of chronological time, the face that offers opportunities for "self-expression" and the development of "skill" under an unyielding rhythm.

The Taylorization of Chronos reveals the extent to which chronological time had penetrated into the smallest physical tasks and most personal emotional spaces of industrial labor. While sociologists have rightly seen this construction of work time as pernicious in the way it shifts control to management, they have tended to overlook the ways workers maintained a sense of agency by building moral order upon that temporal scaffolding. Taylorized labor was made meaningful through the elevation of certain virtues, like perseverance in the face of grinding monotony or the ability to entrain one's body with the rhythms of machines. These notions of hard work, built within a Taylorized timescape, have had an important influence on blue-collar culture more generally and can be seen in numerous ethnographic accounts of working class morality throughout the 20th century (e.g., Burawoy 1979; Lamont 2000; Willis 1981). As in previous historical eras, then, we see that the introduction of new timescapes tends to create moral dilemmas—labor conditions that simultaneously offer new challenges and new forms of self-expression. Workers are not always entirely sure whether or not new forms of work time are wholly good or bad. The heated conversations about the good life sparked by these dilemmas profoundly shape work culture.

CHRONOS PROMOTED

The Taylorization of Chronos at the turn of the 20th century was closely followed by another crucial temporal innovation, again having its most extensive early application primarily in the United States: the bounded career (Cappelli 1999). While not as precisely and mechanically measured, the career is a close cousin to the schedule and mechanical clock because it shares a similar "chrono-logic." Like schedules and clocks, careers are containers for events. They hold the events of one's entire working life trajectory. Unlike schedules and clocks, careers measure broad movements of seniority within and between organizations over a lifetime of work.

What is most remarkable about the rise of the career in the United States in the middle of the 20th century is just how intimately connected it is to the successes and failures of Taylorism from the early 20th century. While the best known accomplishment of Taylorism was the time-disciplining of labor, an equally if not more important outcome was the development of a more powerful, autonomous, and sophisticated class of workers that stood between owners and shop men: middle managers. Emerging from the planning department of the time-and-motion system, this "white-collar" class of workers began to experiment with new ways of boosting laborers' motivation when it proved clear that the "lash" of the clock did not engender commitment and loyalty.[18] This became especially clear as factory jobs boomed during the world wars and workers had less fear of unemployment (Cappelli 1999:59–61). What was to motivate them to tolerate the ratcheting up of piece rates when they could just quit and go to an easier job?

The answer was the "bounded career"—an internal labor market with preplanned pathways of promotion that resided entirely within the company itself. Rather than go to the dwindling pool of unemployed or underemployed workers outside the company, middle managers began to develop

18. The connection between Taylorist time-and-motion study and the career is no more clearly seen than in the work of Frank and Lillian Gilbreth, two of Taylor's most successful students. After spending years developing a more rigorous form of efficiency study, which they called "motion study," the Gilbreth's began to experiment with other temporal manipulations that took place over a longer time scale. They called this the "three position plan" (Gilbreth and Gilbreth 1916). It essentially required employees to be teachers, workers, and learners all at the same time. While carrying out their current responsibilities as workers, the plan required them to teach their current skills to a person lower down in the organization while at the same time entering into a mentoring relationship with the person above them. It was thought that this would generate more internal drive because workers could see their skills develop and understand the implications of their work over a longer time scale. The Gilbreths' ideas about worker motivation through a planned career trajectory, especially those of Lillian, would form the foundation of what would become industrial psychology (Wren 1987).

their own talent and institute systems of promotion that would motivate employees to work hard and refine their skills. As Cappelli (1999:131) notes, this system was based on a different understanding of motivation—a "happy worker model" that could replace the old "frightened worker" model of the Taylorist system. This model was part of a wave of experimentation with new ways of motivating industrial workers—the famous Hawthorne experiments, for example—that were deeply influenced by gestalt psychology and Durkheimian sociology (Wren 1987:245–254).

The bounded career reshaped time discipline in two ways. First, it shifted the focus of time discipline from the externalized "stick" of the clock, to the internalized "carrot" of promotion. In a report entitled "Sales Power through Planned Careers," for example, Andrall Pearson (1966:105) told the readers of the *Harvard Business Review*, "From a study of 30 large companies, a new concept emerges—the career path—which offers businessmen the means for restoring vitality to the sales organization." Throughout his report, Pearson provides a number of graphical representations of such paths (figure 2.3). As Pearson's diagram illustrates, rather than being motivated by fear, career tracked workers can aspire to a position in the distant future. "A career provides a degree of predictability about an individual's future," notes Robert Dubin (1958:279) in his popular mid-century industrial relations textbook, "Predictability about the future is one of the important elements that give stability to society."

Second, the bounded career shifted the "wavelength" of time discipline from the micro scale of hours and tasks to the macro scale of years of seniority. An important means by which this shift occurred was to instill in the career time map an "up or out" norm. As becomes clear in Pearson's diagram, there is only one legitimate way for workers to move through the firm over time: forward and upward. Even the failure to reach seniority by age 55 means an "early" (read: forced) retirement. This is the sense in which Chronos becomes a fully-fledged time-map. Rather than just governing the processes of the immediate work environment, the logic of Chronos could now be used to map out a distant future trajectory in which employees could envision an entire narrative about their direction of travel through the firm and cultivate personal discipline to meet that vision.

Though it is debatable just how widespread extensively preplanned career paths were in practice (Cappelli 1999; Moen 2005), the *idea* of the career took on a kind of aura in American work culture, especially in the context of white-collar work (Moen and Roehling 2004). New conceptions of job security were now thinkable in a way that had not been possible before. American workers became accustomed to "the belief that working hard and putting in long hours continuously throughout adulthood is

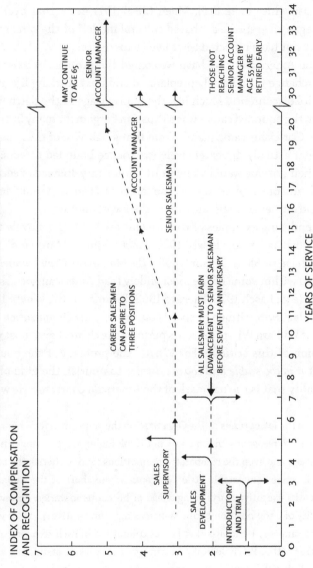

Figure 2.3 A career time map.

the path to occupational success, personal fulfillment, and a secure retirement" (Moen 2005:189). This "career mystique," as Phyllis Moen (2005) calls it, overlooked the fact that regularized and secure employment pathways were rarely if ever granted to women, racial minorities, and low-wage workers. Bounded careers were primarily the privilege of educated middle and upper class white men. Still, Moen (2005:191) notes that over time Americans began to embrace a "shared cultural model" of the career, even though it may not have reflected their lived experience.

While some Americans may have welcomed the promise of existential security in exchange for a heavily preplanned and busy working life, it was not without its discontents. Much like the hourly wage at the dawn of the industrial era, the bounded career was a Faustian bargain for many 20th century workers. Criticisms came mainly from that small slice of the American population that actually did extensively experience bounded careers: elite white men. Their critique went by one word: conformity. Instead of security, predictability, and prestige, critics saw the career as a threat to individuality, autonomy, and authenticity because of its clockwork motion.

The most enduring examples of this critique are in literary novels about working life, such as Sinclair Lewis' 1922 *Babbit*, John P. Marquand's 1949 *Point of No Return*, or Sloan Wilson's 1955 *The Man in the Gray Flannel Suit*. It is also found within some of the most widely read American social scientific literature (e.g., Lasch 1979; Packard 1962; Riesman 1967; Whyte 1965).

In his popular 1956 critique of social conformity, *The Organization Man*, the sociologist William Whyte presents perhaps the clearest and most wide-ranging version of this critique. For Whyte, the problem of the bounded career is that it is *too stable* and *too predictable* to nourish the kind of rugged individuality that is the hallmark of the American character. He writes,

> When he is on the lower rungs of The Organization the young man feels himself wafted upward so pleasantly that he does not think high-pressure competition really necessary, and even the comparatively ambitious tend to cherish the idea of settling in some comfortable little Eden somewhere short of the summit. As the potential executive starts going ahead of his contemporaries, however, the possibility of a top position becomes increasingly provocative. [. . .] He will never be the same . . . He knows that he has committed himself to a long and perhaps bitter battle. Psychologically he can never go back or stand still, and he senses well that the climb from here on is going to involve him in increasing tensions (Whyte 1965:149).

It is in the very orderliness of the successful, executive-bound career trajectory that Whyte sees the deepest existential dilemmas. At the lower levels, the Organization Man feels automatically "wafted" up the status hierarchy. As he continues, things become more complicated. He begins to see more clearly the type of commitment he has entered into, perhaps unknowingly. He begins to see his future *too clearly*. As Nicholas Dames (2003:256) observes, "The career not only domesticates ambition—by placing it in a harness, as it were—but in fact replaces it altogether with a version that desires the career as an end, not a means." So totalizing is the career trajectory, the critique goes, that the worker begins to lose his authenticity in its structure—he becomes a career*ist*. Whyte notes, "The figures of speech younger executives use to describe the situation they now find themselves in are illuminating. The kinds of words they use are 'treadmill,' 'merry-go-round,' 'rat race' . . ." The bounded career trajectory is exhaustingly secure. "It is not the evils of organization life that puzzle [the Organization Man]," Whyte (1965:16) concludes, *"but its very beneficence*. He is imprisoned in brotherhood." In providing relentless security Chronos creates an overly structured future.

Critics like Whyte helped ignite a widespread conversation within professional circles about the fate of the rugged individualist and the future of that enterprising, entrepreneurial spirit that was always assumed to drive American success. In a 1960 essay in the *Harvard Business Review*, for example, Joseph W. McGuire asked 189 of America's "top executives of commercial banks" to discuss how closely they think "real businessmen" fit the images of them portrayed in popular critiques like *The Organization Man*. Do bankers find the "unflattering depictions of roistering, boostering Babbits, insecure Charley Grays in gray flannel suits (by Marquand, Whyte, and Brooks Brothers), or even the range of predators foraging in the executive suite," to be an accurate reflection (McGuire 1960:67)? "Almost 80 percent of respondents," McGuire (1960:71) claims, "said that executives should be risk-takers and individualists rather than persons seeking security and teamwork." He notes, however, that "Over one half of the bankers . . . seem to feel that the day of the rugged individualist, the captain of industry, the business technocrat has passed." "This unanimity of opinion," he concludes "evidences an overwhelming dislike of the trend toward conformity" (McGuire 1960:71). The generalizability of McGuire's survey aside, its very appearance in such a popular business periodical is testament to the degree of interest in the moral dilemmas of the bounded career.

By 1973, the waning days of industrial dominance in the United States, the authors of a congressional research report on the American work ethic, reflecting on the now voluminous literature concerning the "problem" of the bounded career, worried, "As portrayed in a host of official studies, press findings, and industry reports, the increasingly familiar 'blue collar blues' of bored, alienated assembly-line workers have spread to a white collar world of dull, unchallenging jobs" (quoted in Hamilton and Wright 1986:32).[19]

Though the career may have initially been a sought after solution to the problems of Taylorized labor, its critics believed it simply spread those problems over a longer time horizon and to a new class of white-collar workers. Like the schedule and clock before it, the career presented moral dilemmas that had no straightforward answers. The career time map seemed to open the door to predictable and long-term vision at the same time that it closed the door to authentic individuality. The "rat race" versus the "entrepreneur" became familiar cultural tropes that seemed to pit security against creativity in a zero-sum game.

CHRONOS DISRUPTED

In the decades following the 1960s, a number of structural and cultural forces have emerged that seem to be reshaping the way people work. Scholars are just now beginning to understand the significance of these developments. It is still unclear to what degree they are transforming or reinforcing the chronological temporal order.

Demographic changes have been particularly important. As suggested by the historical picture presented above, chronological time has always been primarily about the ordering of *men's* lives. Chronos is a *he* (Odih 1999). Though women have certainly used chronological techniques and participated in the spread of schedules and clocks (Glennie and Thrift 2009), they have historically rarely been the drivers of temporal culture. The Feminist movement, the large-scale entry of women into white-collar and professional work after the 1960s, plus the rise in divorce rates that accompanied these trends, have begun to bring the gendered nature of chronological work time to light. Fewer households are operating with the breadwinner/homemaker model of production, while the duel-earner and single working parent models have become more common. As Jerry Jacobs and Kathleen Gerson (1998) have argued, while it is debatable whether or not *individuals* are working more hours today than in the middle of the 20th century,

---

19. Throughout the 1940s, '50s, and '60s economists and psychologists began to take a renewed interest in the figure of the creative, enterprising individual. Harvard established the Research Center of Entrepreneurial History in 1948 under Arthur H. Cole, which sought an understanding of the enterprising individual as an engine of economic history, spawning a series of publications on entrepreneurial capitalism and the entrepreneurial personality (see, e.g., Cole 1942; Collins and Moore 1964; Hornaday and Bunker 1970).

it is clear that these new types of *households* are working more hours than households on the breadwinner/homemaker model. Women, in particular, have been asked to shoulder a double burden for both home and work responsibilities (Hochschild 1989).

Out of these new household-level time pressures has sprung a new and powerful cultural category: balance. The discourse surrounding balance, however, seems to both challenge and reinforce the chronological tradition of deifying busyness as a badge of honor (Sabelis et al. 2008). Work-to-family and family-to-work conflict have become hot-button political issues, especially for women, which has provided a platform to argue for work arrangements that promote a balanced, rather than just productive, life (Williams 2000). Some forms of flexible scheduling, for example, are a direct attempt to generate more balanced workplaces that can better accommodate non-working life. At the same time, work-life balance rhetoric has reinforced the notion that workers can have it all and do it all, thus fortifying the cult of busyness in some respects (Hochschild 1997). It may be that, in the very act of critiquing the gendered nature of work time, balance discourse has also reinforced other aspects of chronological culture, such as busyness and the use of clocks and schedules to pack more and more activity into one's life.

New technologies have had similarly ambiguous implications for the chronological order. On the one hand, the Internet and the digital revolution have made the boundaries between work and non-work spaces fuzzier. Telecommuting and the increasing use of globally distributed virtual work teams seem to be challenging core binaries, such as work/home and work/leisure (Lee and Liebenau 2002). Among knowledge professionals, for example, the digitization of work may allow them more freedom to work when and where they want. On the other hand, especially among low-wage shift workers, but also among some white-collar professionals, managers are using digital technologies to develop predictive scheduling algorithms and remote productivity monitoring devices that allow them to tweak workers' movements in ways that would certainly impress Frederick Winslow Taylor (Sewell 1998). At the same time that some aspects of the chronological temporal order are being challenged by the digital revolution, then, we may be seeing the simultaneous rise of a kind of neo-Taylorism unleashed by new technologies of efficiency and surveillance (Crowley et al. 2010). Scholars are once again turning their attention to scientific management to understand how the latest attempts to make workers more efficient through close supervision resemble or differ from the past (Ackroyd and Bolton 1999; Conti and Warner 1994; Lomba 2005).

The one area of chronological culture that does seem to be in clear decline is the bounded career. As Peter Cappelli (1995, 1999) has argued, large organizations are increasingly asking workers to strike a new employ-ment deal. In exchange for giving up things like loyalty, long-term commit-ment, and clear hierarchy—structures that, as noted above, were a source of anxiety for some—workers are offered new "opportunities" to become more entrepreneurial and personally responsible for their work trajectories (Moen and Roehling 2004; Smith 2001). Employers increasingly see long-term contracts as a sunk cost, and favor flexible arrangements because they encourage workers to be more entrepreneurial and manage their own employment risks. Management experts have begun to conceptualize a new kind of "boundaryless" career model wherein workers are trained to think of their working lives in terms of a trajectory of employment but not within the secure confines of a single organization or even a single occupa-tion (Arthur and Rousseau 1996).

In America, nowhere has this emphasis on individual responsibility and entrepreneurialism been more influential than Silicon Valley. Already in the late 1960s and early 1970s, pioneering Silicon Valley tech firms such as Fairchild Semiconductor and Intel were experimenting with what would later become standard practices of flexible capitalism: independent con-tracting, the outsourcing of manual labor overseas, alliances with Wall Street venture capitalists, and the use of stock options rather than security and pensions to recruit the most skilled employees. Many of the found-ers and early employees of these companies, such as Robert Noyce, were former East Coast Organization Men who moved to rural California (of all places) to get away from the stifling conformity of bloated bureaucratic firms like Bell and Philco (Lecuyer 2006).

In the last forty years, the quirks of Silicon Valley business culture have evolved into a powerful hegemonic discourse about how all types of work-ers will need to conduct themselves in the coming future (Chiapello and Fairclough 2002; Vallas and Prener 2012). Wildly popular management and advice texts, such as Clayton Christiansen's *The Innovator's Dilemma* and Richard Bolles *What Color is Your Parachute?*, invite workers to embrace risk and anticipate change, even if you think you are secure. For example, in a 1994 *Harvard Business Review* essay entitled "Toward a Career-Resilient Workforce," three management experts note that, "Under the old covenant, employees entrusted major decisions affecting their careers to a parental organization. Often, the result was a dependent employee and a relatively static workforce with a set of static skills" (Waterman, Waterman, and Collard 1994:88). They advocate for a "new covenant" with workers that nurtures,

> a group of employees who not only are dedicated to the idea of continuous
> learning but also stand ready to reinvent themselves to keep pace with change;

who take responsibility for their own career management; and, last but not least, who are committed to the company's success. [. . .] A workforce that is constantly benchmarking and updating its skills is one that not only responds to change but anticipates it. Competitiveness—keeping close to customers, staying on top of technology and market trends, and striving to be ever more flexible—becomes everyone's responsibility, not that of just a handful of executives. [. . .] By looking out for themselves, employees look out for the company (Waterman et al. 1994:89).

These comments harken back to the mid 20th century critiques of people like William Whyte in that they are a direct response to the static dullness and conformity of the bounded career system. But they differ from Whyte's critique in an important respect: they take the perspective of the employer, rather than the employee. In this way, management experts have wholeheartedly taken on the Organization Man critique, but have adapted it to their own ends by exhorting workers to become more involved in shouldering what used to be company risks, such as managing an employee's long-term trajectory (Boltanski and Chiapello 2005). The message to workers, then, can sound tortuously confusing. Be flexible, but one-pointedly committed to the company when it counts. Be an entrepreneurial individual, but fit into the organization's plans. Be disruptable, but don't get disrupted.

In short, there is no question that some things have changed about the nature of work since the 1960s. It remains unclear, however, how workers in diverse structural positions make sense of these changes and to what degree chronological culture remains a salient matrix in which to narrate their lives. Are new experiences of work time engendering new understandings of good work or the good life more generally? Or have the changes simply been met by bootstrapping old chronological understandings of good work to new contexts? How do old and new moral categories interact and sit alongside each other?

CONCLUSION

Work time in America bears the legacy of the chronological temporal order. With its roots in early medieval Europe, this order blossomed most fully in the industrial-bureaucratic workplace of the post-World War II era. Its dominant techniques—the schedule, clock, and career—gave social time a rigid beat and predictable trajectory. These timescapes and time maps are meant to allow workers to construct a life that feels methodical, full of activity, and secure—to unify effort and reward under an umbrella of planning. For employers, they are meant to create the type of worker who is loyal and internally motivated to work steadily for a distant reward. And when internal motivation fails, they function as coercive disciplinary tools to keep the less motivated in line. As Luc Boltanski and Laurent Thevenot (2006:208) observe, clocks and timetables "take advantage of the regularity with which industrial objects function and endow the industrial world with a representation of time . . . in which one can be transported without friction." A frictionless, smoothly flowing, well-oiled temporality is the industrial utopia (Rosa and Scheuerman 2009). One of the basic accomplishments of industrial capitalism, then, was to harness the ancient logic of Chronos to instill on a mass scale timescapes and time maps that produce what Lefebvre (2004) describes as "eurythmia"—when multiple rhythms work together in functional synchrony. Eurythmia orients organizational processes to a measured, steady, long-term trajectory. Perhaps ironically, then, this measured steadiness is precisely the problem of industrial capitalism for its workers, especially when it is deployed as an external disciplinary tool. The worker becomes "a steam engine running constantly under a forced draught" (Edson 1892:282). Work can grind him down with boredom, monotony, and predictability.

Chronological time has not only left its mark on the structure of the American workplace, then, but also on the moral order of work. The meaning of work within this rigid, predictable, and linear temporal order has been built out of the promises and perils of eurythmia. The schedule and clock, particularly in the context of physical labor, have long held the promise of transcending physical limitations, turning the body into an inexhaustible source of creative energy. But in the very act of tethering the body to this unyielding beat, it can easily create exhaustion. Out of this moral dilemma, then, emerged important agents and agendas of social reform: industrial labor unions, the short-time movement, and workplace safety regulations.

Similarly, the career, being the dominant time map of the chronological order, promised a well-oiled and smoothly flowing pattern of progression for ones entire lifetime of employment. For employers, it also promised to solve the problems of self-motivation and long-term skill development that seemed to have gone unanswered by Taylorism. But this security came with its own quandaries, especially for elite male workers. It could just as easily create conditions of stifling conformity, which threatened the very image of rugged individualism that the American success ethic championed. Excessively rationalized temporal trajectories were seen to "stifle inspired outpourings" and inhibit "creative spontaneity" (Boltanski and Thevenot

2006:240). This debate reinforced one of the classic tropes of American work culture—the heroic figure of the enterprising individual—a trope that inspires contemporary thinking about workplaces now more than ever. The legacies of chronological time for the American workplace, then, are both structural and cultural—giving shape to things as mundane as the shift schedule and as elaborate as the myth of the genius entrepreneur.

By virtue of this historical perspective, we are now able to see in greater detail some important general relationships between work time and moral order, which will prove useful in thinking about flexible capitalism. In its long journey from the cloister to the bureaucratic firm, chronological time has continually presented itself as a rational way to synchronize action in space, but also as a cultural scaffolding upon which actors can build meaningful narratives about their worlds. Both faces of chronological time discipline actors to behave in patterned ways, either through external coercion or internal motivation. Social elites, from St. Benedict to Frederick Winslow Taylor, have been interested not only in directing the organization of time, then, but also in shaping the meanings of time so they can gain greater control over mechanisms of intrinsic motivation. Religious, educational, and other institutions that give expert advice pay just as much attention to the kinds of narratives about the good life that are stretched over the scaffolding of social time as they do to the design of the scaffolding itself (Thompson 1967).

If the history of chronological work time teaches us anything, however, it is that the recipients of new timescapes and time maps often find themselves cast into moral dilemmas and Faustian bargains. It is often unclear at first whether new forms of work time are wholly good or bad because these new arrangements may in fact address some of the grievances associated with older work arrangements (Boltanski and Chiapello 2005; Boltanski and Thevenot 2006). Taylorism, for example, was in many ways a reaction to the uncertainties and irregularities of employment under earlier systems of external contracting. The bounded career was, in part, a reaction to the problems of Taylorism. The introduction of these new temporalities, then, asked workers to weigh new forms of economic suffering against new potential freedoms, or the loss of old freedoms against new and unexpected sources of suffering. Workers find themselves pulled between goods and bads that can have precisely the same sources and are thus compelled to debate both the negative and positive futures implied by new arrangements.

The debates that spin out of these tensions, then, create powerful cultural narratives about the good life in capitalism (Bell 1976). Workers seek out political spaces and new languages to articulate their experiences

coherently and figure out where they stand. During the height of the industrial era in the 19th and 20th centuries, labor unions, novelists, management experts, and social scientists were some of the most powerful voices
in these debates. They developed compelling narratives that invited workers to either challenge the economic transformations preferred by elites or
accommodate those transformations, thereby smoothing the way forward
for further institutionalization. There is a great deal at stake in the moral
debates surrounding new forms of work time, then, because of their ability
to either accommodate or challenge the emerging status quo of the new
economic regime (Boltanski and Thevenot 2006).

With this historical backdrop in mind, we can now turn our attention
to flexible capitalism with an enriched understanding. How does this new
temporal regime differ from the chronological regime? Is it a distinct break
from the past, or does it rely on and incorporate elements of Chronos? How
do workers make sense of the introduction of flexible timescapes and time
maps when their dispositions, habits, and expectations may still be deeply
informed by chronological cultural norms? How do workers react to some
of the new freedoms of flexible time if they also in the same moment discover new forms of suffering? What narratives about virtue and dignity do
workers construct in reaction to these dilemmas?

CHAPTER 3
The Financialization of Time-Space

B rent, a 31-year-old senior analyst at a mid-sized investment bank, works so much each week and in such unpredictable stretches that he cannot give me an estimate of his work schedule in terms of hours. After failing to come up with a concrete number, he finally abandons my line of questioning about clock hours and resorts to a curious set of images to communicate his temporal experience.

> There's this line in [the movie] *Fight Club* where Brad Pitt says, "When you have insomnia, you're never really asleep and you're never really awake." And I think about that a lot. In this job, you're never really working and you're never really not working. It's hard to say what's working and what's not. I mean, I'm not a coal miner.

Brent's working life feels like a state of insomnia—that frustratingly liminal space and seemingly endless time between sleep and alertness. To contrast his experience with something else, he alights on an image of work that, in his mind, has a more traditional temporal structure—coal mining. Knowledge work versus hard manual labor. Insomniac hours versus shift work. These distinctions in Brent's imagination capture an implicit awareness that I repeatedly observed among financial professionals from many different areas of the industry: however you want to characterize their temporal existence, it is not normal.

The abnormal timescapes that financial professionals experience are the product of financialization. In its most specific sense, financialization means a shift in the center of gravity of capitalism from more traditional channels of economic growth, such as trade and commodity production, to financial channels—the use of financial instruments and a vastly expanded financial services industry (Calhoun 2013; Krippner 2011). This transformation is one of the core features of the flexible economy (Hutton and Giddens 2000; Sennett 2006). Consumers are now "confronted on a daily basis with new financial products and financial 'literacy' is touted as a core competency" (Krippner 2005:173–174). As a result, financial knowledge has risen from a culturally illegitimate form of knowledge, used primarily for speculation, to one of the most professionalized and highly valued forms of knowledge in contemporary societies (Preda 2009). The advisory services in large commercial banks, the main peddlers of financial knowledge to the business world, have gained greater influence because of this shift. They have grown in number due in large part to massive deregulation in the 1970s, '80s, and '90s, which allowed banks to engage in previously restricted activities, such as underwriting securities (Calhoun 2013; Krippner 2011). As I explore below, a concrete micro-level effect of this trend has been an increase in the "preciousness" of financial professionals' time. Not only is their time highly rewarded economically, but also it is culturally marked as important.

While I will analyze financialization in this specific economic sense, I will also consider it in a more general sense. We can think of the epoch of financialization in terms of the rise of social practices with a unique cultural logic that may or may not apply specifically to economic activity (Jones 2014). Financialization in this sense is characterized by two practices: disembedding and abstraction (Giddens 1990). These practices, especially common among financial professionals who trade securities in the public markets, are connected to the rise of a different kind of financial speculation, known as "quantitative finance" (Bernstein 2005). Quantitative finance relies on complex mathematical modeling, powerful computers, and a new style of "digital deal room," and thus champions a different kind of trader—more scientist than gambler (Zaloom 2006). As Daniel Buenza and David Stark (2005:91) note, "Whereas traders in the 1980s ... were characterized by their riches, bravado, and little regard for small investors," the quantitative traders of today "have MBA degrees in finance, PhDs in physics and statistics, and are more appropriately thought of as engineers. None of them wears suspenders." This new breed of trader, then, is cultivating a different set of habits and skills that are adaptable to the highly abstract and technical forms of trading that dominate today's deal rooms.

In this chapter, I explore how different types of financial professionals experience financialization within their particular timescapes. This task is anything but straightforward. The rhythms of financial work can differ considerably by organizational type, such as between an investment bank and a private equity firm. They can also differ within an organization, such as between the Mergers & Acquisitions (M&A) arm and a trading desk of a large investment bank. But they can even vary a great deal within a single work team, such as between senior and junior personnel in an M&A group, or between a trader and a managing director in a trading group. In short, depending on where an individual worker is located in the complex network of positions that make up the myriad operations of the financial services industry, he or she could experience dramatically different timescapes.

How can we make sense of this complexity? The most significant difference in temporal experience discussed by the respondents I talked to was between those whose work involves "deals" and those whose work involves the "public markets." Dealmakers are involved in managing a large financial object or process, like a huge issuance of stock in an initial public offering (IPO), the acquisition of one company by another (M&A), or the acquisition of capital to facilitate a high dollar purchase. Deals are typically worked by those in "indirect finance," such as the M&A division of an investment bank. Those who work in the public markets, by contrast, buy or sell publicly traded securities (stocks, bonds, derivatives, futures, etc.). The public markets are covered by those in "direct finance," such as financial research firms, sales and trading divisions within investment banks, other asset management firms, and even individual traders who work independently of a company. How do these two broad types of workers differently experience the temporalities of financialization?

DEAL TIME

Deal-oriented financial professionals are essentially knowledge salespeople. Perhaps more accurately put, they sell their attention to powerful corporate (and occasionally very wealthy individual) investors who need knowledgeable advice and business connections to become a publicly traded company, merge with or acquire a competitor, raise capital for a new venture, or make some other major financial move with the help of an intermediary who can lower transaction costs and diffuse risk. They make money largely from the commissions they charge clients on successful deals. Financial advisors' specialized attention is often seen by clients to be irreplaceable. Their time, therefore, is treated as precious. It is common knowledge among investment bankers that, if they become involved in an M&A transaction, for example, it is difficult and undesirable to hand tasks off to another worker mid-deal, even if he or she is equally qualified, because getting this new worker up to speed on a complex transaction of this kind would not only slow down the transaction, but potentially spook would-be investors. Once a dealmaker is in a deal, then, she becomes an irreplaceable part of that transaction, even if other parts of her life need some of that attention.

A common experience for the dealmakers I spoke to is a feeling of being always "on." This mechanistic metaphor, no doubt familiar to many elite knowledge workers, captures the contradictory experience of temporal control they encounter when interacting with demanding clients. On the one hand, because their employers see them as skilled professionals, they can basically work when and where they want as long as the job gets done. They have "flexible" work schedules, in the sense of being able to customize the rhythms of work. On the other hand, because clients see their attention as so precious, dealmakers actually experience very little *meaningful* control over their time. Though they often have the freedom to work when and where they want, the intense expectations to close a deal no matter what it takes encourages them to work constantly. They typically cue their movements more to clients' requests, rather than setting their own pacing and sequencing to the day. No one is necessarily telling them to work constantly, then, but the implicit expectation is always hanging over them.

Above all, being always "on" leads to chronic desynchronization from the normative clock and calendar rhythms of nine-to-five, Monday-to-Friday. This is in large part because deals have their own intrinsic, non-chronologically based temporality. Deals have stages. In the case of investment banking, these stages include creating marketing materials, doing financial modeling, pitching to buyers, and negotiating the terms of a final agreement. Workers are far more keyed to the actions necessary to complete each phase of a deal than to a traditional clock and calendar-based schedule. Dealmakers, in other words, work on "deal time." Their actions, attention, and energy are marshaled according to the tempo, sequence, articulation, and duration of the stages of making a deal.

Kathleen, a 52-year-old senior manager at a small boutique advising firm, says of her job, "I'm basically in the kind of job where you're pretty much on call and available most of the time if there's something going on." As Kathleen indicates, because they live in a state of constant availability, many respondents could not give a straightforward answer about how many hours a week they work. All deal-oriented respondents reported large fluctuations in the start and end times of their days. When asked about her weekly hours, Kathleen, responded,

> It has really varied a lot over the years. I mean, in the past, it's been over 100 hours a week at times. Well, I think it's a little—I think right now, it's a little

bit harder to say because my schedule is varying a lot, but I tend to work—I don't work like 9-to-5. I don't have the kind of job where you have a time you have to be there and a time you have to leave, so I typically work anywhere from eight to ten hours a day, or so.

Kathleen has difficulty describing her week in terms of the duration of clock hours. All she knows is that she does not have any guarantees about when work will end, and she does not work a "9-to-5," signaling the trope of a traditional employment timescape.

Unpredictable long hours that are desynchronized from the clock and weekly cycle particularly affect junior-level workers, such as analysts in an investment banking group, because they are on the bottom of the chain of command within a deal group and have the least temporal control. They are given less control over the decision-making that sets a particular deadline and must therefore react to others' movements. As one former junior analyst in an investment bank noted, "My friends would ask, 'What do you do every-day?' I'd say I come to work and I wait for stuff to happen, and it always does."

Casey, a 25-year-old MBA student, recalled that there were certainly times when her schedule felt manageable working as an analyst in an M&A group.

> But the hard part about that is, it was just hard to predict, so you never really know when your night or your weekend is gonna get blown up. I definitely had weeks, or days at a time where I could leave by dinnertime or so . . . and then it would go back to the 2 a.m. nights and stuff, and it was just kind of unpredict-able in that way.

Casey describes a particularly extreme example of this kind of unpredict-ability. She recalls working three final transactions, or "live deals," at the same time as she was helping senior personnel with pitching new business to potential clients.

> I guess we were working on three live deals at once [. . .] and we were finishing up around like 10 or 11—I'm sorry, maybe it was more like end of the day, end of the main workday, so it might've been like 6. I'm with my boss. We were doing kind of a final turn at the document and he has lots and lots of changes to make, so we're thinking, "Oh, gosh, this is gonna take a while," and then, so I started to make the changes.
> [. . .] So, the associate and I, the person above me, ended up being there until—he probably left at like 2 in the morning. I left at 4 in the morning, and some point between like 6 p.m. and this time I realized that I actually had to travel the next day. [. . .] So, I finish up around 4 in the morning, and you have to print the books, bind them, do all that stuff.

I went home and showered and then went straight to the airport. So, I hadn't slept at this point [laughter]. So, I'm at the airport, nervous, this is one of the first times I've traveled with my bosses and everything. We spent the whole day either in airports traveling to the prospective client's site, going to the meeting, and so then probably got back around 5, 6 the next day. So, I still hadn't slept at this point and then had more work to do when I got back. So that would probably be like the extreme worst-case scenario.

The way Casey uses clock time to narrate her story is telling. In a curious turn of phrase, she obliquely refers to the normative 9-to-5 work cycle as "the end of the main work day, so it might've been like 6," before she goes on to describe the rest of the deal, which then extended into another full "day" of work. Clock hours are not used as a precise measure of duration—as a way to communicate how many hours she worked during this deal. Rather, they are essentially used as a convenient language for placing the different "beats" of the rhythm of deal making.

New Temporal Languages

Dealmakers frequently resorted to using creative language to describe the timescapes of their work when the language of clock hours became inadequate. Kathleen, for example, described her work using the word "flow."

> I think you have to be able to handle a lot of things coming at you at once [in this job], or you really couldn't function. [. . .] That isn't necessarily the amount of time you're working, it's just more the workflow itself.
>
> *That's interesting . . . it sounds like you're more concerned about, or tuned into the kind of intensity or flow of the work. Is that right?*
>
> Yeah, and I think you just—hours is completely independent of that.

Kathleen differentiates "workflow" from "hours," noting that the way work tasks move is salient to her emotional experience independently of how many clock hours have passed. I then volunteer the term "intensity," which Kathleen agrees is an accurate representation of the flow of her work. I pressed Kathleen further:

> How would you characterize that intense flow? What is it that makes it intense?
>
> The volume, and the—yeah, the volume, and then the urgency, and also the importance of a lot of what you're doing. I compare it to when you go to a hospital. They don't work with anything near the level of urgency that we would

work with. It's the importance of the patients getting the right medicine, or the doctor following up on this, that, or the other. That is nowhere near the level of urgency and attention that people put on big business deals.

See, that's almost shocking to me. You would think it would be the other way around, right? [Doctors] have people's lives on their hands.

You'd be fired if you [worked like] most of the doctors and nurses in a hospital.

When pressed to describe "flow," Kathleen first notes that the volume of work is important—how many tasks she has to complete within a particular span of time. "I could have four people standing outside my office waiting to come in, one at a time," she notes later. "At the same time, you've got two conference calls on the phone . . . It's like triage." Beyond volume, however, she discusses the central importance of the urgency of work tasks by invoking the metaphor of a hospital. Kathleen adamantly insists that the degree of importance placed on the types of decisions she is expected to make feels higher than the life-or-death decisions made by doctors and nurses. Kathleen continues,

> It's basically when you're dealing with lots of money, people that pay lots of money, people that have lots of money at stake, that's what drives the expectations. Remember, you're dealing with highly educated people. These are well-paid jobs and the expectations, or the standards are very, very high. But it is because you're dealing with money. That's important [laughs]. We, as a society— money is still valued. It's clearly valued more than people.

The urgency of dealmaking is produced by the preciousness with which high-paying clients treat dealmakers' attention. Many financial intermediary firms make their revenue on just a few major deals per year, so, as Kathleen notes, the money riding on a single deal drives expectations to remarkable heights, especially during the closing moments when months of negotiation are coming to a head.

Tom, a highly successful head of a private equity group in a large investment bank, corroborated Kathleen's insights about the relationship between prestige, money, and urgency, but made it more clear how this urgency shapes temporality.

> When you're in live deal mode . . . a well-identified transaction time is of the essence. Every day is valuable. You're literally doing work to go back to the client and refresh their thinking and your advice to them. [. . .]
>
> *I want to see if you can take me inside that more. What's the mood or what is the feeling like during those particularly fast-paced, intense moments when you're working that many hours? Is there something that triggers your memory there?*

I think during those times there has to be a deep sense that this is normal or at least that you're not the only one doing this, first of all. I think that's pretty important that you sense that this is something that's quite normal. [...] The only thing that comes close to this would be something like a military operation. There's a mission. Every minute is valuable. And so sleep gets pushed to the side. You need to get something done. Sometimes it has sort of militaristic elements to it. It can be a hostile takeover, for example. One company is launching some sort of hostile takeover of another company, or your client is sort of defending himself from a hostile takeover to evaluate different options. It has very much that project or even mission-like feel to it.

The pressure there is partly because of what's on the line?

[...] Billions of dollars on the line. That's why you get rich people, even senior investment bankers, corporate lawyers, to make themselves uncomfortable. Because you literally got many, many millions of dollars on the line in fees that motivate them to do things that would otherwise be unnatural acts. Like staying until ungodly hours doing this work. The economic incentives are there. [...] Not having been in the military, it's what you imagine the military to be like. It's well supported with a very well defined mission that you need to execute through thick or thin. It's interesting that you've got, say, a little bit of a head cold, but if you don't work through this . . .

Tom trails off mid-sentence, realizing that his war metaphor is getting stretched thin. Having "a little bit of head cold" is not exactly comparable to the strain of combat. He continues,

At some point you have to draw the line [on this analogy].

You're not falling down dead or something.

Exactly, the analogy breaks down. But, what I'm saying is, it's mission critical, you've got a high level of stress, and you've got a key role to play that cannot be really filled by anybody else once you're in that seat, or it cannot be filled as well by anybody once you're in that seat. It's intense.

Tom attempts to take me inside the timescape of his work and finds that he can only do so by invoking a (somewhat strained) metaphor that is similar to Kathleen's—the military operation. Like soldiers (or at least how an investment banker imagines soldiers to be), deal-making groups feel the urgency of a transaction as a kind of mission that they will do anything to complete. He notes that money is the central motivator during live deals and that the weight of money creates intensity in the form of a heightened attention and a feeling of urgency. Money can provoke, in Tom's words, even "rich people" to make themselves "uncomfortable" and do "unnatural" things. Consequently, traditional temporal patterns, such as sleeping at night and working during the day, or working in predictable shifts, get "pushed to the side."

The most curious word in Tom's explanation, then, is "normal." During work intensifications, one must summon the conviction that "this is normal." Entertaining the opposite makes one less capable of continuing through the night. Triage and military metaphors are helpful in this regard. They draw on the meanings of the emergency room and the battlefield to justify pushing ones' body and mind past points one might normally go for the acquisition of things like money and customer satisfaction. As Eve Chiapello and Norman Fairclough (2002:186) note, "In many ways, capitalism is an absurd system: [...] capitalists ... find themselves chained to a never-ending and insatiable process." As a result, capitalists must find some means of generating internal commitment— what Max Weber called a "spirit" of capitalism. Associating deal time with the temporality of triage and war is the spirit of financial capitalism for the respondents I talked to. It seems to provide them with a readymade justificatory language for generating this sense of commitment to a radically disrupted temporality in which "normal" forms of time get pushed to the side. So, as much as dealmakers claim that money is the sole motivator of these periods of intensification, we in fact see them drawing on other non-economic cultural spheres to generate commitment to such an unusual experience of time. These spheres share with finance a similarly urgent temporality in which "time is of the essence" and the individual actor is compelled to put aside normalcy and personal comfort for the sake of a higher goal.

In sum, the timescapes of dealmaking disrupt what workers think of as a more normal temporality because of the perceived preciousness of their time from demanding clients. Deals involve wild swings between desynchronization, unification, and crisis that are brought on by clients' intense needs to complete timely transactions. Long stretches of uneventful pitches, for example, which involve multitasking among sometimes incredibly boring activities, like fixing the font on a spreadsheet and answering dozens of emails, can be punctuated by the high stakes mini-drama of closing a deal. Whether they go well or poorly, deals allow for the merging together of the workgroup into a battle weary but noble band of survivors. To make sense of these wild swings, and to justify the incredible personal commitment they require, dealmakers translate the "abnormal" temporalities of finance into a more recognizable form by associating them with more familiar timescapes, such as battles and emergencies.

It is important to note, however, that the disrupted timescape of deal-making emerges from what looks like a workplace that gives a lot of control over time to the worker. Individuals can generally work when and where they want. This highly flexible workplace, however, masks the intense expectations from needy clients that actually shape the timescape (Blair-Loy 2009). Dealmakers can work when and where they want, but clients demand they work all the time, in London one day and New York the next, because they need to achieve "good timing." They need to capitalize on opportunities to close a deal while they last. The flexible timescapes of financial capitalism, then, manifest on the ground among dealmakers as unpredictable urgency that demands they adapt to wild swings between boredom, crisis, and sublime achievement.

MARKET TIME

Most mid-level employees who work in the public markets, such as analysts and traders, do not sell their attention to time-hungry clients, as is the case with dealmakers.[1] Rather, market workers are engendered to interact with the complex and often mystifying movements of "the market." More accurately put, they are required to interact with digital representations of other market-oriented workers who are also (it is assumed) interacting with the same set of digital representations of market activity.

Unlike deal time, then, what I will call "market time" is the timescape created by the cycles of a particular market. It is composed of rhythms nested within rhythms. On the level of the year, markets tend to fluctuate into more and less active months. As Don, a bond trader in his forties mentioned, "Over the years I've learned that the market gives you time, and you have to take it when it is given. You can't fight the market. It's a bear, and it will bite you if you try to go against it." I asked him to clarify what he means by the market "giving you time." He replied,

> There are certain times of the year when—if you try to take a vacation or something, it is practically impossible. If you try to get away in May or September, the market will keep drawing you back in because there is just so much going on. So, you gotta take vacations when the market gives you time, like in August or January.

1. There are exceptions to this. Sales desks within "sell side" trading operations have a lot of client contact. Also, managers on the "buy side" have a lot of client contact when they are pitching portfolios to existing clients or convincing new clients to let them manage their money.

Nested within this yearly cycle, is a daily cycle constituted by the specific time window of the financial exchange in which one's work resides. Most financial market work in the United States, for example, occurs between 9:30 a.m. and 4 p.m. Eastern Standard Time. Clock and calendar times thus have somewhat more relevance to those working in the public markets than dealmakers because, with some exceptions, once the exchange in which one is trading has closed, there are relatively few "live" tasks left to complete.[2]

On an even smaller scale, market time is also colored by the rhythms of different types of securities. Traders working in over-the-counter derivatives, for example, might only book one or two trades per day while currency traders might execute hundreds.

That the experience of market time is different from deal time became readily apparent to me when I asked market workers how many hours a week they work. They could not only answer with ease, but virtually all respondents gave the same answer, give or take a few hours. Most reported coming to work "about 7" in the morning and leaving "about 6 or 7" in the evening. Traders are also expected to engage in professional networking outside of market hours a few times a week—typically going to dinner with colleagues. Aside from business dinners, then, most reported sending a few emails at night and perhaps reading a few business-related reports or pieces of news, but nothing near the extent of weekend and night work reported by dealmakers.

Still, an 11 or 12-hour workday plus, for traders, a few hours at a business dinner is certainly a long day by many Americans' standards. Much to my surprise, the duration of work was the least of market workers' complaints. In fact, many I interviewed reported that a predictable 11- or 12-hour day seemed like a blessing. This makes sense when we understand the frame of reference for their assessment of a good schedule. Most market-oriented professionals have either worked in a more deal-oriented position or have colleagues and friends who work in those types of positions. Many also have friends or spouses who work in other time hungry professions, like corporate law or medicine. Compared to the unpredictable, marathon workdays they see there, market-oriented workers' schedules are easy.

2. This is changing as I write. Exchanges are increasingly opening up to Extended Hours Trading (EHT)—trading that occurs outside the time window of the major exchanges. As of this writing, EHT is seen as a somewhat riskier timeframe for trading. Nevertheless, the rise of EHT points to the possibility that clock hours are becoming increasingly irrelevant to market workers who could, in theory, trade in any of the major exchanges at any time of day.

Nick, a 47-year-old project manager in a large investment bank, notes that his 55- to 60-hour workweek, "doesn't really feel like a lot. [...] Because I have kids, I sort of benchmark it by that—if I'm seeing my kids in the morning, I'm seeing them at night pretty regularly through the week, then 11 or 12 hours at the office does not feel like a stretch for me." He continues, "Now if somebody says, 'Gosh, that's a lot of hours,' I'm like, really? [...] For me it feels like—I really have the luxury of having my cake and eating it too." Nick means that, for a job with the kind of salary that his provides, he is lucky to be able to see his kids at all, let alone twice a day. "So you sort of say, 'Well, like if I can actually get this kind of comp, and still get to see my kids a lot during the week ... it's pretty hard to argue with that combination.'"

Though market-oriented financial professionals did not report problems surrounding the duration of work, other dimensions of time in their work environment certainly did feel problematic. Elizabeth, a 32-year-old MBA student, worked as a sales analyst on a trading floor in a large Wall Street investment bank for three years in her late twenties. When I talked to her, she was completing her MBA after a short detour trying to start her own clothing label. She recalls the schedule she kept while working on the trading floor with mixed emotions.

> The hours were fine. [...] That being said, I think that the—whatever it is, 10 and a half to 11 hours a day, understates a little bit what the day actually felt like sometimes. [...] In terms of actual time commitment, I don't think it was necessarily excessive, but from an energy commitment, that was certainly a lot more.

As I heard from many other market workers, the number of hours one spent in, for example, a deal room is a poor way to describe the subjective experience of work time. Clock hour allocation and physical energy expenditure should not be conflated. Elizabeth continues,

> I mean you basically, from the moment that you get there at 7 in the morning ... you are really expected from the second that you walk in the door—I mean, there were definitely days I would walk around the corner to be walking to my desk, just from the door [of the elevator], and you'd already have people screaming at you to call certain clients and do certain things and—especially when there was news. I lived through some relatively insane markets too, so the emotional swings throughout the day—you really have to be on all the time.

Elizabeth describes the energy commitment of the job in terms of feeling constantly "on." But she seems to mean something different from what dealmakers mean by "on." Even though she could predictably leave work at a reasonable hour, unlike many of her colleagues in investment banking, this relief was nearly outweighed by the temporal *density* of work tasks. She notes, "You can't leave for lunch. You can go get food quickly, but you're pretty much chained to your desk for that particular time. You have to be able to keep up with the traders. You have to be able to disseminate information quickly—sort of be ready for anything." Elizabeth invokes a common theme among market-oriented respondents I talked to: working in the public markets requires remarkable skills of concentration because of the sheer volume of tasks required during market hours. Maintaining this penetrating focus for 11 or 12 hours can be exhausting.

Bill, a 62 year-old veteran asset manager working for a wealthy Louisiana family, corroborated Elizabeth's assessment of the job's intensity. When I asked him, "How many hours a week do you think you work?" Bill sidestepped the question entirely. "That's an interesting question," he replied, "because here's the thing: It's like being a fireman. You don't go to too many fires, but you have to be ready for any fires at all times." Again, while being "on" for dealmakers referred to the intense duration, irregularity, and urgency of time, then, being "on" for market workers seems to refer to the intense density of time—the notion that energy and attention must be compressed into a small window of opportunity for profit. Time is shaped not necessarily by clients' demands, then, but by the fact that "fires"—that is, emergency situations—breaking out in the market must be dealt with within a fixed temporal window (market hours). Having a more fixed schedule frees market workers from the strains of a fuzzy work/non-work boundary but in the process compresses the intensity of work into a smaller space.

Despite these small differences, both dealmakers and market workers seem to be discussing a similar overall texture to social time: wild fluctuations between desynchronization, unification, and crisis. In fact, they never discussed moments of simple, unremarkable, functional synchronization. In the case of market work, these fluctuations are brought on by an almost paranoid anxiety about bad timing—the imperative to maintain vigilant attention in order to pounce on narrow windows of opportunity. When the market is slow, work can involve long stretches of chaotic multitasking, such as continually updating one's view of a digital space with few opportunities for profit while taking calls from colleagues, instant messaging, and answering emails. When things pick up and are going in one's favor, market time invites moments of compelling unification in the form of a flurry of lucrative trades that invite one into an absorbing flow state. And when things fall apart, market time creates the conditions for crisis. Both groups of workers, then, reach for the semiotics of cataclysm to make sense of and justify financialized time. Given the extensively male dominated nature of finance, it is not surprising that this semiotics is also hyper-masculine. Triage, battle, and firefighting frame the desynchronization-unification-crisis dynamic with meanings that are recognizable and ennobling, and that also reinforce the gendered nature of financial time.

THE TECHNOLOGY OF MARKET TIME

The financialization of time is not only the result of the rising power of financial services but also stems from a set of cultural practices that have grown up around the digital exchange of financial instruments in the new era of quantitative finance (Zaloom 2006). The effects of these techno-logical innovations on work temporality are difficult to observe simply by listening to the way financial professionals talk *about* their jobs because they are so deeply embodied and habitual. Examining the more subcon-scious, corporal dimension of financialization, then, requires me to look more closely at the physical and cognitive tasks needed to work with the technologies of today's "digital deal room," which involves using comput-ers, paper, telephones, and the other apparatuses of trading. Following this line of thought, I will consider the notion of financialization in terms of two essential cultural practices: disembedding and abstraction. They are responsible for producing social time in the deal room and reveal some crucial insights into how financial capitalism influences cognition and emotion.

Disembedding

Disembedding is a term coined by Anthony Giddens (1990) to capture the ways in which globalized social relations and social action are increasingly oriented to extra-local networks of interaction. Globalization, Giddens claims, means that individuals' daily activities are increasingly subject to influences that are stretched over large distances and long times. Market workers' workplaces are a prime example of this. Though they physically exist in a local context—such as lower Manhattan—the activities going on there are oriented primarily to processes happening across the globe. During the epoch of financialization, financial markets have taken on a more and more global scope (French, Leyshon, and Wainwright 2011; Knorr Cetina 2007; Leyshon and Thrift 1997; Sassen 2001). As Karin Knorr

Cetina (2007:7) notes, "The financial system can arguably be considered a structure of the world rather than of national societies." Financial markets are concentrated in global centers, such as New York, London, and Tokyo, "that are interconnected across time zones and continents." Since the global debt crisis that swept the world's major economies after 2008, the debt and equity markets have only become more global, requiring traders and analysts to keep track of many more processes that are stretched over larger tracts of time-space. When market actors make decisions to buy or sell a security in the contemporary financial economy, then, they typically do so with an image in mind (and on screen) of other actors spread across the globe.

The older and more experienced traders I spoke to seemed to have the most awareness of this shift toward the global within their particular market sector. Chuck, for example, a high-yield bonds trader in his mid forties, made explicit mention of the word globalization without prompting from me. When I asked him how things have changed since he first started trading bonds in the late 1990s, he reflected, "Because of globalization, I think, we pay more attention to so many more different things. The world of high yield bonds used to be mostly high yield bonds market driven. But now, we are looking at, for example, Spanish debt, or the German Ten-Year Bond." Even within Chuck's fifteen years as a bond trader, he has noticed a distinct shift toward a more global perspective. He also notes, however, that the source of this shift is difficult to pinpoint. "It's funny though. I mean, it has kind of become a self-fulfilling prophecy. Traders look at all of this stuff [global financial data] because it matters, but it matters because traders look at it."

Bill, a 64-year-old asset manager who specializes in the bond market, had an even greater awareness of an increasingly disembedded workplace, given his nearly 30 years of experience. He tied this transformation to technology.

How much does distance or space matter to you in your work?

Is that metaphoric?

I think I mean literal distance and space.

None.

None? Okay. Why? [He holds up his phone]. Because of that—your phone?

The tech stuff, all of it: iPads, phones, computers. You can be anywhere. [. . .] You can be on a boat, on a mountaintop, anywhere.

Bill's initial response to my question about space is telling. His implicit understanding is that space could mean either an actual physical distance or something more abstract. In terms of the former meaning, space matters little because he can observe the market from anywhere with an Internet connection. However, I then asked Bill about the latter meaning of space as "metaphoric." By metaphoric, Bill says he means "cultural distance."

Cultural distance is important?

That's a very important investment.

Yeah? So, when you interact with, like, Japanese markets, you have—

Oh, my goodness, yeah. Because you think a certain way, and particularly in a non-Western culture, you better be trying to get into the mindset of those investors. Because at the end of the day, with any investment product, you might say, you're looking for somebody else to pay you more for it. Somebody else is going to bid it up knowing what your price is, and what would make them do that is part of the analysis.

"Metaphorical" distance seems to have more salience for Bill than actual physical distance. As a trader who takes positions in several different exchanges, such as the Tokyo Stock Exchange, Bill may not be aware of the physical distance between his office in Louisiana and Tokyo, but he is highly aware of the many local factors that might influence Japanese investors, and thus Bill's positions in Japanese debt securities.

Let me give you a glimpse, then, into the types of "disembedded thoughts" that go on in Bill's mind as he contemplates buying or selling Japanese debt. A few months before I talked to him, the coast of Japan had been struck by a tsunami that destroyed a nuclear power plant, triggering one of the worst nuclear disasters in history. I asked Bill what that day was like for him sitting in his office in Louisiana.

A typical day is that I might start looking at the markets at seven in the morning and just see what happened over in Europe, in Asia, so on and so forth. You kind of check that off—nothing happened. Well, one morning: boom, there's a tsunami in Japan. How bad is it? The news usually unfolds in that case kind of slowly because no one is really sure.

Then comes this nuclear reactor stuff. At first, oh, so what? Some houses got knocked down; tsunamis happen. But the nuclear thing and the power outage and the lack of power production, that goes on for a long time. In that case it was really just seeing what are the effects of this, and so your wheels start to turn. How does this run down the line—effect the things [trades] we have on, and what even might be ways to take advantage of it?

At this point, Bill begins to inundate me with facts and figures about Japan. I have a hard time keeping up, and begin to feel like Charlie Brown listening to his teachers' disembodied squawking voice.

> Japan already has one of the worst fiscal situations in the world . . . debt exceeds GDP by more than . . . that does not count unfunded liabilities like pensions and social security . . . low birth rate, only like 1.1 child per . . . Japan is also very, very sectarian . . . almost xenophobic in their investment culture . . . their five year JGBs yield about 50 basis points . . . yen is really at fairly high levels . . .

After several minutes of analysis, Bill continues,

> That's the backdrop for: Along comes a wall of water. How it runs down the line in my thinking is that they're going to have to do a major rebuilding project here, and where are they going to get the funds? You're just about at the equilibrium level now where the big pension funds are starting to sell. They're not savers anymore; they're spenders because of the baby boomers retiring. That's when we put on some trades that would take advantage of Japan's negative fiscal situation.

In one sense, Bill has cultivated extensive knowledge of how his financial actions are embedded in a local context—Japan's demographics, economics, history, and even some cultural proclivities. In another sense, his knowledge of this embeddedness is expressed almost entirely in disembedded abstractions—rates, ratios, averages, and other statistics, as well as a blunt understanding of Japanese investors as "xenophobic." Through the abstract language of numbers and stereotypes, Bill's disembedded cognitions of the flow of debt around the Japanese economy can become re-embedded from a distance, allowing him to "look in" on Japan while keeping it at arm's length.

Abstraction

Abstraction goes hand-in-hand with a disembedded workplace. An abstraction is something that does not have a physical existence. It is a knowledge object that can be considered apart from the world of concrete entities, though it may refer to, or may have at one time referred to, that concrete world. Abstractions are the primary drivers of disembedding because in order to conduct oneself in a delocalized action environment, one must learn to interact with and have deep trust in the reality of things that are occurring in another room or on the other side of the planet (there is little difference) and therefore cannot be directly apprehended by the senses (Giddens 1990). Abstractions are the foundation upon which market time is built.

Financial instruments—stocks, bonds, futures, options, spots, swaps, and the like, as well as other types of financial data, such as a research report on a company's capital structure—are abstract in at least two ways. First, unlike traditional production markets, the objects of financial markets are (and are increasingly) decoupled from concrete economic objects in the world—for example, a company (Buenza and Stark 2005). As Alex Preda (2009:53) notes, "Financial markets are a second order construction, based on the observation of producer markets. Yet, since financial actors primarily observe each other, they monitor only internally generated (or second order) representations of producer markets." Financial data (including financial instruments) are representations of other financial actors' representations of the real objects and activities that make up production markets (i.e., the entities producing things in the economy). The "objects" of the financial economy, then, are related to the world of concrete entities only obliquely. They are second-order (even third- and fourth-order) abstractions, thus creating a kind of abstract "financial economy" that hovers above and indirectly refers to the "real economy." This economy of representations has become the most important space of economic growth for many of the world's powerful companies (Krippner 2005).

The primary representations of objects in the real economy that feed into an initial picture of the financial economy for market workers are typically produced by intermediary groups, such as securities analysts, whose job it is to tell those working in the public markets "what's going on out there." They do this primarily by publishing research reports on particular sectors of production markets, which are then (at least in theory) read by investors (Preda 2009:54). Analysts are often found working right alongside traders and managers in trading groups, but there are also entire firms solely dedicated to producing real-time and in-depth financial data for other firms and individuals to use in making their investment decisions.

Financial data are abstract in a second sense: *as objects*, they have an insubstantial material manifestation. As Knorr Cetina (2007:6) notes, financial instruments "may not even be pieces of paper, but merely an entry in the books of relevant parties." If there is a sense in which financial instruments have a material manifestation, then, it would be pixels. Since roughly the 1980s, when the epoch of financialization began to accelerate, traders have interacted with the market predominantly through computer screens. Prior to computer trading, most financial instruments were exchanged face-to-face. In the case of exchange trading, for example, traders physically assembled in so called "open-outcry" trading "pits" and shouted bid and ask prices to one another (Zaloom 2006).[3] Open outcry pits are basically gone. The vast majority of markets are now conducted in office buildings in large "deal rooms" or "trading desks" within high-rises in the major global financial centers. Rather than shout and gesture to a co-present person, traders today now use phones, chat applications, and specialized proprietary trading software to see, hear, and feel what other actors are doing in the market.

The Digital Deal Room

How does this disembedded and abstracted workplace shape the experience of time? In order to take a closer look, I observed the trading floor of one of the world's most powerful asset management firms. I primarily observed two groups of "buy side" debt traders—a high yield group (focused on debt securities with a low credit rating—often called "junk bonds") and a distressed debt group (focused on debt securities from entities that have filed or are about to file for bankruptcy). These are high risk, high reward financial instruments that are popular in leveraged finance portfolios. Large institutional investors, like pensions and mutual funds, invest in these portfolios and ask firms like the one I observed to manage that process. In order to make money for these investors, then, the traders I observed are primarily responsible, not for interacting with investors, but for managing the risk-return ratios of the firm's portfolios.

Like most bond traders, these traders operate in an over-the-counter (OTC) style of trading. That is, they do not trade directly on one of the major financial exchanges, such as the NASDAQ, a style known as exchange trading, but trade "internally" among a more exclusive network of dealers and brokers located in multiple geographic locations and connected by a digital trading system. If all this sounds complicated. It is. In my experience, without developing a more advanced understanding of financial capitalism in general, it was difficult to understand even basic things about traders, such as where they work, with whom they are interacting, and what they are actually doing at a given moment.

---

3. In the case of OTC trading, networks of traders and brokers talked to one another on the phone. Traders worked alongside traders' assistants, who ran calculations on paper and shouted bid and ask prices over a microphone (Bernstein 2005).

The whole situation becomes easier to understand, however, when we simply describe what can be seen with the naked eye. The deal room I observed occupies an entire floor, approximately 50 yards by 20 yards, in a modern New York City high rise. It is filled with workstations. There are no cubicles and only a few short dividers separating major blocks of traders. Each row on the trading floor is composed of a desk, approximately 20 to 30 feet long, which features about 6 workstations. The stations are very close together, giving each trader roughly four feet of personal workspace. Teams of traders typically sit together in these rows.

What was most arresting to me about seeing a deal room is precisely how normal it looks. Aside from the fact that there are more computer monitors per capita than most offices, the deal room essentially looks like any other open plan professional workplace. Traders work in relatively intimate, face-to-face conditions, which facilitate verbal communication among members of the trading group. As Don put it,

> That's why this trading floor is so open-air. That way when Steve or Chuck is getting killed, I'll know about it. I don't need to remember or be prompted to go over and ask them, because I can just hear it in their voices. So, hearing that tells me that I should be paying attention to certain things in my area [of the bond market] that might be affecting them in their area.

As Don indicates, the underlying logic of the digital deal room as a workspace is to facilitate a kind of group mind, which allows greater sharing of information and the tighter coordination of decisions. Perhaps ironically, then, this disembedded and abstracted form of trading, so different from the old open-outcry style in many ways, still relies on timeless things like physically co-present bodies and voices to be effective.

Each trader's workstation features a telephone, a bank of three computer screens that surround the trader in a slight arc, and a keyboard.[4] Traders organized their computer desktops slightly differently, but the content of the desktops is much the same from trader to trader. This firm operates on the Bloomberg Professional Service, a state-of-the-art software and hardware system, which many of the leading financial firms lease from the Bloomberg Corporation. "The Bloomberg," as traders sometimes refer to it, provides streams of real-time financial data on any financial instrument

---

4. Analysts, by contrast, tended to have two screens rather than three, reflecting the comparatively smaller number of applications needed at any one time to conduct their work. The number of screens at one's workstation is also seen as a kind of status symbol. A stereotype in the trading world is the hotshot trader surrounded needlessly by ten screens just to convey how big his—ahem—account is.

from any company in any country in the world. It also gathers financial news from hundreds of information sources—newspapers, television broadcasts, the myriad indices of various exchanges, etc.—and allows users to search this stream of information using keywords. Users can also assemble a list of securities that they are either currently trading or are interested in trading, thus allowing them to compose a targeted picture of the market. The system also allows traders to communicate through instant message with any other Bloomberg user anywhere in the world.

These services are integrated with many other applications that one would find on a common personal computer, such as Excel, email, and a calendar application, but also with a set of specialized software applications designed in-house by the firms' information technology department, which occupies a floor of a high rise next door. Rather than get tools from someone else's workshop to do some of the core functions of trading, then, this firm has designed its own tools that can be tweaked and refined as the business and the market change.

Traders run all of these trading and communications applications simultaneously, distributing them across the three screens in front of them as they see fit. At the same time, they place and receive calls on a multi-line telephone, which allows them to communicate verbally with brokers on the "sell side" of the market and other traders and analysts outside the firm. On top of all this highly customized text and audio information, the trading floor is also equipped with televisions tuned to various financial news broadcasts, which allow traders to see important news developments, such as speeches by the Federal Reserve chairman. Lastly, traders are provided with hundreds of pages of research and analysis by the army of securities analysts assigned to each trading desk, most of whom are recent graduates from prestigious universities. For all the emphasis on the digitization of financial markets, then, I was surprised to see that most traders are inundated with paper. They had several piles of paper documents on their desks, on a chair next to them, at their feet below the desk, or wherever space would allow.

In short, it was not uncommon in a single day for one trader to receive several hundred emails, hundreds of digital pages of financial news, hundreds of digital pages of instant messages from colleagues outside the firm, hundreds of paper pages of research analysis, all while conducting dozens of phone calls, listening to and talking face-to-face with their fellow team members about trades, keeping an eye on their existing trading positions, and, of course, booking actual trades on the computer. When traders leave their desks to use the restroom, get food, or go to a meeting, these streams of information continue on without them. They must be careful about when they take breaks. They often eat breakfast and lunch at their desks, so as not to miss important developments in the market.

Traders are clearly inundated on a second-by-second basis with thousands of abstract representations, which, when added together, constitute their vision and feel of the market. It would be physically impossible to engage in any substantive way with all of this information. As an outside observer, one feels compelled to ask: What's the point? Why so much information from so many sources at such a high speed? It was difficult for traders to communicate what they do with all of this information and precisely how they use it to assemble a picture of the market, but they all agreed that they could not do their jobs as effectively without it. Many had to resort to metaphors, similes, and other forms of creative speech to communicate their experience to me.

Steve, a 33-year-old high yield trader, worked his way up into this position from being an analyst and junior trader. He describes trading as a "constant circle of information flowing." "I am constantly looking for the pieces of information that are important for different companies that I'm tracking, different trends in the market that I think might be important." Tracing a narrowing spiral shape in the air with his finger, he describes his main task as trying to "slow that circle down so that I can get at the information I need exactly when I want it." I asked Steve,

What kinds of things do you do to slow down the circle?

I don't know what it is that enables me to do that. I just do it.

Maybe you can you give me an example?

Well, basically what happens is, I have a bunch of things that I'm interested in keeping track of that I'll notice when I get a sense of the market in the morning. As the day progresses, I'll see another piece of information that triggers my memory about one of those things. I make the connection. If it's the right piece of information, it might mean that I take action and make a trade. But, usually I've been thinking about doing that trade earlier in the day.

So most of what triggers your memory is something you read?

Yeah, usually something on the newsfeed, or I'll get a message from a colleague—that kind of thing. Basically, you have a lot of trends, names of companies, stuff like that, working in the back of your mind all the time. Then along comes something on your screen that triggers your memory of that trend or company, which kind of brings it back to your mind. Then you can assess whether or not to take action from there.

Steve compared this process to the popular children's card game *Memory*, where players try to find pairs of matching cards that have been turned face down using only their memory of where each card lies.

With these metaphors, Steve reveals an important insight about the underlying logic of the digital trading system. It takes for granted that a single individual would never be able to use, or be interested in using, all of the information the system provides. Rather, the system inundates thousands of users across the globe in a swirl of information. When everyone views these data simultaneously and in real-time, the chances that important pieces of information will be lost are slim because of the sheer number of perspectives. Also, because Bloomberg users are connected by instant communication technologies, the system enables them to discuss information of potential importance with colleagues interested in the same market trends in real time.

Rick, a 45-year-old veteran trader in the distressed debt group, said similar things. After telling me that he gets "probably a thousand or so pages of messages from different people over the course of a day" just through the Instant Message application alone, I asked Rick if he would rather there be less information for him to feel responsible for.

> We are information junkies. I would much rather have too much information than too little. I mean, I can always use the search function on any of these feeds, if I want to make sure I haven't missed something on a company. Really, when it comes down to it, this is a relationship business. So, if something important comes up and I miss it, I have enough confidence in my contacts to know that someone will probably catch it for me and let me know.

> *So, it's a collective effort?*

> Exactly. It's a collective effort. By having so much information out there all at once, you won't miss what's important, because there are so many other people out there watching.

As Steve and Rick point out, working in the public markets involves engaging with a globally distributed, short-term working memory. It is a kind of "collective working memory" made up of computers and human brains linked together by information cables that stretch over vast distances. Like on the individual level, working memory on the collective level assists in reasoning and decision-making concerning "live" tasks that are immediately at hand. Unlike individual working memory, collective working memory is distributed among thousands of group members who share a common focus of attention—in this case a digital representation of the market. In order for traders to construct an individual working memory that produces good decision-making, they must become immersed in the collective working memory that is streamed to them via the digital trading system. As Daniel Buenza and David Stark (2005:86) note, "The trading room distributes intelligence." Becoming immersed in this distributed intelligence allows them to extend their individual capacity for working memory beyond their physical bodies.[5] When a potentially important piece of information needs to be attended to, then, it is often the collective working memory that catches it first. Traders have a great deal of trust that, via the real time temporality of the Bloomberg system, this piece of information will be streamed to them exactly when they need it—just in time. It is then up to each trader to do something innovative—to use that piece of information creatively in order to make a trade that others do not see (Buenza and Stark 2005).

Liquidity

Market workers are immersed in a screen world—a collective working memory of the global economic system, shoehorned into three 24-inch monitors. An interesting question to ask about this world is, "When is it?" The screen world is not really a depiction of the present financial economy. As Knorr Cetina (2012:128–129) notes, it is a "rolling projection of change," which creates an "analytic time" made up of "the streaming aggregate patterns of algorithmically processed transactions and contextual activities." Rather than depict the present or past, the screen world seeks to capture the region of time-space just over the horizon that divides the future from the present. Through continual updating of expectations in real time, the screen world is meant to project the immediate future back into the present in order to gain some kind of strategic advantage. It is a projection that is meant to help the user control the near-term future rather than sit back and wait for it to arrive. As a result, the image of reality that matters—the unfolding market—is never fixed. It is a portrait of a constantly changing just-about-to-happen future.

A common experience of time described by traders that results from this orientation to the future is what I will refer to as "liquid." By the liquidity of time, I mean the "frictionless-ness" of the interactions that make up one's lived experience of duration, pace, sequence, tempo, articulation, and so on. Through disembedding and abstraction, virtually anything that has been represented as an object for interaction can be moved or exchanged without having to manipulate the physical proprieties of the actual object

5. What I am calling collective working memory is similar to what cognitive social psychologists have called "distributed social cognition." Technology plays an important role in extending the already social foundation of collective cognition (see, e.g., Dror and Harnad 2008).

that is being represented, such as its weight, height, color, or texture. There are very few limits on the number, speed, size, and distance of the objects that one can interact with at a given moment. This slick and constantly shifting experience of the movement of work objects creates an enticing absorption affect (Knorr Cetina 2012; Zaloom 2012).

Financial instruments are a prime example of objects that create a liquid experience of time, so much so that "liquidity" has taken on its own special meaning within finance. I am using the term liquid here in a more general, non-economic sense (Bauman 2000). Financial instruments create liquidity in the sense that they move in the relatively frictionless procedure of a digital communication. Therefore, unlike more concrete objects, they are not affected by terrain or weather conditions, are not so heavy they cannot be lifted by hand, or so fragile they could be crushed. Using such physical descriptors for digital objects, in fact, sounds absurd.

Compared to the flow of less liquid objects—for example, freight on the trailer of a semi truck—the flow of financial instruments through a trader's action environment is almost infinitely customizable. This was especially the case at the asset management firm I observed, whose proprietary trading software is designed in-house. One day I overheard Cynthia and Rick, both in the distressed debt group, complaining about the usability of their custom-built trade booking application, which is used widely by many trading groups throughout the company. "Why don't you just make my job as difficult and inefficient as fucking possible," Cynthia sarcastically exclaimed to her computer screen as she attempted to book a trade. Rick turns to Cynthia to see what is wrong. They comment on how one of the tabs they use in one screen of this application disappears when they change to another screen. This "disappearing tab" slows down their workflow by a few seconds. After commenting on it several times throughout the day, Rick calls the IT department and, within a few hours, is engaged in a long face-to-face conversation with a programmer from the building across the street about reconfiguring the screen to fit his needs. The programmer shows Rick another way to do this task, but Rick insists that he wants to do it his way. The programmer agrees to make the changes over the next few days. In this small way, Rick is able to customize the pacing and sequencing of his workspace, making the trading terminal (and its temporality) fit him like a pair of old shoes. Once their screens are customized to their liking, then, the number and speed of the objects traders interact with is limited not by the physical properties of the objects themselves, but almost entirely by traders' capacity for attention and concentration. It is a relatively frictionless action environment that is also almost entirely customizable by the worker and expansible to his or her capacity for attention.

One concrete result of the liquidity and customizability of time on the trading floor, then, is a kind of absorption effect among traders (Knorr Cetina 2012; Zaloom 2006).[6] This was demonstrated to me most clearly by Steve from the high yield group. When I asked him about his experience of working all day in front of the screens, he said,

> When I'm in here [pointing to the screens and phones in a sweeping motion with both arms] I'm in a circle and it's taking up all of my attention. I some-times go the entire day without talking to my wife and kids. It's not that I for-get about them, it's just that I'm so involved with this stuff [pointing again to the screens], conversations with all these guys [pointing around him to his col-leagues], before I know it, it's 5 o'clock. [. . .] I was driving home last night, and it suddenly dawned on me that I hadn't spoken to my wife all day.

As Steve is explaining this to me, he is suddenly interrupted by Regina, the group's secretary, through the intercom telling him he has a phone call. He yells across the room that he will take the call, and, within seconds, he is deeply engaged in a phone conversation about a trade with a broker. Chuck, who sits next to Steve, turns to me and says with a grin, "There you go." I watch Steve as he gets spun off into a sequence of actions. The initial call from the broker triggers a conversation with Chuck and another trader about their positioning. This spins Steve into a series of activities on the computer, then more talking to colleagues in the office, then more actions on the computer. After about half an hour, he has reached a stopping point with this spiral of activity and notices that I am still there watching him. We lock eyes and he gives me a half smile, realizing what had just hap-pened. "Yeah, so there you go," he says.

During particularly active markets, which require long periods of star-ing at the screen, traders' minds are running at hyper speed, but their bodies, perhaps ironically, remain relatively still, becoming like an extra appendage one must keep running in order to support the mind. Chuck, for example, notes that when the markets are at peak volatility, he typically notices strain "more in my body than in my mind. Mostly my neck and

6. This absorption effect is identical to the psychological states described by Mihaly Csikszentmihalyi (1990) as "flow." It was noticeably absent among the securities analysts I interviewed. Because their work primarily involves researching the recent past—that is, companies' business performance—their tasks are less "live" and time-sensitive, and therefore require a less absorbing style of attention. That said, analysts' jobs can be performed the same way outside of market hours as during market hours. Consequently, they typically stayed a few hours longer at the office than traders. Clock time is less salient to their jobs, compared to traders.

back." He continues, "When things are really intense, I notice that I'll wrap my legs around the legs of my chair like this." He demonstrates by kicking off his shoes and curling the tops of his feet and toes around the back legs of the chair, which fixes him extra tight to the seat and positions his body in a forward lean, his head now closer to the screens. "When I get home at the end of the day, I'll notice that my back hurts. When I stand up, my entire neck is tense all the way down." He traces a line with his hand from the bottom of his neck all the way down his spine.

Chuck notes that taking a vacation is the only thing that really helps relieve this strain. "Before we had kids, my wife and I would take trips to the Caribbean for a few days or a week every few months. She would be all excited to get out and do stuff, but I would end up just sleeping. I would sleep like 12 or 14 hours because I felt so drained." As Rick puts it,

> Every day, by the end of the day, I'm wiped. I need to work out or do something physical just to get my mind clear. I've got to do something to get my head away from this world for a second. That's why at night I try to read something light— like a mystery novel or something. Just something to get my mind to calm down before I hit the pillow.

Cynthia had similar thoughts. "You have to find a way to decompress when you get home every night. If I don't get a workout in every day, I go crazy. I like routine." She says she feels "blessed" because, "I am an incredible sleeper [laughs]. When I hit the pillow, I am out like a light. I know other people in the office who have more trouble with that, and that can be hard."

These respondents all point to a common experience: engaging with the collective working memory of the financial markets requires traders to entrain their cognitive rhythms with the rhythms of objects that have very few physical limitations on the speed and volume of their movement. Time feels liquid. This requires a great deal of mental energy. Merging with the rhythms of the market leaves an echo in one's mind at the end of the day, which one must then attempt to dampen, tame, or block out in order to get refreshed for the next day of work. The most common way that traders report being able to achieve this dampening is by engaging directly with the body at the end of the day through some sort of physical activity.[7]

---

7. I occasionally noticed this during the workday as well. When the markets were less active traders would pick up a toy football and toss it around the trading floor. When the markets were more active, requiring extended engagement with the screens, traders would often, most likely unconsciously, begin to fidget their legs and hands, allowing them to remain engaged with the screen even though their bodies clearly wanted to get up and move.

The digital trading floor, with its globally distributed network and the thousands of human brains that are used to attend to its abstract representations, produce a form of social time that is built around an obsession with timing. Traders virtually connect to one another through their computers to look for opportunities that they can exploit creatively and, most importantly, before their competitors. "Like the fashion-conscious or like nightlife socialites scouting the trendiest clubs," note Buenza and Stark (2005:87), "[traders] derive their strength from obsessively asking, 'where is everyone going?' in hopes of anticipating the hotspots and leaving just when things get crowded." Digital trading platforms, in essence, distribute the risks of "bad timing" across a global playing surface so that individual traders can more effectively see opportunities for "good timing" and compete over who sees them first.

We can now see more clearly why market time feels so dense. Within the window of opportunity of market hours, there is a virtually unlimited number of smaller micro opportunities that traders worry are being exploited by others before them. Especially when the market is highly active, then, there is almost no upside to disengaging from the screens. But even when the market is slow, there is a sneaking suspicion that, with just a little more attention, one can find something everyone else has missed. The entire architecture of the digital deal room is designed to create an obsession with finding moments of good timing within a constantly changing portrait of the near-term future.

Phantasmagoria

One's experience of temporality is always colored by one's experience of spatiality. Time and space are not separate things but facets of the same four-dimensional reality. The disembedded and abstracted nature of the trading floor, then, not only shapes the temporality of traders' work environments, it also creates a peculiar experience of space, which I will refer to, following Giddens (1990), as "phantasmagoric." A phantasmagoric space is one in which its visible form conceals more than it reveals. As Giddens (1990:19) puts it, within highly disembedded and abstracted action environments, "what structures the locale is not simply that which is present on the scene; the 'visible form' of the locale conceals the distanciated relations which determine its nature." In the case of the deal room, the physical experience of it as a place—an air-conditioned office populated with computers, desks, and people—conceals more than it reveals what is really going on there—the exchange of billions of dollars among the world's most powerful financial players. The reality that matters on the trading floor is not given in the physical experience of it as a concrete place. Thus, one must learn to see the disembedded abstractions that structure action there—such as the German ten year treasury bond, or a line of text on a screen reporting widespread rioting in Greece because of austerity measures, or an almost unimaginable sum of money like 3 billion dollars— as "really real," even though one cannot directly apprehend these objects with the full spectrum of the senses. Learning to see and engage with this concealed reality as really real is a fundamental part of becoming an experienced market worker.

I found some of the younger and less experienced members of the trading group still in the process of learning to see and experience the reality of their workplace as really real. Trevor, in his late thirties, joined the distressed debt team as a trader from a consulting firm in the Midwest during my fieldwork. He was initially assigned to derivatives and portfolio trading, which involves booking trades that apply to an entire portfolio, rather than a single bond holding. This is a slower paced type of trading—he typically books one, perhaps two trades a day—but is more abstract. In a typical day, Trevor uses complex algorithms to seek out particular bonds or loans that fit the type of across-the-board derivative trade he wants to put on. As he attempted to explain to me the type of trading he does, I remarked to him how difficult it is for me to understand the process.

The information on these screens doesn't seem real to me. But I imagine you see a lot more concreteness behind these numbers.

Well, actually, there's not a whole lot of difference between doing a one hundred thousand dollar trade and a three million dollar trade. The amount and type of work is almost exactly the same for me. Sometimes you can get too into the numbers and forget what you're dealing with—which is actual money. [. . .] I mean, I deal with a *lot* of money. Like, millions of dollars. But, you know, it doesn't feel like it sometimes. And it's not my money either so . . .

He trails off and pauses for a second. He adds, reflectively, "You have to be careful and step back and remember how much money this is and how much responsibility that entails."

I discussed this experience of the unreality of money with some of the junior-level securities analysts, many of whom have come to the firm with a limited finance background. I talked to Melinda, for example, in her first month as an analyst straight from an Ivy League university. She recalls how she had been doing research on a particular company and saw that, "the company had gone up like six percent in a single day. And, for some reason,

I decided to actually look it up to see what that meant, you know like in terms of actual money. It was like *twenty million dollars*." Melinda's surprise reflects the fact that though working in the financial markets is ostensibly about the exchange of money, there is actually scant physical manifestation of money anywhere in the office environment. Especially if things are going well, one could easily forget exactly what is going on underneath the physical locale of the office itself.

Older and more experienced traders, then, seemed to have a less phantasmagoric experience of the office. They had many more opportunities and a greater depth of understanding in which to learn how to apprehend the screen world as really real. Traders often used highly evocative textural language to describe the otherwise intangible abstractions found on their screens in more tangible terms. For example: "Look how frothy high yield is right now," or "That's pretty tight pricing," or "Equities volume looks pretty chunky."

Not only had more experienced traders developed a language for "feeling" the market in more concrete terms, but all of them had gone through the painful experience of losing a lot of money on a trade that did not go their way. When I asked Chuck, for example, in very generic terms, "What it is like to be a trader?" He mused,

> It's like—and this is a really bad metaphor but pretty accurate—it's like, have you ever seen films where they show kids in a war zone playing soccer or something? The place is like all bombed out, but, since there aren't any planes overhead, they think, "Hey, I'm not hearing any bombs right this second, so why don't we go out and play some soccer." It's kind of like that. After awhile, you just become so used to hearing bombs dropping that it doesn't bother you anymore.

A few months later, I asked Chuck again about this fantastical imagery in the hopes that he could help me understand what "bombs dropping" means. Turning to his screen, he pulls up a chart of the equity value of a company called Cengage, which owns Thompson-Reuters, a leading academic textbook publishing company. Chuck explains to me that the firm, mostly under his direction, invested heavily in these bonds with the expectation that their price would increase over time (i.e., they bet long). He and the other high yield traders had the theory that, even though a lot of higher education is "going electronic," professors are unlikely, in the short run, to completely rearrange a curriculum around a new book (electronic or otherwise), because this requires a lot of work. "Why would a professor do that when he could just stick with the same book he's been using for years?" Chuck reasoned. If professors are as conservative as he thinks, then Cengage should continue to do well as a company.

Chuck then pointed to the chart of the company's value: a precipitous drop. Over the last three days, against Chuck's prediction, there has been a huge sell off, causing the price of Cengage's AAA debt to drop. Chuck bet wrong. The losses, he tells me, have been on the order of 25 million dollars, practically overnight. Pointing to the screen, he notes, "Yeah. I couldn't sleep after I saw that one." Fortunately, Chuck notes, "No one has given me much shit about it. We've all been there. We've all taken big losses when things didn't go our way." He pauses, and then reflects, "But still, you can't help but feel bad after something blows up on you."

As we are talking, Steve and Daniel, high yield traders who sit on either side of Chuck and have been eavesdropping our conversation, turn their chairs toward us.

STEVE: What do you mean when something blows up on you, Chuck? Are we talking about Cengage right now? That was not a blow up, buddy. You need to bring it down.

DANIEL: Cengage was not a blow up, man.

CHUCK: [looking a little hurt] It was like 25 million.

DANIEL: But that was over three days, man. It's not that bad.

Interviewer: [To Steve] I'm sure this kind of thing has happened to you before too. How do you deal with it? Does it still affect you when you go home at night?

STEVE: No. You totally downshift. You downshift. You gotta downshift.

CHUCK: [Looking more hurt now, turns to Steve] But could you do that like five or six years ago when you first started? Can you honestly tell me you can downshift when something blows up on you? Can you just lay your head on the pillow, no problem?

Steve, looking a little uncomfortable with answering, sidesteps these questions by needling Chuck again about how, "Cengage was not a blow up, man." This spins them into a discussion about the academic textbook market and how they should be positioning themselves now. Steve, finally returning to my question, says coolly, "I find it easy to switch off from this world when I leave work. There is really no need for me to check the market after hours, except to maybe send a few emails in the early evening." Chuck just shakes his head, and says to me, "I guess stress is all relative. It's all about what you're used to. For my wife, for example, she gets stressed out by our daughter yelling at our son. [. . .] I'm like, 'Whoa, take a step back. It's not that big a deal.' Because to me, real stress is losing 25 million in three days."

This exchange is about whether or not losing a lot of money in a short time is a "big deal," and whether that loss should register emotionally—seemingly easy questions to answer. The answers, however, are anything but clear. On the one hand, despite his earlier claim that, "You just become so used to hearing bombs dropping that it doesn't bother you anymore," the loss of 25 million dollars in three days feels like a real emergency for Chuck. He feels like he has performed poorly at his job, and the reality of the loss manifests itself materially in Chuck's body as insomnia. On the other hand, Chuck's colleagues seem to easily dismiss the loss as "not that big a deal," and indicate in subtle ways that Chuck should be able to easily shrug it off, like switching off a light—"you just downshift." So, was the loss big or not? How should one feel about such an event? Within the phantasm of the deal room, the answers are not clear because the objects of interaction in the work environment— namely, millions of dollars—are artifacts of trust in the reality of abstract representations. This is not to say that traders do not experience money as really real; as Chuck demonstrates, they certainly do. However, it takes trust and the use of one's imagination to conjure this reality into being.

Many experienced traders I talked to, then, noted that one must learn to treat money—or, more accurately put, the risk of losing it—neither too lightly, nor too seriously. They must be continually reflexive about the reality and unreality of risk. As Buenza and Stark (2005:95) note,

> Traders are acutely aware that the reality "out there" is a social construct consisting of other traders and other interconnected instruments continuously reshaping, in feverish innovation, the properties of that recursive world. In this coproduction, in which the products of their interventions become a part of the phenomenon they are monitoring, such reflexivity is an invaluable component of their tools of trade.

Bill, the most experienced trader I talked to, was the most poetic about the importance of being reflexive about risk and of toeing a careful line in regard to one's emotional relationship with risk. He says,

> A pro racecar driver probably knows many people that have been maimed or killed, but he doesn't think it's going to happen to him. He might even know that it could, but he really just doesn't. At the least, it doesn't bother him. It doesn't impair his ability. Because you cannot be afraid if you're a racecar driver or you'll have your foot just a little bit off the gas, and then the other guy is going by you, and you lose. [. . .] I think for what I do, it's the same kind of thing. I just don't really ever think it's going to happen to me.

Yeah, what is "it?"

"It" means blow up; go out of business and hurt a lot of people.

Other people will say, "I just can't believe the kind of risk that you can take." And I don't feel it, though. I don't feel the pressure at that level. Other people would just—"How do you sleep? You've got how much risk going on?" I don't like it as much as I used to, but when I was younger, I remember I would do this for nothing. I loved the thrill of it.

Over-lightness leads to recklessness, which can have potentially cataclysmic consequences for the firm and its clients, or in some instances the economy at large. Over-seriousness leads to a paralyzing fear that prevents one from capitalizing on high-reward opportunities. In the case of the "Cengage blowup," then, Steve and Daniel evaluated Chuck's emotional response as over-serious. Chuck had become *too* convinced of the reality of the screen world, and he was potentially "letting off the gas," as Bill would put it. Talking to Daniel later in the day about the stress Chuck was feeling, he mused, "You gotta try to keep in mind that this isn't reality. We traders are less than one percent of the population, and we don't live in the real world. Our problems aren't real problems. So, if you get too into this job, you can forget that."

The phantasmagoric experience of place that traders discuss is part and parcel of the liquid temporality of the deal room. In order to create the forms of strategic time that allow traders to come up with ever more creative ways of beating their competitors and making value for their clients, the financial industry has created a disembedded and abstracted version of reality that can be manipulated with greater ease. Abstracted objects, with their slickness and lightness, free concrete reality from its fixity. But this new freedom comes with some unanticipated emotional complications. It creates a world of abstract objects that can transform in the very act of looking at it. It requires a curious combination of efforts to see this world as real but also not to take that reality so seriously that it leads to a paralyzing fear of risk. Traders feel an emotional tension, then, between an abstract reality (the market) and a concrete phantasmagoria (the deal room). The market world thus invites workers to painstakingly build a stable cognitive and emotional life on a foundation of shifting sand.

CONCLUSION

Financialization is not just about how financial capitalism has come to dominate the global economy (Krippner 2005), nor how finance increasingly makes us "think in terms of finance"—debt, return on investment, risk, and so forth (Martin 2002). Finance is also a form of movement in time-space. Financial timescapes are built on the premise that successes emerge from extremely narrow windows of opportunity in which hundreds of actors are organizing themselves to capitalize. If you are not perfectly positioned to pounce, you lose. Dealmakers experience these timescapes as stretches of often chaotic and time-pressured "pitching," the majority of the cases ending in dead ends and failed deals. But when everything goes right, all the frustrating multitasking is forgiven in an intoxicating night of negotiation and triumph. For market workers, the density and pace of financial time is contained within the rigid boundaries of market hours, but a similar rhythm holds. The simultaneously frantic and tedious task of staring at the market through the portal of the trading platform is punctuated by a few spectacular trades that go your way or a few tragic trades that undermine your efforts. The timescapes of finance, then, require wild fluctuations in energy and attention. Workers swing from stretches of cluttered desynchronization—producing spreadsheets and reports while tracking thousands of market actors in real time—to moments of transcendent unification—the closing of a big deal, the completion of a big trade—to moments of crisis—a big deal goes flop, bad positioning brings big losses. Workers must learn how to cope physically, cognitively, and emotionally with these wild fluctuations. They develop temporal languages to justify the expenditure of energy required during intensifications. In the case of traders, they develop cognitive capacities that allow their working memories to be expanded beyond what a single human brain can produce and develop emotional strategies to be simultaneously serious and nonchalant about risk (see also Zaloom 2012).

These financialized timescapes are also inflected by different relationships to chronological time. The contrast between dealmakers and market workers bears this out. Dealmakers have almost no fixed clock time markers in which to contain their work. Like a lot of well-paid knowledge workers in the flexible economy, they are essentially on-call 24 hours a day (Kunda 1992). The sometimes bizarre military and triage metaphors they use to describe their work seem to be ways of putting a recognizable cultural frame around these temporal conditions in order to make them seem somehow more normal, or at least "thinkable." Market workers, on the other hand, have the distinct luxury of chronologically bounded work. The markets open and close at specific clock times, and the wider cycles of the market have relatively predictable hot and cold spots. These provide a set of comparatively fixed and immovable temporal boundaries to what is otherwise intense work. If market workers were to keep a time diary, then, they would appear to have relatively normal schedules, though slightly longer than average. Within the chronological windows given to them by the market, however, they have experiences of time that are just as exhausting as working long hours because of how the actual *doing* of work shapes their bodies, minds, and emotions.

Though financial professionals work in what seems like a special and unique workplace, then, it exemplifies, perhaps in a more dramatic fashion than most workplaces, the flexible timescapes that many elite knowledge workers face today. Corporate lawyers, IT professionals, researchers, analysts, and other "data junkies" are all similarly required to interact with digital representations of things out there in the world and to work toward big deadlines driven by demanding clients (Ancona and Waller 2007). As many scholars have noted, these professionals tend to work long hours because they have difficulty drawing lines between work and non-work. This phenomenon has often been connected to a particularly pernicious "culture of overwork" that exists in (especially American) elite workplaces, which pushes knowledge professionals to engage in a total immersion in their working lives at the expense of their personal lives (Wharton and Blair-Loy 2001). But by analyzing the rhythmic textures of financial workplaces, we see other hidden dimensions of overwork among elite knowledge professionals that are far less ideological and explicit. These dimensions relate less to the way being "always available" uncomfortably pushes against other non-work demands (Blair-Loy 2003; Jacobs and Gerson 2004) and more to the actual physical and cognitive experiences of laboring in a flexibilized temporal environment. Dealmakers, for example, show us how having total control over when and where one works can actually create opportunities to overwork because client demands can become all encompassing. They also illustrate how the perception of ones time by others as "precious," no doubt a common experience among well-paid professionals, makes time feel more urgent. Every second carries the extra weight of expectation. Market workers show how the abstraction and disembedding of the objects of work can create experiences of time that are particularly dense and liquid, so that even short work hours can still cause exhaustion (Southerton and Tomlinson 2005). Even more subtly, these practices create phantasmagoric experiences of place, which make it difficult to judge the reality of work stress. On top of long hours, liquid hours, and urgent hours, then, some knowledge workers may also have difficulty linking the incredible expenditures of energy required to meet these demands with outcomes that feel "really real." The linkage of effort to reward is dependent on faith in the reality of abstractions.

When Brent, whose words opened this chapter, gives a curt response like "I'm not a coal miner" to my question about how many hours he works, then, he is essentially saying that I have asked questions belonging to a different regime of work time. The whole language of hours, temporal boundaries, and work objects is almost meaningless to him. Other words are more important to his experience—pace, intensity, density, liquidity, and urgency. Knowledge workers may put in long hours—perhaps they are aware of it, perhaps they are not—but this is not the only or even the most important problem. The problem of work time stems from the total immersion in urgent rhythms and objects of work whose very reality is sometimes difficult to pin down. The space of work is slick, fluid, and shifting. Getting some sort of cognitive and emotional fix on this space, then, requires massive attention and energy expenditure if one is to be perfectly positioned to pounce on the moment of profit when it arrives.

CHAPTER 4
The Deregulation of Time-Space

lvaro and I follow Interstate 40 east as it carves a wedge-shaped channel through the Smoky Mountains. He has just spent the last five hundred miles of our trip telling me how stressful long haul truck driving can be. Tight deadlines, an erratic sleep pattern, short-tempered shippers, traffic, weather—his work involves navigating myriad contingencies in order to do one thing: be on time. After several hours of talking about stress, I ask, "what brings you back to the job?" "I like the rush," he replies. "Like when you've been driving all night, and pushing and pushing, and you get there, and your body and your hands are shaking, and your vision is just like. . . ." He can't find the words to describe his feelings, so he gestures forward with both hands to make the image of a narrowing passage. "I love that feeling." Like many truck drivers I met, Alvaro has a unique knowledge of the limits of his body. Having worked in the trucking industry off and on for nearly a decade, the job has tested the limits of his attention and alertness many times, giving him frequent glimpses of the fragile balance between fatigue, speed, and efficiency that fuels the flexible production economy.

In this chapter, I examine the timescapes of American solo long haul truck drivers. Often referred to as Over-The-Road (OTR) drivers, they are primarily responsible for moving large volume freight (upwards of 80 tons in a 53 foot trailer) over long distances, often driving for weeks or even months before returning home. Because they work alone, they cannot keep their trucks constantly moving, as with teams of drivers, so they

Portions of this chapter appear in Snyder, Benjamin H. 2012. "Dignity and the Professionalized Body: Truck Driving in the Age of Instant Gratification." *The Hedgehog Review* 14(3):8–20.

must stop between shifts to sleep—typically at one of the thousands of truck stops and rest areas that dot the American Interstate system. I conducted interviews with both "company drivers" and "owner-operators." Company drivers have relatively little control over the process of driving. They are fulltime employees of a motor carrier firm, which tells them when and where to drive and even stipulates what route they must take to get to their destination. Owner-operators, by contrast, typically own or lease their trucks and contract with companies who provide them with dispatch service. They are responsible for doing their own route planning and managing running costs. My ethnographic observations, in contrast to the interviews, focus solely on owner-operators because, as I explain below, they exemplify many of the changes going on in the industry due to deregulation.

Like financial professionals, OTR drivers work in an economic context that has been shifting since the 1980s. Rather than financialization, however, the trucking industry exemplifies the remarkable push under flexible capitalism toward the deregulation and acceleration of production markets. Deregulation has caused companies in a variety of industries to shift to more casual employment agreements, such as the increasing use of contract work, in order to reduce costs in the face of narrowing profit margins (Kalleberg 2003; Standing 2011). The trucking industry officially deregulated in 1980, but even prior to this had experimented with forms of deregulated competition (Hamilton 2009).

In addition to tighter competition, the trucking industry has also had to adapt to the changing needs of the companies that are clients of the industry, such as Walmart and Amazon. These "fast companies" have become increasingly interested in streamlining their logistics operations in order to make speed a source of competitive advantage (Harvey 1991; Pache 2007; Stalk and Hout 1990). In response to these pressures, trucking firms have relied not only on flexible employment arrangements but also on new forms of logistics and worker surveillance that force drivers in an erratic pattern of shift-work that operates 24 hours a day, 7 seven days a week (Levy 2015). While truck driving looks from the outside like one of the few stable and traditional blue-collar jobs still available to working class Americans, then, from the inside of the cab things actually look very different (Belzer 2000). In this sense, the trucking industry highlights the fact that the face of flexible capitalism is not only to be found in quirky forms of flexible labor, like "gigging" as an "itinerant expert" in the knowledge economy or the so-called "sharing economy" (Barley and Kunda 2004), but also hidden in plain sight within occupations that we might assume are the same today as they were in the mid 20th century.

While I will discuss deregulation in an economic sense, as with financialization, I would like to expand the meaning to include more mundane, micro-level, and cultural phenomena. Deregulation in this more general sense refers to the habits, strategies, and skills that workers cultivate to adapt to the speed and intensity of cutthroat competition. Examining embodied adaptations to the intensifications of labor within a free market is especially interesting in the context of the trucking industry because at the same time that drivers are required to drive more "flexibly" within deregulated markets they are also required to comply with a rigid set of federal regulations on their work time that is based on the chronological model of the Taylorist factory. OTR drivers thus literally embody in a single person the tension between deregulation at the company level and "re- regulation" (Standing 2011) at the worker level, as well as tensions between flexible time and chronological time.

THE DEREGULATION OF TRUCKING

The imperative for truck drivers to become more flexible has come from two sources: one internal and the other external. Internal transformations in the trucking industry are like a microcosm of changes in the American economy at large. According to Shane Hamilton (2009), truck driving prior to the 1930s probably looked more like it does today than to the period between 1930 and 1980, an observation that rings true in many other areas of the production economy (Cappelli 1995). Early trucking was an unregulated "dog eat dog" world (Keeshin 1983). Between the 1930s and 1970s, however, New Deal preferences took hold of the industry and turned it into one of the most strictly regulated, monopolistic, and unionized sectors in the country.[1] Like in so many other areas of the production economy, the 1970s proved to be a watershed decade. Following the global oil shocks, which triggered a worrying period of "stagflation," the Carter administration began to champion deregulation in trucking and many other industries as the way to deliver lower prices to consumers (Hamilton 2009:163). Backed by a growing chorus of "independent" truckers who had become tired of the restrictive environment of New Deal regulation, Congress pushed through the Motor Carrier Act of 1980.[2] Champions of the free

1. According to Shane Hamilton (2009:148), by the mid 1950s nearly 1.5 million drivers belonged to the Teamsters Union, making it the largest union in the nation, and the industry had consolidated to include just a handful of quasi-monopolistic firms.
2. The push to deregulate the trucking industry was not simply a reaction to stagflation following the 1970s oil shocks, which most observers point to when discussing

market, independent truckers, and American consumers who wanted cheaper grocery bills all got what they asked for: a "chaotic and cut-throat competition reminiscent of the 1920s" (Hamilton 2009:169).[3] Heightened competition has lead to increased pressure on motor carrier firms to reduce fixed costs.

From outside the industry, other pressures to flexibilize have come from the companies that use trucking firms and truck drivers in their logistics divisions, such as retail and manufacturing companies. Since the 1980s, the speed with which a company can get products to market before competitors has become an increasingly important lever of competitive advantage (Pache 2007). Competition over the temporality of production manifests at every level of activity, from eliminating idle time in production processes, to reducing the lag time between the creation of an innovative product and its launch on the market, to the distribution of products at the precise time-space coordinate that meets consumer demand. Firms have developed a variety of so called "time compression" strategies to gain control over temporalities at each level, such as "Just-in-Time" warehousing systems and "Supply Chain Management" (Harvey 1991; Stalk and Hout 1990). In these ways, the new regime of flexible production is reconfiguring the classically modern temporal order of the factory system (Harvey 1991). "Speed, flexibility, and incessancy of market activity have replaced the scheduled rhythm of the factory floor" (Ciscel and Smith 2005:429).

The trucking industry, being one of the major modes of distribution in the United States, is a linchpin in this system of "flexible specialization." The industry has been under increasing pressure from retailers,

---

deregulation in general. It also arose from a small group of "independent" truckers who had been operating in a completely unregulated parallel trucking industry that had managed to escape the stiff regulations of the 1935 Highway Motor Carrier Act. Operating in a completely unregulated market, which was paradoxically protected from any real competition from the rest of the industry, these drivers made fortunes while drivers for the big regulated companies saw their earnings potential capped by anti-competition legislation. Lead by neo-populists like Mike Parkhust, the owner of *Overdrive* magazine, these independent drivers marched on Washington and pushed for the massive reforms that eventually returned the trucking industry to its "dog eat dog" roots (Hamilton 2009).

3. Deregulation appears to have achieved many of its stated goals. The price of shipping freight has dropped overall, as more motor carrier firms compete to get those products to their destination with ever-greater precision of timing (Belman and Monaco 2001; Belzer 2000). For drivers, however, deregulation has meant that the overall volume of freight has increased, while real wages have fallen considerably, especially with the declining influence of trucking unions (AASHTO 2007; Monaco and Habermalz 2011). Thus, though drivers are making less than their pre-deregulation counterparts, their jobs have arguably become more important to the vitality of an economy that is increasingly run on a just-in-time basis.

especially large firms like Amazon and Walmart that could not dominate their markets without a flexible logistics system, to reduce costs and increase precision. They need freight to get to its destination, not necessarily as fast as possible (though that is typically the default status), but with precision timing—neither later nor earlier than the customer needs it. Creating this kind of precision requires reducing the number of friction points that might delay freight toward its destination. It has also meant doing away with older techniques of trucking that flourished in the regulated industry, which involved the use of hubs and warehousing (Viscelli 2010).

To adapt to this changing environment, the industry has introduced a number of flexible techniques to create a workforce that is both cheaper and nimbler. To reduce employment costs, firms have begun to rely more heavily on casual employment contracts (Belzer 2000; Viscelli 2010). A popular form is the so-called "lease-purchase," which has given birth to a new breed of owner-operator who may look similar to the classic "independent trucker" of the 1970s but is very different in practice.[4] Like the kind of arrangement one might find in a rent-to-own home furnishings store, lease-purchases offer drivers the "opportunity" to lease an older model truck from a motor carrier firm and slowly pay off the truck through monthly installments. To meet this obligation, they work as an independent contractor for the company. Drivers thus become responsible for fuel, maintenance, insurance, tolls, paperwork, and other costs once born by the employer. Employers also become exempt from payroll taxes, insurance, and the other legal requirements of a full-time employee (Viscelli 2010:49). In return, the company provides trailers and dispatch services to match drivers to freight, essentially acting as a contracting agency. From the driver's point of view, he becomes a kind of small business with an employee of one. Unlike a company driver, he is free to accept or refuse the load given to him by a dispatcher and he can run that load in any way he sees fit, so long as it arrives on time. These types of arrangements mirror the wider trend in flexible capitalism of giving more autonomy to workers at the same time that they ask them to shoulder more of the risks that were once absorbed in a tighter and longer-term internal contracting system (Cappelli 1999; Kalleberg 2003).

4. While lease arrangements have been around in the trucking industry for decades, there was a sharp rise in their popularity during the 1990s when other forms of coping with shrinking profitability proved ineffective for motor carrier firms. Where only 50% of owner-operators used leases in the mid 1970s, roughly 90% of owner operators in 1997 used such arrangements (Viscelli 2010:48).

While arrangements like these seem to give a lot of autonomy to drivers, then, other flexible work practices ensure that autonomy is coupled with powerful market incentives to drive as efficiently as possible. To motivate drivers to move with the kind of precision and speed demanded by clients, the industry uses a pay-by-the-mile system (Belzer 2000; Viscelli 2010), which resembles the increasingly common pay-for-performance schemes used in other sectors of the flexible economy (Cappelli 1995). Drivers are paid either a certain number of cents per mile driven or a percentage of the freight bill upon delivery. Either way, only a moving truck "pays the bills." The commodification of distance, rather than time, encourages drivers to move freight quickly from origin to destination rather than put in hours on the job regardless of how far they have driven. Time is money for truck drivers only insofar as it relates to space. It is probably more accurate to say that, for them, space is money.

THE REREGULATION OF TRUCKERS

The great irony of the deregulation of the trucking industry is that at the same time that restrictions have been lifted on companies and their operations—a request that many truckers themselves encouraged—more and more regulations have been heaped on drivers. The turn to flexibility in the global economy "has not been one of *de-regulation*," observes Guy Standing (2011:44), "but of *re-regulation*, in which more regulations were introduced than in any comparable period of history." The trucking indus-try is a clear case of this. As elsewhere, reregulation has meant a *downward* shift of regulations from markets and firms to the individual worker. If left to their own devices, the combination of casual employment and pay-by-the-mile encourages drivers to drive more miles than their bodies can safely handle. As Michael Belzer (2000) has observed, drivers begin to voluntarily "sweat" their own labor. Drivers are seen to need some set of regulations on their time because the cutthroat competition of a deregu-lated industry encourages them to push themselves to exhaustion. If the industry is to be both productive *and safe*, drivers cannot work on their own time. Hence, since the early 1990s the industry has greatly expanded the Hours of Service Regulations (HOS), which dictate how many hours drivers may work and sleep.

Drivers are held accountable for these rules by keeping logbooks. Violations are met with hefty fines. In the firm I observed, drivers' log-books were going digital. As I describe below, all types of drivers were required to use a device that employs GPS surveillance to automatically calculate logbook hours. This device makes it nearly impossible to cheat the regulations, a notoriously common activity during the era of self-reported paper logbooks (Levy 2015).

The Development of the HOS Regulations

The HOS regulations have been around since the 1930s, but have seen a number of dramatic revisions and expansions, the most recent changes occurring during my fieldwork between 2010 and 2012, followed by another raft of changes in 2013 and 2014 that occurred after my fieldwork.[5] These expansions have been, in large part, based on the perception that deregulation has created a kind of fatigue crisis in the industry, which is leading to poorer driver health, higher driver turnover, and an increased likelihood of fatal collisions (Belman and Monaco 2001).

Today, the HOS are drafted by the Federal Motor Carrier Safety Administration (FMCSA). Given the dramatic shift toward flexibility discussed above, what is most startling about the logic guiding the FMCSA's management of driver fatigue is just how much it is indebted to the "chrono-logic" of Taylorism. Much like a factory work schedule, the HOS regulations provide a standardized, scientifically derived, clock-based temporal framework that seeks to achieve a routine of shifts. Routinization, in theory, gives drivers' movements a degree of predictability that facilitates surveillance and coordination, thus preventing overwork by increasing efficiency. The FMCSA's reliance on an older industrial temporal logic to achieve the new goals of "post-industrial" flexibility is a telling example of how intimately connected flexible capitalism is to the era of mass production.

The FMCSA has been one of the leading institutions pursuing scientific research on the relationship between sleep duration, work duration, and fatigue. They have encouraged and often commissioned dozens of independent survey and laboratory studies, which attempt to measure the exact duration (in clock hours) of "on-task" alertness after which a driver's performance begins to degrade and the likelihood of a fatigue-related accident increases. Their findings have been very clear: "Performance begins to degrade after the 8th hour of [driving] and increases geometrically

---

5. It is telling that although my observations were made within a few years of writing this chapter, already the regulatory context has changed for drivers. As of this writing, the FMCSA has added a rule requiring drivers to take a mandatory 30-minute break within the first 8 hours of driving (FMCSA 2013).

during the 10th and 11th hours" (FMCSA 2003:22471). Recognizing that drivers rarely spend an entire shift driving—they often stop to deliver or load freight, get fuel, take breaks, and perform other non-driving related work tasks—other studies have attempted to determine the optimal duration of a shift. Again, the agency's findings are very clear. "After 14 hours from the start of the work period, it is time to stop driving, as the risk of fatigue-affected incidents is increasing rapidly" (FMCSA 2003:22473). Finally, understanding that "human beings are subject to a circadian, biological clock of about 24 hours, which controls natural wake/sleep cycles," the FMCSA has pioneered studies on sleep and circadian rhythms. These studies are unequivocal that "humans require about eight hours of restorative sleep daily" (FMCSA 2003:22460). Guided by these quantitative data, the FMCSA has designed a core set of rules that regulate how long (in clock hours) drivers may be on-duty, how long they may drive within that shift, how long they must rest before starting another shift, and how long they must sleep. These rules are known as the "14-hour rule," "11-hour rule," "10-hour restart," and "sleeper berth provision" (FMCSA 2003).

14-HourRule. Also known as the "14-hour clock," this rule stipulates that drivers can work a maximum of 14 continuous hours before they must go off-duty, thus creating the functional equivalent of a shift-work system. Drivers punch in for a "shift" of driving when they start their vehicles and must shut down their vehicles, or punch out, after 14 hours. Importantly, the 14-hour clock is a continuous countdown timer. It counts down the minutes that have passed since punching in, even when the truck is stopped, even if unforeseen events occur, such as traffic jams, bad weather, mechanical failure, or delays at shippers.

11-Hour Rule and 10-Hour Restart. Within the time "window" created by the 14-hour rule, drivers may drive a maximum of 11 hours, at which point they must take a minimum 10-hour break. After completing this "restart," drivers regain, as they call it, "a fresh clock," meaning they may work another 14-hour shift and drive another 11 hours. Unlike the 14-hour clock, the 11-hour clock is a "task oriented" timer—it counts down the minutes when the truck is moving and stops when the truck is stopped. Remote calculations of this requirement have become increasingly easy to achieve because of GPS technology, which can detect exactly where, when, and for how long a truck is moving.

Sleeper Berth Provision. Within each shift, drivers must log a minimum of 8 hours "in the sleeper berth"—the rear section of the truck equipped with a bed. Drivers may take these hours whenever they wish, but they must take them consecutively. They may not break that time into smaller periods of sleep. Most drivers plan to take their sleeper berth time during their 10-hour break so as not to cut into their revenue-producing hours during their 14-hour shift.

Frederick Winslow Taylor would be impressed by the HOS. Much like scientific managers, the FMCSA has proceeded by breaking trucking down into its component movements—driving work, non-driving work, waiting, sleeping, and recovery. Through experimentation in a controlled lab setting, stopwatch in hand, they have discovered apparently consistent and naturally arising temporal boundaries beyond which the body cannot function safely. Designing rules around these emergent laws, they have invented shifts of movement that will allow drivers to extract the maximum amount of effort from their bodies while reducing the likelihood that they will crash their vehicles. The entire consideration of the relationship between effort and reward, then, is based on the clock hour and the concept of the routinized shift.

To summarize, even though the industry as a commercial enterprise has been deregulated, drivers have actually seen a dramatic expansion of regulations over their daily lives. And, even though drivers are paid by the mile, those regulations are designed around the hour. Under the current rules, a driver's day should ideally consist of 14 hours on duty and 10 hours off duty—a structure that is meant to mirror the 24-hour circadian rhythm of the human body. On-duty time can consist of a maximum of 11 hours of paid driving and 3 hours of non-driving (non-paid) work. Off-duty time should consist of a minimum 8 continuous hours of sleep, plus 2 hours to eat, shower, do laundry, and get refreshed for the next shift. This is the ideal scenario. During my observations, however, I rarely saw a driver use all 11 hours of available driving time (his revenue-producing hours) because of the numerous delays that can occur while driving long distances. Thus, drivers frequently work many hours within a given shift that are functionally unpaid. If all of this sounds complicated; it is. As with financial professionals, it is much easier to understand truck driving by looking at how work actually gets done.

THE PROBLEM OF INFLEXIBILITY

Though truck driving is regulated by the hour, drivers consistently emphasized in interviews that their jobs are not easily understood in the language of clock time. "My time isn't so much time as it is miles," one driver told me. "I don't look at time as hours." Pointing forward toward his destination, he continued, "We're 22 miles away. At this speed, that's 20 minutes. So, our ETA is 4:15. Hours aren't just hours. It's distance and the HOS, and speed—that's how we experience time." As I discuss more below, in addition to the hours on the clock, drivers must be attentive to any number of rhythmic patterns that figure into a particular driving scenario and impinge on their speed and efficiency. These rhythms include the speed of shippers and receivers to load and unload freight, fluctuations in traffic, the availability of safe parking at truck stops and rest areas, the effect of terrain and weather on fuel consumption, and the rhythms of the body. From the drivers' perspective, truck driving is thus better understood in terms of the rhythms of "freight time" than in terms of shifts of clock hours.

A frequent complaint about the HOS regulations, then, is that they are too rigid and inflexible. These complaints apply particularly to the 14-hour rule. Though designed to provide a rigid limit to the number of hours drivers are awake and working, and thus limit fatigue, drivers reported that the 14-hour rule actually produces new work scenarios that they find fatiguing anyway. I will describe two of the most commonly discussed scenarios.

You Have to Stop When You Want to Go

Drivers experience the 14-hour clock, which cannot be stopped, and the 11-hour clock, which follows the movements of the truck and marks a driver's "productive time," as pitted against each other. Especially when one is delayed by traffic, weather, or problems at a shipper, the 14-hour clock can begin to "cut in" to one's productive time (the 11 hours allotted to make money by driving), thus creating a fatiguing feeling of urgency. Rick, a driver and owner of a small fleet in Kentucky, says that he "appreciates the [10-hour] rest period" that is built into the HOS rules, but finds that it often falls at the wrong time in the rhythms of delivering freight. "Sometimes factories are open eight to five. Sometimes you haul to grocery stores and warehouses that are [only] open at night." In these common situations, Rick reports, he may drive 3 hours to deliver freight during the middle of the night but not be able to pick up his next load until the next evening. As a result, he "wastes" the remaining 8 hours of his 11-hour clock waiting to pick up his next load. While waiting, his shift has come to an end, even though he has only driven 3 hours that day. "I have to wait an extra 10 hours to reset [e.g., take the required 10-hour rest break that will give him a "fresh" driving clock] when I've used only maybe a couple of hours [of the 11-hour clock] . . . on a night time delivery."

Time spent waiting is emotionally taxing, Rick notes, because he feels like he is "losing" productive time. Even though he has technically worked a 14-hour shift, only 3 of these hours have made money. "I'm waiting and I'm getting tired waiting. [. . .] Waiting can make you more tired than working. And that's what more flexibility [of the 14-hour rule] would allow you to do better." Like most drivers who spoke about the 14-hour rule, Rick suggests that one should be able to stop the 14-hour clock during forced down times in order "protect" revenue-producing hours. As another driver put it, "I get paid by the mile. My sit time kills me. It kills my paycheck. So when my 14-hour clock is up and I've only driven for five hours, that inhibits my ability to earn a living for my family." It would be easy to interpret this sentiment as drivers wanting to work more because they want to make more money, even if it is not safe. A more accurate interpretation, however, is that they want the freedom to work *when* it is most profitable. They want more control, not over *how many* hours they drive, but over *which hours* they drive.

You Have to Go When You Want to Stop

Another common (and more concerning) complaint was that the HOS rules sometimes force drivers to drive when they want to stop. Drivers discussed many reasons to stop during a typical shift, including tiredness, traffic, weather, and the availability of safe parking. Many noted that because the 14-hour clock is inflexible—it cannot be stopped when one encounters problems related to these factors—they feel pushed to keep driving until their 11-hour clock has been used, even if it would be safer and more efficient to stop. Hank, a former driver and current vice president of a mid-sized Illinois trucking firm, says,

> I've been driving down the highway in the truck—and I know my drivers do the same thing—they have hours on the 11-hour to reach they're destination. They're currently within their 14 hours to reach a destination, but they get fatigued. They have a choice to keep driving fatigued or stop and take a two or three hour nap and get up. But then, if they do that two or three hour nap, they're out of their 14 hours.

Drivers often reported that sleepiness can arise at unexpected times and that a simple "cat nap" would be sufficient to allow it to pass. Because the 14-hour clock continues to tick down no matter the circumstances, however, a few hours of unplanned sleep can work against a driver's productivity. As he sleeps, his 14-hour clock continues; the time "window" in which he can drive and make money gets smaller and smaller.

Other sources of fatigue, such as rush-hour traffic, are more predictable. The inflexibility of the 14-hour rule is also a problem in these situations.

"When we come into a large city," notes one driver, "we [often] hit it at the height of rush hour. We can avoid it by taking time off and getting much needed rest and continuing on afterwards." Unfortunately, this driver reports, the 14-hour clock encourages drivers to push through rush-hour traffic in order to log as many miles as possible in their available on-duty period. "You know when the hours—the peak hours of congestion in the major cities are going to happen," notes another driver. It would be much better, he advises, "if you can stop your clock for that one or two hours while all this traffic goes away, and then you can leisurely drive in, do your loads, and get outta Dodge."

In general, then, drivers seem to be arguing that more flexibility in the HOS rules represents greater control, not over how many hours they may drive and sleep, which has been the focus of the FMCSA's research, but over "which hours" and "what kind" of temporality—fast or slow, languid or rushed, staccato or legato—they can create within these rules. Having greater control over the placement and quality (rather than duration) of driving and sleeping within a given shift would enable them to better synchronize their workflow with the flow of traffic, weather, their bodies, the schedules of shippers and receivers, and the myriad other contingent processes that constrain the creation of "good timing." In short, drivers find that because the HOS is designed from a "chrono-logic," it is at odds with the temporality they are trying to achieve, which features irregular and unpredictable rhythms.

ENTRAINMENT AND RHYTHM EXPERTISE

Confronted by chronological shifts on one side and a flexible logistics system on the other, drivers' essential task is what I will call, following Deborah Ancona (Ancona and Chong 1996; Ancona et al. 2001; Ancona and Waller 2007) "entrainment." Entrainment originally described the principle in physics where two pendulums swinging in different phases side-by-side will incrementally begin to swing in phase together. Organizational theorists, responding to the growing use of work teams in flexible capitalism, began to use this term to understand the movements of groups of workers through project cycles (Ancona and Waller 2007; Slocombe and Bluedorn 1999; Standifer and Bluedorn 2006). As Deborah Ancona and Chee Chong (1996:251) note,

Entrainment presents organizational life as cyclical and rhythmic, where there is an active interplay among paces, cycles, and rhythms of different activities at different levels of analysis, where windows of opportunity come and go, and where speed and timing are critical to understanding the nature of organizational life.

With its focus on rhythm, timing, and the interplay of processes, entrainment is an apt descriptor for flexibilized organizations.

In the context of flexible trucking, entrainment helps describe one of the most important skills drivers must master: the incremental synchronization of two desynchronized rhythmic systems—clock time and freight time—which must occur during the period between pick up and drop off. Entrainment allows drivers to slowly align the "downbeats" of the HOS and freight deadlines, thus delivering freight "just in time" without breaking the rules of their logbooks. Rather than become routinized shift workers, then, in order to achieve entrainment drivers must become "rhythm experts." They must develop a specialized ability to synchronize the beat of clock time, which governs both the HOS regulations and the appointment times of shippers and receivers, to the complex patchwork of rhythms that affect the speed of freight as it travels through the logistics system. More often than not, this task falls upon the driver's body. Drivers use their body rhythms—wake-sleep cycles, digestion cycles, shifts in adrenaline and cortisol, etc.—to convert clock time into freight time.

A Long Night

I witnessed many demonstrations of entrainment while riding alongside drivers, but one stands out. On an afternoon in October 2010, Alvaro and I arrive at a poultry plant in northwest Arkansas to pick up a load of frozen chicken due in Crawford, Virginia, by Sunday afternoon. Alvaro is an owner-operator and contracts his work to a large firm that provides him with trailers and dispatch. He owns his own truck, which is looking a bit worn and outdated on the inside, but on the outside sports a gleaming burnt orange paint job and a custom decal of a phoenix rising from the ashes on the door. Across the front of the cab, just above the windshield, are the words, "Money Making Machine."

We find a space to park in the freight yard. Rows of loading docks puncture square holes in the side of a featureless building. A chain-link fence topped with barbed wire cordons off acres of cement with truck parking. Alvaro and I get out and walk across the yard toward the shipping office, dodging clumps of chicken feathers as they float across the ground in the breeze. We enter to find the clerk, who sits behind a glass window, visibly frazzled. It is Friday, and he is probably anxious for his shift to end so he can get on to his weekend. Alvaro politely asks if his load is ready, which has been scheduled for pick up between 2:00 p.m. and 5:00 p.m. (it is now 2:00 p.m.). The clerk sharply barks, "I've got seven things I gotta do right now before I even get to you. Wait in your truck and I'll let you know when it's ready." Alvaro takes his paperwork and politely asks, "Any idea how close the load is to being rea—" The clerk cuts Alvaro off before he can finish, "I'll let you know. Just keep your CB on."

Alvaro says nothing and backs out of the office. "I won't be talking to him anymore today," he says to me. He explains, "When I was younger, I used to get pissed off about that kind of thing. But now, I just stay cool. What's the point of getting my adrenaline up for that guy? If he gets mad at me, he might screw me by putting me at the back of the list [to get loaded]."

We get back in the truck and sit with the cab facing the loading dock door, which has two lights. A flashing red light means the load is not ready. A green light means it is ready. Right now, the red light is flashing.

4:45 p.m. Alvaro and I have been passing the time in pleasant conversation. He makes a few phone calls to his wife in Mississippi just to check in. The appointment window is nearly closed, but there are no signs of the load being ready. I ask Alvaro if we should check with the shipping clerk again. "Nah. What's the point? He'll just get pissed again. They'll call us when it's ready." I ask him how he is able to avoid boredom while he waits for a load. "I don't get stressed about waiting," he says. "I got everything I need in here—satellite TV, Internet, bed. I guess you'd say I'm a patient person." We continue to chat, occasionally checking to see if the red light has turned green. It hasn't.

7:00 p.m. We are now far past our scheduled pick-up window. If the load is not ready soon, Alvaro's 14-hour clock will run out, and he will have to take a 10-hour break, even though he has only done a few hours of driving today. That means he will have spent the majority of his shift waiting here without pay. Moreover, by being forced to take a long break, he will then have trouble making his appointment time on Sunday.

Since we first parked at 2:00 p.m., Alvaro has been logged as "in the sleeper." While his logbook says he has been sleeping, though, he has actually been awake. This is a strategy that drivers frequently use when they encounter an unexpected wait. By logging himself as in the sleeper, he is, as drivers call it, "protecting my clock." In this case, if Alvaro ends up waiting so long that his 14-hour shift runs out, by being logged as in the sleeper that whole time, he will at least have gotten a jump start on fulfilling his requisite 10-hour break and 8 consecutive hours of sleeper berth time. Thus, he will be that much closer to being able to legally start another shift, even though his body has been up most of the time.

It might look like Alvaro is taking a big risk here by not sleeping. But a closer look at the load scenario reveals that sleeping during this moment is actually just as risky as not sleeping. First, because there is no indication of when this load will be ready and because Alvaro is incommunicado with the shipping clerk, there is a chance that by going to sleep now he will miss the call on his CB that his load is ready. If that happens, the clerk will likely not come out of his office to follow up, but will just let Alvaro sit there and waste what are becoming precious minutes of driving time. Second, Alvaro has sleep apnea, which has been brought on by a decade of sedentary work that has made him dangerously overweight. He says, "I should probably try to get some sleep right now, but because of my sleep apnea I have to be careful." The company that contracts with Alvaro paid for him to see a doctor, who prescribed the use of a special mask, called a CPAP. The CPAP, which Alvaro jokingly calls his "space mask," covers the nose and mouth to keep the airway open and promote deep sleep. Alvaro says that if he goes to sleep with the CPAP on, he will sleep so deeply that it will be difficult to wake up again if the shipper calls after, say, an hour. He will have to wake up from a deep sleep and then drive in a more groggy state than if he had just stayed awake. Given the unique spatio-temporal constraints of this moment, then, deep sleep is inefficient and potentially dangerous.

8:33 p.m. We get a call from Brian, Alvaro's dispatcher, who wants to check on the load. Sitting in the dispatch office at the company headquarters in Missouri, Brian can see through his computer screen, which is tracking Alvaro by GPS, that he has not moved in a while and the load is getting close to becoming a problem. Alvaro complains that he is starting to get tired and that he needs to get going soon if the load is going to be on time. Brian suggests, "Well, maybe you should try getting some sleep now so you can get rolling again right away when the load is ready." Alvaro gives a long pause and responds, slightly annoyed, "Brian, you know I don't work that way, man. When I go to sleep, I go to *sleep!*" Brian says, "I know, I know. You run it however you see fit." They hang up. Alvaro and I continue to wait, now staring at the blinking red light praying that it will turn green soon.

9:30 p.m. Alvaro finally crawls into the sleeper berth against his best wishes. He looks back at me in the passenger seat and says, "I gotta try to get some sleep, man. I could be screwing myself right now, but it's either sleep now and drive groggy or not sleep at all and drive tired." Since he does not know if he will be leaving sooner or later, he has to at least attempt to sleep in order to create a somewhat functional body state. He decides to make a compromise with his body. He will take a nap without the CPAP so that he does not sleep too deeply. He settles in and quickly falls into a shallow sleep that is characteristic of sleep apnea. He begins to snore loudly. The snoring is interrupted periodically by a shallow breath and then silence. No breathing. Then a kind of loud snort as his body tells itself to keep breathing. This wakes him slightly. He shifts positions. Repeat.

11:30 p.m. Green light! I cannot believe my eyes. A green glow fills the interior of the truck, replacing the red pulses that have been marking the slow passage of time since this afternoon. I can feel a tension in my chest lighten that I had not noticed until just now. I wake Alvaro and tell him the load is ready. He sits up and looks at me through slit eyes. He groans and, without speaking, slides into the driver's seat and starts the engine. He looks very groggy but manages to expertly back the truck to the freshly loaded trailer. After some paperwork, we finally pull out just after midnight. We have just waited for 10 hours.

On the way to the interstate, Alvaro says, "we had better try to at least get some miles in today, otherwise we'll be late." Although Alvaro has had just 2 hours of shallow sleep, his logbook reads "in the sleeper" since 2 p.m., which means he has "slept" at least 8 hours and has taken a 10- hour "break." According to the logbook, then, he is now eligible to start another shift. "We'll just see how far we get before I feel like we need to stop," Alvaro says. "That sleep did not make me feel good, man. I am *tired*."

1:50 a.m. After nearly 2 hours of driving, Alvaro says he thinks he should probably shut down for the night, even though he has 12 hours left on his 14-hour clock. He would like to get more miles in, but he is feeling too tired. I am feeling exhausted too, barely able to keep my eyes open over the last hour.

We pull into a tiny truck stop somewhere along Interstate 40. It quickly becomes clear, much to my horror, that every space is occupied. I cannot believe what happens next. Without saying anything, Alvaro pulls back onto the interstate to see if we can find another truck stop with available parking.

3:32 a.m. Over the last hour-and-a-half, we have stopped at three more truck stops and one rest area. They have all been completely full. We pull into another truck stop—a fifth attempt at parking tonight. Yet again, it is full. Alvaro tries to remain optimistic. He turns to me with a wry smile and says, "Looks like we're going to Little Rock, man!" The chances are slim that there will be any parking between here and Little Rock (another 120 miles away). So, Alvaro decides to push on to a bigger city where there will be more parking. Plus, he informs me, by that time spots will begin to open up as other drivers start their shifts.

Alvaro pulls back onto the highway. My head is bobbing up and down as we drive. I can barely keep my eyes open for more than a few minutes at a time. Alvaro keeps complaining that his eyes are burning. "That's how I know when I'm at my limit. But we don't really have a choice [to stop] at this point." I look over at Alvaro periodically. I never see him doze off, but he eventually positions himself so that his right elbow is resting on the steering wheel, allowing him to prop his head up with his right hand and steer with his left hand. I assume this keeps his head from drooping. He rolls down the window and lets the cold autumn air stream into the cab. The chill is bracing and forces our eyelids open. Every now and then the truck veers slightly, but Alvaro keeps it going remarkably straight.

At some point (I do not record the time in my field notes) Alvaro pulls into a gas station. He gets out and starts walking around the truck. He hops back in after a few minutes and says, "Now I'm just working with my body. Sometimes you just gotta get out, take a walk around, breathe some fresh air. You gotta get the blood pumping again." We drive on.

5:08 a.m. Dawn approaches. We finally pull into a small truck stop on the outskirts of Little Rock. Alvaro does a lap around the lot and at first I get the sinking feeling that we are again out of luck. But then we see one spot in the corner of the lot. It is a tiny spot, and Alvaro pauses in front of it. "I don't know if I can do this right now, man," he says. He eases the truck into position and starts to back in slowly just inches from the two trucks on either side of us. The angle is a little off, so he pulls out and repositions himself for a second attempt. Success! Despite having just driven 5 hours in the middle of the night on 2 hours of sleep, Alvaro has managed to safely maneuver his 53-foot trailer into the tiniest of spaces without a scratch. He shuts off the engine, crawls into the sleeper berth, and throws on his CPAP. I follow closely behind, climbing into the top bunk. We fall asleep in seconds knowing that, despite the risky drive tonight, we are now well positioned to get this load of frozen chicken to Virginia right on time.

As Alvaro clearly demonstrated, through the conduit of the body drivers turn late loads into on time loads. What I am calling entrainment, then, involves the transmutation of one set of rhythmic patterns into another set of rhythmic patterns using the vigilant body as a medium.[6] As Alvaro describes it, "You have to get your body into the rhythm. You have to get into that rhythm of riding. The rhythm of driving and changing." By carefully timing his sleep, by skillfully propping his head up while driving, by knowing when to open the window or step out of the truck to "get my blood pumping," Alvaro demonstrated rhythm expertise—a professional knowledge of his body's capacity for attention, fatigue, and alertness. This

6. This corporeal transmutation is similar to the emotional transmutation described by Hochschild (2003) in her ethnography of emotional laborers.

knowledge allows him to convert the illiquidity and imprecision created by friction in the logistics system—in this case, the rigidity of the HOS, an inefficient shipper, and a national truck parking scarcity problem—into liquidity and precision. The body transforms chronological time into flexible time.

THE STIMULUS SHIELD

Because entrainment is so important to their jobs, drivers surround themselves with both high- and low-tech ways to manipulate their body rhythms. Unlike the technologies that surround financial professionals, which primarily enhance individual working memory by increasing the number and speed of stimuli that an individual can receive, drivers' technologies are designed to filter and block. Trucking technologies create what Wolfgang Schivelbush (1979), following Sigmund Freud (1922), has called a "stimulus shield"—a set of buffers and filters that protect one's senses from being overwhelmed by traumatic stimuli.[7]

The most obvious component of a truck drivers' stimulus shield is the cab of the truck itself, which can include a variety of high-tech tools, depending on the sophistication of the motor carrier firm one is working for and the degree to which the driver has invested his own money in upgrades. Drivers' seats, for example, feature an air-cushioning system and a forward-backward rocking mechanism designed to mitigate the characteristic up-down, forward-backward rocking of a tractor-trailer combination. This system is fully adjustable, allowing drivers to feel the truck on the road with greater or lesser sharpness.

7. In *Beyond the Pleasure Principle*, Freud attempts to describe how human consciousness protects itself in environments of heightened (and potentially traumatizing) stimulation, such as a war zone. I have found this imagery helpful for thinking about the technologies of truck driving, but I imagine it would be applicable to many other chaotic and risky timescapes in which technology is used to filter and block a harsh environment. Freud (1922:30–31) invokes the image of an organism suspended in an environment of intense and chaotic stimuli that must learn how to protect its "inner layers" by creating a *Reitzschutz* (literally, stimulus protection). As Freud (1922:29) describes it, "a rind would be formed which would finally have been so burned through by the effects of stimulation that it presents the most favorable conditions for reception of stimuli and is incapable of any further modification." Working from Freud's metaphor of an "encrusted vesicle," we can think of a stimulus shield as a system of filters that protects the body and psyche from exposure to both chronic and sudden or jarring stimuli. Rather than allow more stimulus in, it allows in only the right amount and kind of stimulus necessary to protect a person's sensorium from fatigue, while still allowing him or her to experience the environment.

Many newer trucks are also equipped with a lane departure warning system. This gadget detects the left-right movement of the truck. Before the truck can begin to cross the side or centerline of the road, speakers located at head level project a loud rumbling sound, meant to mimic the sound of the rumble strip carved into the side of American interstates. Should a driver become distracted or nod off and begin to depart his lane, this system is meant to jolt him to attention.

Some trucks also have a Collision Mitigation System, which projects a radar signal forward of the truck to detect the speed of vehicles directly in front. Like submarine radar, this system gives a sharp, repetitive "ping" that increases or decreases in frequency relative to the speed of an oncoming object—in this case, a slower vehicle heading in the same direction as the driver. Not only does this allow drivers to detect the onset of a forward collision before it happens, but it also provides a digital readout featuring the distance and speed of the closest forward vehicle, giving the driver precise information about the space-time ahead of the cab. When on cruise control, the system automatically adjusts the speed of the truck to maintain a safe following distance.

Together, these technologies create, to paraphrase Jack Katz (1999:33), a humanized truck or, alternatively, an automobilized person. They allow the truck to become an extension of the body, connecting the driver to the rhythms of the driving environment, while shielding the body from direct exposure.

A well functioning stimulus shield is only partly effective in facilitating drivers' efforts to entrain rhythms. Just as important as mitigating chronic and jarring stimuli, is producing enough stimulus in the work environment to avoid boredom and remain alert. The techniques drivers use to produce this ideal level of stimulus are as varied as drivers' personalities, but I observed several common techniques. The most notorious are legal and illegal stimulant substances. While the truck driving population is well known for illegal stimulant drug use, after the institution of mandatory randomized drug testing in the 1980s, use has declined (Couper et al. 2002). Aside from illegal stimulants, though, drivers have ready access at truck stops to a variety of legal stimulants, such as coffee, caffeine pills, and specialty caffeine drinks, like *Monster* and *5-hour Energy*.

While many drivers I talked to reported occasional use of legal stimulants (none reported currently using illegal stimulants), they always noted that these substances only provide a short-term fix. If used improperly, they can be more dangerous than helpful because, as one driver put it, "Those things come down quick, and when they come down, you come down with them." Paul, a 55 year old driver who has worked in the industry off and on for nearly 30 years, discussed the best way he has found to use caffeine pills, something he has given up in his older age.

> Now, in my very early years—I started drivin' when I was 26, 27, and I tried the NoDoze things [a brand of caffeine pill]. I found out if I was absolutely *tryin'* to stay awake, that what I needed to do was take that *before* I got tired, cuz it don't take long to find out that once you get tired, then the only thing's gonna help is sleep. Period.
>
>   Only if I *knew* I was gonna be up all night [. . .] I would just take a couple of NoDoz. Then I would never get that tired feelin'. But once that tired feelin' comes on ya, there's nothin' out there that's gonna help but some rest."

As Paul noted later in the interview, the number one thing a driver should avoid when using stimulants is "to push their body into doin' something, rather than just layin' down and tryin' to get some sleep."

Randy, a 57-year-old driver with nearly 40 years of experience, shared Paul's opinion, having made mistakes with stimulants earlier in his career.

> You have to know when enough is enough. A lot of guys don't.
>
> *Yeah. That's when they get in trouble?*
>
> Years ago, it used to be, okay—well, I never did it, but I know guys that would be popping pills [i.e., amphetamines] all day long. You can't do that no more. Now, you got guys that, I don't know, do one of those *5-hour Energy* bottles. I don't do that 'cuz that's too much sugar, caffeine, so I walk and I get a cup of coffee, then I'm fine. But that's for me personally. Everybody else has their own little system that they do, but my rule of thumb is: if I'm fatigued, and no matter what I do, I can't change it, I'm done. Because too much can happen when you don't know what's going on. I've already had that happen to me, and I got away with it.
>
> *Yeah?*
>
> I was working for another company, and I was up all day because something was going on, and I didn't get sleep. I told my dispatcher, "I can't go." "Well, you're gonna have to go. Just get there and tell 'em just to put you in the hotel."[8] All right well, I had one of those energy drinks: I fell asleep behind the wheel. Next thing I know, I was up against the guardrail.

Paul and Randy demonstrate an intimate knowledge of their capacity for alertness. Though they do not shy away from stimulants, they note that

---

8. Some companies will occasionally pay for or reimburse drivers for staying in the limited number of hotels along the US Interstate system that have truck parking.

these substances must be precisely entrained with the rhythms of the body—in Paul's words, prior to the onset of "that tired feelin." Stimulants work but only if one has enough expertise to make them work.

More frequently, I observed stimulant practices that had nothing to do with ingesting substances. Many of these techniques were mundane, such as listening to the radio or getting out of the truck to stretch and breathe. Most interesting among these techniques was the way drivers use cell phones. Cell phones have become an indispensible tool for drivers to maintain a state of constant availability for and connection to the flow of freight. Where communication was once limited to CBs and truck stop pay phones, drivers today use cell phones to communicate with their dispatchers as well as shipping and receiving offices. They also use cell phones, I noticed, to stay awake. This is especially useful when driving at night. As many drivers told me, driving at night has the up side of lower traffic volume and less chance of surveillance from the DOT. The down side, however, is that fatigue is much closer at hand because the body reacts to the lack of sunlight with lowered energy.

Alvaro, for example, frequently drives at night. Over the years, he has developed friendships with several other Hispanic drivers from different companies. Calling themselves the "Spanish Club," these drivers hold occasional conference calls during the night. "We talk and relax and keep ourselves awake," Alvaro notes. When I asked him why talking on the phone makes it easier to drive when he is tired, he replied, "It motivates your brain. When you're tired, you need something to get your blood pumping. What makes you tired is sitting here, driving. So we argue a lot and get our blood boiling and that keeps you awake." In the early evenings, I also observed Alvaro call his wife and extended family back home. On several occasions, Alvaro told me that his wife had placed the phone on the kitchen table so that he could listen as she interacts with the children, grandchildren, or anyone else who is around the house. As another driver put it, "I may call my wife [at night] or somethin' and kinda see if she's up. Cuz again that is another one of those things that'll just break that cycle of— I've been drivin' here for four, five, six hours and the brain is—I'm woke but seem like the brain's tryin' to go to sleep."

The sum total of a well functioning stimulus shield and a system of stimulant practices is still not enough for drivers to accomplish entrainment. The most important form of expertise for converting chronological time into flexible time, then, is sleep. As one driver said of creating an authentic feeling of freshness and alertness, "I'll tell you one thing I've learned: coffee don't work, energy drinks don't work. Sleep is the only thing that works." Riding with Kevin—a 27 year-old lease-purchase operator with just a year's experience behind the wheel—gave me a particularly good look at the skills necessary to sleep effectively within the ever-shifting timescape of the logistics system.

Being a relatively new driver with the new responsibilities of being a small business of one employee, Kevin approached route planning with a greater degree of consciousness than older drivers I met. He had not yet developed a stock of strategies for negotiating different load scenarios. One night, Kevin received new load information at around 7:30 from his dispatcher just as he was pulling out of the freight yard somewhere in New Jersey upon completing a previous delivery. "Looks like the next load will be 1,460 miles to Rolla, Missouri, at $1.20 per mile," Kevin comments to me. "Pretty shitty, but not unexpected."[9] I can see the excitement in Kevin's eyes as he begins to plan. He has told me many times on our trip how much he likes truly long hauls like this one, which give the driver freedom to run the truck as fast and continuously as it can go. He begins to work through an array of scenarios. "Let's see. We could either run this in two really long and fast shifts—worse gas mileage but it will get us there quicker. Or, we could run it in three shorter and slower shifts." Kevin says that he is tempted to do the first option, because, "I just really want to run fast right now. I just enjoy it more." But, doing that would potentially get us to our destination too early, which would mean a longer wait, not to mention the extra cost of poor fuel economy. The load picks up in the afternoon tomorrow, which means there is no way to start the next shift of driving right now. "It looks like we need to sleep now and then start running a little after midnight," Kevin says. "That would be [he checks the clock] about four, five hours of sleep." He pauses and contemplates that scenario. "I can do 600 miles on four and a half hours sleep. As long as I get a shower in there sometime to wake my ass up . . ."

After figuring out the locations of several truck stops along the way for fuel and sleep, we hop in our bunks around 8:20. Kevin pulls closed a blackout curtain between the front cab and sleeper berth area. This cuts off the waning sunlight of the summer evening that is streaming through the front windows, creating a more ideal sleeping environment. A few minutes after we are settled in, I hear Kevin rustle around in the bunk below me, then get up and pull open the blackout curtain to hop into the front of the cab. "I should be sleeping right now," he says to me. I can sympathize. This sleep feels like it is coming at the wrong time. I am feeling awake and ready

9. Generally speaking, loads running east to west pay less because they deliver freight from the "consuming" areas of the country in the East to the "producing" areas in the West and middle of the country.

to run, but Kevin's nearly spent 14-hour clock will not get us to our next pickup location. He takes a look at the load information again, obviously still turning over in his mind how best to run tomorrow. After another half hour of double-checking his calculations, Kevin is satisfied that we should, indeed, sleep now and crawls back into the bunk around 9:15.

1:00 a.m. As I have learned over the course of our journey together, Kevin is, to put it mildly, a heavy sleeper. He typically sets eight separate alarms, knowing that he will often turn several of them off unconsciously. Having had several instances of sleeping through all eight of his alarms, he recently purchased a special alarm called the *Screaming Meanie*, which is marketed to long-haul drivers. Much like a fire alarm, this device shrieks at precisely the right decibel level and alternating pitch to agitate one's ears. It is so loud and so irritating that it simply cannot be ignored, especially given the fact that the alarm can only be turned off by simultaneously pressing three buttons, which requires the use of both hands. Kevin affectionately refers to this alarm as "the bitch."

On this occasion, Kevin runs through all eight of his normal alarms. Being a light sleeper myself, I hear him turn them off and then fall immediately back to sleep each time. As expected, only the dreaded "bitch" manages to wake him. But it still takes Kevin a full minute of deafening shrieks to be moved to turn off the alarm. Through now ringing ears, I hear Kevin mumble, "Fuck" in my direction. "Is it time to get up?" I mumble back. "It has been for the last half hour," he replies. I am expecting him to get up now, but we remain in our bunks for another half hour contemplating the idea of work. We both succumb and fall back to sleep. It is just too early; the timing is completely off.

3:45 a.m. Kevin finally rises, this time on his own without an alarm, and makes his way to the front of the cab. I follow behind shortly. "The alarm went off and I was just like 'No way,'" Kevin reports. "I'll sleep a little more and then get up. I can't run 600 miles today like this." Like me, Kevin tells me he was not ready to sleep last night. He wanted to run, but didn't have the log hours to do it smartly, given our afternoon pickup time today. With a yawn and through groggy eyes, he peers into the darkness and reluctantly starts the truck. We roll out.

5:00 a.m. The last hour has been difficult for me. I am hungry, having had to skip dinner last night, and dead tired. Like me, Kevin looks bad off. He does not appear to be falling asleep, but is periodically yawning. He stares ahead at the road with a zombie-like blankness. We drive along in silence, both of us too tired to talk.

5:30 a.m. In an uncharacteristic move, Kevin decides to stop quickly at a rest area to go to Starbucks. As he has told me before, he normally drinks only water and juice but, "this is an occasion when a little coffee could really do the trick," he says. Kevin gets the largest size latte on offer, as well as a muffin. I get a regular coffee and something resembling a bagel. Back out on the road, I start to feel a thousand times better. The caffeine kicks in. The "bagel" temporarily pushes back the hunger. The sun peaks over the horizon and fills the cab with orange light. I can literally feel the sun fill my body with energy. I look over at Kevin. A mask of alertness has replaced his zombie-like stare. We get chattier. Things are better.

As Kevin demonstrates, in order to create a seamless bridge between his logbook hours and the flow of freight, drivers must become vigilant sleepers. They use the ancient technique of the alarm clock to spring to action when work requires it. This technique, however, is put into the service of a highly irregular and unpredictable rhythm that is characteristic of the flexible logistics system. Drivers frequently use a curious phrase to describe this activity: "I sleep when I can." Drivers must continually switch from a "night shift" to a "day shift" and back again, depending on the rhythms of the flow of freight. I heard drivers have long debates with themselves, their dispatchers, and other drivers about whether or not they should sleep or drive at a particular moment.

When drivers become more experienced, they gain a more precise understanding of what works for their bodies, not just in terms of sleep duration—for example, I can do X number of miles on Y hours of sleep—but also in terms of the timing of sleep with the rhythms of the earth. Paul, for example, the most experienced driver I talked to, said, "One of the things that over the years that's appealed to me about drivin' at night is—actually, I'll try to do this with an alarm clock: If I get up at 10, 11, 12 at night and start drivin', then at 6, 7 in the morning when the sun's startin' to come up, it's like I'll feel a little source of energy that comes along with it." By timing his drive so that the sun rises in the middle of his shift, Paul is able to smooth out the inevitable dip in energy that he has come to know through experience. "A lot of that [knowledge] is probably what makes us, or what should make us professionals. Knowin' what it is we have to do to be responding properly," Paul notes. Of course, having this kind of control over the timing of a particular shift changes from load to load, but, as Paul highlights, knowing when to implement this stock of techniques is precisely what differentiates rookie drivers from experienced drivers.

Rhythm expertise, a high-tech stimulus shield, a system of stimulant practices, and a professional relationship to sleep constitute the flexibilized driver. They allow him to engage in entrainment and transmute clock time into freight time. Desynchronizations between clock time and freight time—where the downbeats of the HOS, the rhythms of freight, and the rhythms of alertness are not matching up properly—are buffered, absorbed, and redirected by these practices. Through them, drivers are able to bring the HOS, freight flows, and body rhythms into line at precisely the right moment for picking up or delivering freight. They turn desynchronization into precious moments of unification—a state of perfect merger between rhythmic systems. From this perspective, flexibilization is not just a set of employment arrangements or production processes, but a stock of strategies to create a body and mind that are available for disruption so that "bad timing" can be transformed into "good timing."

A HEAVY PHANTASMAGORIA

As discussed in Chapter 3, one of the central characteristics of the timescapes of flexible capitalism is their disembedded and abstract character, which produces "phantasmagoric" experiences of place. Being a lynchpin in the flexible logistics system, truck drivers are certainly a fundamental part of these new timescapes. But, as we have seen, drivers engage with them through a more rigid temporal structure than knowledge professionals— the HOS. This rigid quality also extends to their experience of space. Drivers live in a concrete environment of real objects that are subject to all the frictions of the material world as they move through space. Consequently, there is a kind of solidity and hardness to the workplace that lies in stark contrast to the digital deal room.

The concreteness of truck driving was made most clear to me when drivers discussed crashing the truck. Dax, a 37-year-old rookie driver who would only give me his CB handle when I interviewed him, says that during the one year he has been driving, "there have been just so many crazy experiences. I've had near-death experiences and so many close calls, it's hard to pick out just one." When pressed further, Dax discussed a time when he was driving north on Interstate 95 from northern Virginia into Maryland near the notoriously dense traffic corridor between Washington, DC, and Baltimore. "You know that area and how crazy it can get," he comments. Dax was in the center lane of a three-lane road and a car had just sped up and passed him, then cut dangerously close in front of him as they crested a large hill. "We come up over the top of that hill and there's just a wall of traffic. A dead stop." Dax realized that he was going way too fast to stop without rear-ending the car that had just cut in front of him, surely causing a massive pileup and loss of life. Fortunately, another truck driver in the far right lane saw what was about to happen. Reacting quickly, he slowed down just enough to create a gap for Dax to slide his truck into and find enough distance in front to stop safely. "I sort of locked eyes with this other driver and fortunately I saw what he was doing and was able to get over real quick."

Dax says that this experience "absolutely terrified me. If it wasn't for that other driver looking out for me, I would have been in serious trouble." He says that it highlighted how, in order to do this job, "you gotta remain calm and slow everything down. You gotta be able to slow everything down in your mind."

Later that same day, Dax began to feel extremely tired, even though he still had ample time left on his logs. Rather than push through it, he, "decided to pull over anyway. I was so tired; I basically just fell right to sleep and started dreaming. In my dream I thought I was still driving and that I was falling asleep at the wheel. I had forgot that I had pulled over and was taking a nap." The image of the truck beginning to career off the side of the road in his dream startled him awake. Experiences like these have left Dax, as he puts it, "burned out." He is ready to quit. "Some guys are built for trucking and some aren't. I'm still trying to find my niche in life, even at 37, and trucking isn't my niche. You need to like being busy and rushed, or you need to have it in your veins, and I'm just not like that."

As Dax demonstrates, exchanging economic objects is not an achievement of the imagination for truck drivers, in which they must learn to see and feel abstract representations of the objects they exchange as though they are "really real." The reality of economic exchange in truck driving is given in the aesthetics of the work environment itself. Consequently, as Dax's account of his horrible day illustrates, when exchanges "go bad" for drivers, they do not need to conjure up the emotional consequences. Compare Dax's account to Chuck, the bond trader, whom you will recall was haunted in his sleep by a trading "blowup"—losing 25 millions dollars in three days. Though Chuck deeply felt the emotional consequences of his loss, the severity of this event was debatable, and thus his colleagues were able to talk him down to see this event as "not that big a deal." The blowups that haunt Dax's dreams, by contrast, cannot be debated. Serious mistakes with the truck cannot be imagined away. Help from colleagues can only take the form of the kind of quick, potentially life-saving reactions that Dax received from an anonymous fellow driver in the lane next to him. Though drivers form an integral part of the timescapes of contemporary global capitalism, then, there is nothing phantasmagoric about their sense of space. The road has a certain clarity and hardness that cannot be disembedded and abstracted.

There is an important caveat to this. There are at least two senses in which the concrete material places and objects that populate the trucking environment—bodies, roads, traffic, towns, truck stops, shipping and receiving facilities, and the like—have a certain ethereal unreality to them. Drivers frequently commented to me that, though many of them were lured into the industry, in part, by a promise to see the country, they slowly come to realize that, as Kevin put it, "In this job, you will see everywhere and stop nowhere. I've been by the Grand Canyon countless times; never been there, never really visited." As Kevin hints, though drivers certainly have the sense of traveling to different *spaces*, they do not necessarily experience different *places*. This is primarily because they are either disincentivized or forbidden by their company to travel outside the logistics system to see the sights, as one might in one's car, even in their downtime. They must stick to the roads and parking facilities that can accommodate a tractor-trailer.

Many drivers I spoke to reported remarkable experiences of adventure as they circumnavigated the entire country over the course of several years of hard driving, but after awhile, this excitement wears off. Tommy—48 years old, sixteen years behind the wheel—told me that he has been trying to get out of the industry for almost a decade now, but cannot seem to find any better employment. In the beginning, though, his attitude was different.

Did you enjoy it when you first got into it?

Loved it. I wanted to see every state in the United States and I did. After about five years I had my fill of it and after that it wasn't fun no more.

What made you get fed up with it?

It became a job instead of an adventure after about five years.

As Tommy notes, the adventure of traveling cross-country quickly becomes "a job"—a routine of, as another driver put it, "the same sections of interstate all the time." As another driver put it, "Everything gets boring because you've seen every inch of interstate eight thousand times. It has nothing to offer you, nothing new."

What gives drivers this experience of monotonous routine? For one, the shipping and receiving yards in which, as we have seen, drivers spend many hours of downtime, are highly utilitarian spaces. Shipping/receiving facilities are designed to be as interchangeable as possible in order to facilitate a frictionless routine of pick up and delivery. A typical shipping yard is a concrete patch on the side of a featureless building surrounded by a barbed wire fence (figure 4.1). At best, shipping facilities include a sparse room attached to the shipping clerk's office for drivers to sit in while they wait. It may even contain a television.

Figure 4.1 A shipping yard in rural Pennsylvania.
Photo by Benjamin H. Snyder.

More so than these workspaces, though, drivers discussed the boredom and monotony of truck stops. This is especially the case today, drivers reported, now that the vast majority of America's truck stops are owned by just three companies, which have merged through a series of massive buyouts: Pilot Flying J, T/A Petro, and Loves. Like other forms of convenience franchising, corporately owned truck stops aim to provide exactly the same customer experience regardless of location. Drivers thus see a monotonous set of "choices" in their downtime as they travel through the diverse geography of the United States. During my fieldwork, Pilot Flying J began replacing all of its restaurants with Denny's franchises, thus further reducing the variety of dining options available on the road.

Not surprisingly, then, I rarely saw groups of drivers congregate in truck stops during their downtime. Even in the rare cases that I observed larger truck stops that include forms of entertainment, such as coin operated arcade games or big screen television rooms, they typically sat unused. Rather than places of community, then, drivers primarily experience truck stops as oversized convenience stores. As one driver noted, "Most guys just sit in their trucks [during their downtime]. There's not really anything to do at a truck stop, and plus if you're not driving then you should probably be sleeping anyway." Taken together, the spaces outside the truck in which drivers spend most of their time do not ground them in a sense of place because these spaces are designed for fleeting, utilitarian interactions. Though drivers physically pass through the American landscape, they do so within a closed system of relatively placeless spaces that keep that landscape at arms' length.

The trucking environment is phantasmagoric in a second way. This is best seen not from the drivers' seat, but from the perspective of dispatchers— the men and women who direct and oversee drivers' movements by providing them with load information and tracking the progress of freight. I observed the dispatch operation of the same company whose drivers I rode with on two separate occasions, far less time than I spent with drivers. These brief periods, however, gave me a feel for the basics of life on the other side of the cab.

What was most remarkable to me about seeing the dispatch operation for the first time is just how similar it looks to the digital trading floor I observed in New York City. Much like financial traders, dispatchers work in a large, open-plan office environment, at computer terminals with two or three monitors, and in close quarters with their fellow dispatchers (figure 4.2). Each dispatcher is assigned a fleet of drivers with whom they match loads of freight located throughout the country. Dispatchers' primary motivation is to achieve a perfect "on-time rate" for their fleet. The higher the rate for each fleet, the higher the average on-time rate for the

Figure 4.2 A dispatcher at his terminal.
Photo by Benjamin H. Snyder.

company. Companies with the best rates tend to attract more clients due to a reputation for fast and reliable service.

When dispatchers start a shift—typically 11 hours, which mirrors drivers' shifts—they spend the first hour or so, as one dispatcher put it, "tapping" each driver to check his or her status. "Problem loads"—that is, those that are running late—are followed up using a set of communications technologies that, again, are similar to those used by financial traders. Dispatchers primarily communicate with drivers using what are officially called Electronic On Board Recorders (EOBRs), but which workers colloquially call "the Qualcomm," referring to a popular brand name of EOBR (figure 4.3). The Qualcomm system tracks drivers' precise GPS location, instantly streams their logbook activity to dispatch, and features a messaging application that allows drivers and dispatchers to communicate in real time. Dispatchers also frequently talk to drivers on cell phones.

In much the same way that financial professionals observe the movements of financial instruments, then, dispatchers gain access to drivers' movements mainly through disembedded abstractions: letter and number codes that represent information about each driver, such as his available drive time, hours logged in the sleeper berth, current GPS location, estimated time of arrival, etc. This information is streamed to them in real time to two or three

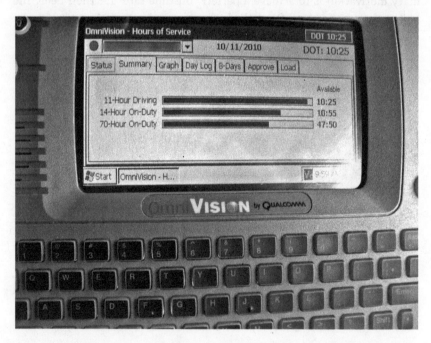

Figure 4.3 An Electronic On Board Recorder (EOBR) displaying real-time logbook data. Photo by Benjamin H. Snyder.

computer monitors. The dispatchers I observed also use specialized logistics software, which runs algorithms that calculate the ETA of each load and flash warning signs to the dispatcher when a load is predicted to run late.

I sat with Brian, who is Alvaro's dispatcher, on a typical day. He began his shift at 8 a.m. by pulling up basic statistics on his entire fleet. He immediately notices that a load being run by a team of drivers from Southern California through the mountains toward the Midwest, is running late. Yesterday, he had seen this coming and had communicated with the drivers that they needed to pick up the pace. "I was hoping that they would have made up some of that time last night, but . . ." Brian trails off as he clicks through some screens to see the drivers' logbook information. He looks at the time and GPS coordinates recorded each time they switched their logbooks from driving, to off-duty, to sleeping. This allows him to gain a rough estimate of their average speed, which, he tells me, looks to be somewhere around 40 miles per hour. "They've been dogging it," he sighs. "Granted, they are moving through the California mountains, but if they had just pushed it a little harder last night, we could have made this happen."

Now Brian has to find a way to prevent this load from being late. He comes up with two options. The first is to contact the Walmart distribution center, where this load is due in less than a day, to see if he can push the appointment window back. He quickly calls the receiving clerk and finds that she is amenable to changing the appointment. He hangs up and tells me that, though they now have a later appointment time, "I'm not going to tell the drivers that yet. If I tell them now, they might be tempted to run slower. I want them to think they need to keep pushing hard right now just in case something else holds them up."

Though Brian is feeling satisfied that the load is back on track, he decides to look at a second option just in case. He can also choose to "repower" the load—hand it off to another driver who has enough time left on his logs and is in the right location to deliver the load on time. Looking at the overview screen of his entire fleet, he finds a solo driver who, according to his logbook, is just finishing a 10-hour break and coming on to a fresh 14-hour clock. He is located in an ideal position to intersect with the late team and take their load. Brian uses the instant messaging application to ask the driver about his status (figure 4.4).

BRIAN: morning sir! You ready to run?
DRIVER: pls be gentle today. Am on 3 hrs sleep since I was trying to
    get loaded last night.
BRIAN: gentle? Never! Get ready to work:)

Figure 4.4 Using the EOBR to communicate with dispatch.
Photo by Benjamin H. Snyder.

Brian sends the driver the information for the repower, but tells him it is not a sure thing yet and to get back in contact when he finishes his current delivery. Having found two solutions to his problem, Brian finally feels satisfied that he can move on to his next task.

Like traders and the financial economy, dispatchers have a disembedded and abstract relationship to the production economy. Unlike traders, however, the underlying referent of the abstracted objects they manage can talk back. This can create some tension because drivers, as we have seen, tend to experience the timescapes of the production economy in a more concrete way than their dispatchers. A typical complaint that drivers lodged against dispatchers was, as one driver put it, "sometimes they treat us like machines." Dispatchers sometimes see drivers as their logbooks, rather than considering the many physical and emotional challenges that come with the flexibilization of the body (Levy 2015).

For example, while riding with Jeff, a 32-year-old former insurance salesman who had been driving as a lease-purchase operator for over a year, we encountered a difficult transition from a relatively steady routine of day shifts to a shift of night driving and then back again to a day shift, all within the span of 50 hours. After receiving the bad news from Brian over the Qualcomm that he would need to make this transition, I commented to Jeff that, "Maybe Brian will feel bad and give us a good load next time that's on a better schedule for you." Jeff laughed, saying, "No. He won't feel bad. That's the general attitude from people in dispatch—that we're robots and can just turn it on and off whenever we want." I pressed him further to describe what he means by "we're robots."

> Because Brian can see everything that's going on with my logs and he can see, "Oh, it says you've been in the sleeper for 15 hours, why can't you drive tonight?" And I say, "Well, Brian just because I'm in the sleeper doesn't mean I can just switch like that [snaps fingers] from one cycle to another."

> *And what does Brian say to that?*

> Well, then he turns it around on me and says, "Well, maybe you shouldn't be in this line of work if you can't be flexible, and yada yada yada." That's when we start to get in fights and feelings get hurt. Fortunately, he's a good guy and we always end up making up in the end.

As Jeff so clearly articulates, tensions can run high between dispatchers and drivers because of a confrontation between a concretized worker, who experiences economic exchange in his body, and a disembedded manager, who experiences it through the manipulation of abstract symbols. When dispatchers mistake the symbolic representations of drivers' body rhythms that they encounter on their screens—that is, logbook data about sleep— to be the real thing, drivers experience their own bodies as machine like. Dax, who after only a year is more than ready to quit, put it succinctly, "I am always being monitored. I don't feel and think. It's like I know I'm in my skin, but I don't feel like I'm in my skin. I'm like a human robot. I have to move at someone else's pace. I'm on someone else's time."

Trucking timescapes are inflected by a peculiar experience of space that is a kind of "heavy" phantasmagoria. What is given to the senses in the trucking world is not all that it seems. Though their work is physical and the objects of their work are heavy and concrete, the efficiency and surveillance systems designed to make that world move with more precision and liquidity, which are based on the practices of disembedding and abstraction, end up reconfiguring the experience of concreteness. Drivers can move through space without moving through place. Their bodies and cognitions can be directed and controlled without anyone sitting over their shoulder looking at them directly. Perhaps surprisingly, then, truck drivers share with financial traders the sense that the technologies of work leave few other options than to tailor their bodies and minds to the chaotic rhythms of the market.

CONCLUSION

Like financial professionals, truck drivers are immersed in a flexible timescape. But the degree of control drivers have over this timescape is dramatically different. Truck driving is characterized by stretches of work that involve a welter of intersecting processes that are mainly out of their control. Drivers must use creative strategies, especially their own body rhythms, to synchronize all this chaos. They turn desynchronization into unification—brief windows of "good timing" in which all the chaotic processes come together in sublime coordination for a moment of exchange.

From one perspective, there are stark contrasts to how these two groups of workers experience this temporal regime. Unlike financial professionals, for drivers moments of unification are not particularly profitable and are only rarely physically or emotionally invigorating. Drivers often find themselves sitting around waiting for this moment to arrive. While waiting, they are essentially volunteering their attention and energy for the sake of the two companies who will most profit from the exchange—the motor carrier firm and the shipping/receiving firm. What is most remarkable about this situation, then, is just how *unimportant* some of the massive inefficiencies in the flexible logistics system seem to be for the profitability of the companies involved. How can a system whose very purpose is to create smooth exchanges continue to be profitable with things like parking scarcity, frequent miscommunication between shippers/receivers and drivers, and the types of risky driving that routinely occur because of these erratic rhythms? The answer is that drivers, especially those involved on an independent contracting basis, are doing a good job of shouldering these risks themselves so that companies do not have to. What would be the economic incentive to get rid of these inefficiencies when they can just as easily be absorbed in drivers' bodies, thus creating that perfect moment of exchange anyway? Desynchronization, it seems, is actually perfectly profitable as long as companies have ways of displacing that friction somewhere else. Unlike financial professionals, whose workplaces are molded to their every specification like a pair of warn-in shoes, the trucking industry leaves it to drivers to manipulate their own bodies to suit the needs of the work environment.

Another difference between the worlds of finance and truck driving is the much more heavy-handed use of chronological temporal practices. Taylorism is alive and well in the trucking industry, but has been bootstrapped to a more irregular and deroutinized work environment using more advanced systems of surveillance than a simple stopwatch. Where Chronos has an almost benevolent face among some financial professionals—it provides a helpful fixed temporal barrier for market workers to contain an otherwise chaotic timescape—Chronos is used as a taskmaster among truck drivers. The FMCSA pretends that truck drivers are factory workers and use the ancient technique of the shift to discipline their behavior. What other way could one manage an "unskilled" worker, their logic suggests? Chronos the taskmaster, then, is a convenient external disciplinary tool that can be repurposed even within a flexible temporal environment. It is an awkward marriage. Drivers are constantly stretched between these antagonistic temporal systems. Especially with the introduction of GPS surveillance, they have few ways of working around these antagonisms, so they must find creative ways to filter and absorb them. Unlike the world of finance, then, chronological time in the trucking industry is not a stopgap for the speed and intensity of flexible capitalism, but a mechanism by which risks are passed down to the worker.

From this perspective, the truck driving industry is perhaps an extreme example of the new world of flexible scheduling and irregular hours that are becoming an increasingly common feature of "unskilled" work in the flexible economy (Presser 2003; Sewell and Wilkinson 1992). Just like truck drivers, a growing number of fast food, retail, and other types of service workers are asked to make themselves always-available (Halpin 2015; Kantor 2014; Lambert 2012). They often find themselves setting time aside for employers that goes unused when demand does not move with the anticipated rhythm, preventing them from being fully engaged with the rest of their non-working lives (Williams 2006). As Guy Standing (2013:12) notes, contemporary capitalism no longer sees waiting *during* work or waiting *for* work as worth paying for. Even though these workers spend a lot of time in a working frame of mind—thinking and worrying about when the next shift will arrive, for example—they are not being paid for the expenditure of that emotional and physical energy. Low-wage flexibilized work, then, is certainly physically and emotionally exhausting, but not primarily because of the old problems of industrial repetition, that is, boredom and monotony from constant routine (Roy 1959). Rather, boredom and monotony are the product of unpredictability. Workers swing from aimless waiting to hurrying without much warning. Truck drivers' experiences reveal that what appears on the outside to be "unskilled" labor, then, actually takes a great deal of skill, creativity, and improvisational genius to do successfully. Many low paid flexible workers, such as single mothers who are juggling on-call scheduling and young children or undocumented workers in the "gig" economy, for example, have to become rhythm experts too (Ehrenreich 2001; Halpin 2015). They have to understand the contingent micro-movements of their worlds in excruciating detail so that they can figure out how to synchronize that chaos into something that works.

From one perspective, then, trucking and financial timescapes are very different inflections of the same temporal order. From another perspective, however, there are some curious and unexpected commonalities between these two groups that shed interesting light on the relationship between worker independence and flexible time. Both types of workers are engaged in employment arrangements that give them certain kinds of freedom and autonomy. Financial professionals can typically work when and where they want as long as they are getting the job done. In the trucking industry, lease-purchase and owner-operators feel especially lucky to have found blue-collar work that does not involve a heavy-handed manager directly looking over their shoulders (Viscelli 2010). Even company drivers, who have less control over the labor processes than owner-operators, are still afforded the distinct luxury of long stretches of time alone when managers cannot see exactly what they are doing.

Upon further inspection, however, we see that what is given with the right hand is taken away with the left. Financial professionals' license to work when and where they want is coupled with intense client demands and unpredictable market swings that actually give them little meaningful control over time. Similarly, drivers' apparent autonomy is constrained by new abstract and disembedded systems of "remote control" that actually give them very little room to do what they want. In fact, given that drivers rarely use paper logbooks anymore, which can be easily forged, there are actually fewer opportunities in today's industry than in the past to bend the system to one's preferences (Levy 2015). This is an important improvement in some ways as it prevents bad drivers from cheating the system and overextending themselves. But in the process, it creates new kinds of scheduling complexities that may actually be both more fatiguing and less efficient.

Both cases suggest, then, that looking at workplace conditions from a purely macro and structural perspective—that is, some employment arrangements are structurally flexible while others are more rigid—may actually mask the lived sense of temporal control going on there (Blair-Loy 2009). In both trucking and finance, having some increased control over the labor process has actually opened the door to other sources of market-driven time pressure that make it difficult for workers to stop, switch off, and recover. Many of the techniques that give workers more autonomy, moreover, also pass more risk down to workers. As Michael Belzer (2000) and Steven Viscelli (2010) have observed of the trucking industry, the new freedoms of working independently can also be thinly veiled strategies to get workers to "sweat" their own labor. Employers can encourage their employees to be in a working *mindset* all the time; they just do not have to pay for it.

Flexible time delivers workers into a confusing environment of control, both more and less free than a rigid, routinized, and standardized environment. It asks workers to be better at working improvisationally and entrepreneurially, but couples that imperative with other incentives and remote forms of surveillance that ensure they work obsessively, perhaps even by their own volition.

CHAPTER 5

Precarious Futures

Unemployed. Among the mainly middle class white-collar workers I talked to, this was almost a dirty word. They preferred phrases like "between jobs," "seeking employment," "looking for my next opportunity," or "in transition." While early on in my fieldwork I did not find this language particularly significant—perhaps they are trying to shun a stigmatized label, I thought—as I learned more about the experience of job loss among white-collar workers, I began to see it as crucial. The word unemployed implies a certain backward looking, negative attitude that does not adequately capture the temporal and emotional structure in which they preferred to see themselves. They saw themselves as "transitioning," not from a loss located somewhere in their recent past into a new present, but from one understanding of the future to another. The past, which for many years had served as a relatively reliable source of information about the future, had ceased to be of much use. Unemployment, then, was primarily a future-oriented process.

In this chapter, I focus on one of the most notorious aspects of flexible capitalism in America: numerical flexibility. Numerical flexibility is a set of employment practices, ranging from the increasing reliance on layoffs and outsourcing to temporary contracting, which make it easier for employers to quickly adjust the composition of their workforce.[1] This results in rapid

Portions of this chapter appear in Snyder, Benjamin H. 2016. "The Disruptables." *The Hedgehog Review* 18(1):46–57.

1. There are several types of firm-level numerical flexibility that I do not discuss at length here for the sake of simplicity (see Kalleberg 2003 for a good summary). *Internal* numerical flexibility refers to things like overtime and irregular hours. It relies on adjusting labor input within the firm to meet shifts in need. *External* numerical flexibility, which is what I focus on in this chapter, refers to things like outsourcing,

cycles of hiring and firing. These practices have become especially popular in America's large corporate firms since the 1980s (Cappelli 1999). If there is one major source of disruption to the chronological temporal regime on the level of time maps—that is, the bounded career, loyalty, status, and security—it is numerical flexibility. I look particularly at white-collar workers because they sit on the latest frontier of this expanding preference for unstable, short-term, and unpredictable trajectories of employment. Once one of the most stable and secure areas of the American labor market, white-collar jobs are becoming increasingly "precarious"—a term popularized by Arne Kalleberg (2009) and Guy Standing (2011) to describe the conditions of uncertainty and unpredictability in the life course created by flexible economic practices.[2]

While we now know a great deal about how the life course is being restructured by these practices, little is known about how workers subjectively discover for themselves that their lives have become precarious, how they make meaning of that crisis, and, most importantly, how they continue to plan their lives in the face of existential disruption (see Lane 2011; Pugh 2015; Sharone 2014; Smith 2001 for important exceptions). I suggest that we think about the rise of precarious work not as an outcome of restructured employment contracts, but as an ongoing interactional process that transforms a particular dimension of time: the future. Precarious work practices induce *repeated* bouts of job loss and job seeking, which require workers to continually renegotiate their relationship to the future; both an "old future"—how things were once supposed to look before—and a "new future"—how things are supposed to look from now on. When the old construction of the future they once assumed to exist crumbles beneath their feet, how do people pick up and carry on?

---

automation, short-term/casual contracts, and the like. The focus here is on using the external labor market (and technology) to achieve the optimum workforce size to match fluctuations in need. Both internal and external numerical flexibility are particularly popular in the United States and tend to result in rapid cycles of hiring and firing. They can be contrasted with "functional flexibility" models, which are more popular in Europe. Functional flexibility refers to things like moving workers with diverse skillsets to different parts of the company, multi-tasking, and job rotation. Unlike numerical flexibility models, functional models tend not to result in intensive hiring and firing.

2. Precariousness is a term *du jour* that refers to a whole host of disruptions to the forms of security once promised by industrial society (see Standing 2011:17). Here I am using it in a more limited sense to refer only to insecurity associated with one kind of flexibility (external numerical), which particularly affects the employment contract. This source of precariousness has generally received more attention than others in the literature (Kalleberg 2009; Osterman 1999; Standing 2011).

The time I spent with white-collar job seekers was a particularly important historical moment that brought these issues into stark relief. I conducted my fieldwork just a few years after the 2008 meltdown of the American housing market, which triggered one of the worst recessions in history. The job seekers I talked to, all of whom had lost their jobs after or just months prior to the "Great Recession," were delivered by job loss into an atmosphere of intense national introspection about the future of work (e.g., *Time* 2009). The main cultural category around which this national conversation took place was the traditional "bounded career." Respondents were bombarded with narratives about what the career was in the past, what has become of it now, and what is arising in its place. They were given advice on what to do to get their lives back on track within the new order of things.

As I discuss below, I describe their engagement with this information, following Anne Mische (2009), in terms of "projectivity"—the dimension of social action oriented to the construction of expectations (see also Emirbayer and Mische 1998; Tavory and Eliasoph 2013). I examine how job seekers shift from an old future to a new future by going through a patterned set of transformations in their capacity for planning, imagination, and future-oriented action. This places a different frame around the problem of precarious work and lays the foundation for an explanation, which I take up in chapters 6 and 7, for one of the puzzling findings in many studies of precarious workers: Many Americans accept and sometimes even embrace the disruption of secure employment (see, e.g., Halpin 2015; Kojima 2015; Pugh 2015; Sharone 2007; Smith 2001). Why do American workers not have more resentment toward the economic elite's decision to use insecure employment as a *purposeful* business strategy? Are they somehow blind to this transformation? Or do they see what is going on, but simply lack the language to understanding or critique it? Or do they see what is going on and somehow believe that precarious employment is good for them?

I began my research by interviewing a variety of white-collar workers, from a 23-year-old call center worker fresh out of college to a 61-year-old executive assistant with decades of experience. As my fieldwork progressed, however, I began to focus more on older white-collar job seekers. Statistically speaking, this demographic was the least likely to lose their jobs during the Great Recession (Elsby, Hobijn, and Sahin 2010), but that is also precisely what makes them the most interesting in terms of understanding how precarious work shapes social time. Older white-collar job seekers are uniquely positioned to understand what it means to transition from a world where bounded careers are the (aspirational) norm to a world where that norm seems to be disappearing. Because of their age, older job seekers have clear personal and intergenerational memory of older time maps, which younger job seekers lack. The data I present here, then, are not meant to represent the average job seeker, but to reveal what sort of moral work goes into transitioning between the old bounded career time map and the new precarious time maps offered to white-collar workers.

HOW ARE FUTURES MADE?

Precarious employment practices are nothing new. Many of the insecure, flexible arrangements we see today have precedent in the late 19th and early 20th centuries. The "golden age" of employment security in the post World War II era was likely a mere blip in an otherwise long history of insecurity (Cappelli 1995; Polanyi 1944; Wallerstein 2011). Today's precarious work, however, is different in a few key respects. It is more global in scope, has spread to a wider area of the labor force—not just "unskilled" jobs—and is a *built in* business strategy. As Kalleberg (2009:5) puts it, "Layoffs and involuntary terminations from employment have always occurred and have fluctuated with the business cycle. The difference now is that layoffs have become a basic component of employers' restructuring strategies." The increasing use of mass layoffs, outsourcing, downsizing, and temporary contracting is not just an inevitable outcome of the business cycle, but also an *intentional* competitive strategy that employers increasingly rely on even in good times (Standing 2011).

But how does precarious work look subjectively? I start from the position that, within people's everyday lives, the cultural backdrop against which they experience the turn to numerical flexibility is primarily based on their perceptions of employment compared to when they were younger and compared to the preceding historical periods of which they have closest intergenerational memory—in this case, the post World War II era. Though secure employment may be the historical exception rather than the rule, from the perspective of today's white-collar job seekers, and especially the older ones, it may in fact be the opposite. For them, security has always been the way things are, or at least the way things are supposed to be.

The analytical language of "projectivity" or "future making" can help us make sense of this situation. Theories of projectivity show us how people construct meaningful images of the future from a variety of possible trajectories. They show how social action works when older constructions of the future, which function as the cultural backdrop against which change is noticeable, interact with and are (perhaps) superseded by newer ones.

Projectivity is a basic aspect of social action (Emirbayer and Mische 1998). Anne Mische (2009:696) calls it "the open, indeterminate, 'polythetic' perception of the field from the point of view of the actor surveying the future in terms of multiple possibilities." It is what humans do when they get themselves to move "forward" in social time-space by constructing sets of expectations, prognoses, and plans.

A major part of engaging in projectivity is storytelling. People construct narratives that link past and present, thereby allowing them to gather a set of expectations, turn toward the future, and make a move. Mische (2009) notes that future-oriented narratives are shaped by a wide array of cognitive dimensions, including reach, breadth, clarity, contingency, expandability, volition, sociality, and connectivity. These dimensions interact in different configurations, which give images of the future different shapes and trajectories. As they are more widely shared and refined, Mische (2014:445) suggests, futures can congeal into highly standardized narrative genres—"recognizable, schematized templates of dramatic storytelling"—that become common sense ways of understanding what to expect of the future.

The dimension of reach—the degree to which future narratives extend into the short, medium, and/or long term—is a crucial aspect of projectivity for examining the time maps of flexible capitalism. I will draw on Iddo Tavory and Nina Eliasoph's (2013) theory of anticipation to understand this more clearly. They argue that actors can engage in short, medium, and long term forms of reach simultaneously. In the short term, they explain, there is basic "protention." Protention is future-making on the small, moment-by-moment, day-to-day level. It is the "socially located 'feel' for the immediate future, a future that actors constantly calibrate in interaction and that requires mastery of interactional complexities that actors take for granted" (Tavory and Eliasoph 2013:913). Things like the way a person gestures with her body, a facial expression, or the way she pitches her voice, signal the direction of action in the micro-future. Actors are typically unaware of their competency with these mundane signals and that they share them with others.

The middle-range future is composed of things like narratives and projects, which actors place themselves in as they assemble discrete protentions into longer strips of action. These middle-range futures are always under construction and revision. They "tend to change as [actors] tinker with them and re-imagine their trajectories in midflight" (Tavory and Eliasoph 2013:914). Unlike short-term protentions, which draw on actors' unconscious and embodied habits of interaction, middle-range futures are often quite consciously and deliberately constructed through shared narratives.

When actors have the time and attention to "stop and think," they engage with others in conversation about what has happened in the past, what is happening now, and what will happen in the future (Mische 2014).

In terms of the long-term future, Tavory and Eliasoph discuss "temporal landscapes," which I take to be identical with what I have been describing as "time maps" (Zerubavel 2003). These are the foundational temporal structures upon which actors may not even realize they are standing, but which allow them to imagine and have conversations about a shared future in the first place. "Actors assume that the path is already laid, and all they need to do is take the expected or even required steps on it." Seemingly natural and taken-for-granted, these structures are often only seen and understood when they begin to disintegrate. "When actors retrospectively see this, they realize that those 'plans' worked only because actors 'got it,' performing them both on the level of protention and by planning their trajectories within it" (Tavory and Eliasoph 2013:916).

In what follows, I examine the introduction of precarious time maps into the white-collar workplace in terms of a disruption of the links that actors had always taken for granted between the short, medium, and long-term futures. How do people become aware of this disruption? How do they know that the old arrangements for the long-term future are falling apart? Once they become aware of it, how do they generate creative action—that is, reconstruct their habits of protention and restructure their medium-range narratives—in the confusion created by disruption?

OLD TIME MAPS

Because the job seekers I talked to were mainly white-collar corporate employees, many in their 40s, 50s, and 60s, they typically began to relate their stories to me, and generally understood their life histories within, the framework of an institutionalized chronological time map: the bounded career. This map took the form of a linear, vertical march from a lower to a higher rung in a single organization or occupation—what Phyllis Moen and Patricia Roehling (2004) describe as a "lockstep" pattern. As I discuss in Chapter 2, much like the mechanical movement of the clock, the bounded career has a rigid, predictable beat, which holds some promise of increased security, status, and power once one submits to it. This deeply naturalized time map was often taken for granted by respondents as they moved (or imagined themselves to be moving) securely on its tracks, becoming noticeable only in retrospect as it began to falter, or, more often, after it had long since crumbled.

Colleen is a 40-year-old former television broadcasting professional who had worked her way up to a middle manager's position in a prestigious network television studio in Boston. She had been raised by a career-driven, single African-American mother, who had always stressed that, in Colleen's words, "For a woman of color, [education] is not optional, it is mandatory." Recalling her mothers' advice, Colleen says, "The mantra I was given was, 'Go get your education. Be your own woman and have your own.'" By the age of twenty-four, Colleen seemed to be living her (and her mother's) dream. She recalls, "I worked my way up from entry level. I was a production assistant all the way to associate director. [. . .] To go from undergraduate Radio, TV, and Film [school] to being in a top ten market and establish your career was like unheard of, and a dream come true for most people that aspired in that field." She adds, "My career progression was such that, by the time I got the promotions, I was already performing the job that was ahead of it."

Between 2005 and 2006 Colleen says she "hit the glass ceiling." Despite having given her heart and soul to her job, which included getting up at two in the morning and working eleven- and twelve-hour days, her movement upward in the company began to stall. She was passed over for promotions and given undesirable work tasks that signaled her lower status in the eyes of the news director. At the same time, several members of her family, including her only brother, became sick and passed away, but she was so busy with work that she was unable to be there for her family through this difficult time. "So it just—it was chaotic," Colleen recalls,

> I mean, the draw for [working in] media is people are like "Oh, my gosh. You get to meet so many exciting people and go to so many places around the world." And that's the glitz and glam and the window dressing we put on it. But a lot of people are cogs in a wheel and have that supposedly high profile, or the impression of having the ability of power. But you pay profoundly personally. [. . .] Yes, I had a gorgeous condo split-level in the suburbs of Newton [laughs]. But the thing is, I was living on such a level where I would come home, literally dress there, sleep there, eat there, but I really wasn't able to enjoy my home anymore. And just—it just got to be very cannibalistic.

In early 2006, Colleen performed "a holistic review of my life," which led to an epiphany; it was time to quite. "It's just like, you're doing this for what?" she recalls. "You're not moving forward and your career is no longer giving you the high, or the promise of the high, that it did in years before. And look how much has disappeared from under your feet on a personal level." So, in late 2006 she "made the very profound decision to resign."

I felt like to stay in my job, it was the equivalent of being on a freight train going at top speed that you knew was heading for a collision. And I had two choices: I could either collide with the train that I was on, or I could jump off and possibly break a leg or arm. So I chose to jump, thinking that, okay, well, we can repair this and move on. Not having the—not being aware of this tremendous blind spot of what was going on in the economy. [. . .] So I sold my home, turned a nice profit, decided, "Oh yea, I'll explore another career."

It is only in retrospect that Colleen can see a "blind spot" in her life trajectory—the immense risk she had taken by resigning in 2006—a particularly inauspicious historical moment. However, on an emotional level there was simply no other option. Having turned her vision of an empowering media career into a reality, she began to see it for what it was—an empty status game that unsustainably pitted her personal life against her professional life.

Even more so than Colleen, Henry, a 58-year-old former customer service specialist for a multinational communications corporation, could narrate his past as a linear progression upward through a chain of positions with growing status. Henry originally joined the firm directly out of high school when it was a large printing company.

I worked for my company there for 25 years. Started right out on the ground floor as a press helper. That was 1973. June of '73. I progressed through my career at the plant. I was promoted to quality control technician, and then, about four years after that, I was promoted to quality control specialist. And then, after that, I was promoted to production planner. Then, in 1999, [the company] sold the division that I worked for to a competitor.

Henry's narrative moves fluidly through this period, despite there being a major change. "I didn't want to leave the company," he notes. "I spent a lot of my career there, built a lot of relationships." So, in 1999, he applied for and was offered a sales support position within the company that required him and his wife to move to Maryland. Henry worked in this position from 1999 to 2007.

The transition to new surroundings within the same company was one of the best things that ever happened to him. He recalls, "It was a tremendous growth period for me. In September of 2007 I was promoted to customer service supervisor. Again, from 2007 to 2011, my career continued to just boom and grow and . . ." Henry's voice trails off as his narrative reaches the present. He pauses and looks away. Turning back, I can see his eyes begin to water. Looking me directly in the eye as though to make sure

I see the importance of his next point, he says, "I am *very* passionate about customer service. I love what I did." The curious mix of present and past tenses in his speech signals a coming temporal confusion.

Henry remembers that "Unfortunately, in July of 2007 our company had merged into [name of Fortune 500 company]. They—you know, our senior management was looking to cut costs. They began a process where they were starting to outsource our customer service." This process of, as Henry calls it, "workforce reduction," eventually led to him being laid off. It is important to pause here to notice a narrative sleight-of-hand in Henry's storytelling. In retrospect, he sees that the merger in 2007 with a larger corporation was "unfortunate" for him. However, just moments earlier in our conversation, he had described the period between 2007 and his job loss in 2011 as a major period of growth in his career, which featured an important promotion. Perhaps unconsciously, Henry provides a glimpse of the difficulty of reckoning his long, linear, upward career trajectory with the fact that the temporal foundations underlying this life narrative had been eroding beneath his feet for some time, perhaps as early as 1999 when the original company had sold his position away, forcing him to reapply and relocate.

The bounded career time map was not the only one that respondents described. Those who had been in lower level white-collar office jobs had often experienced multiple rounds of layoffs, downsizing, and outsourcing throughout the last several decades. Linda, for example, is 57 years old and describes herself as a "seasoned employee" who has "been in transition since October of 2011"—fifteen months at the time of our interview. She notes that her "original career" was in education as a teacher of "business subjects." This eventually led her to seek employment in the business world "looking for administrative assistant [positions]. Back then it was called secretary *[laughs]*." She eventually found employment with a mid-sized regional bank as an executive assistant to the senior vice president. She entered the company "hoping to get into the training department." Shortly after being hired, however, the bank began to outsource. Her position was dissolved. Foreshadowing things to come, Linda mentions offhandedly, "Outsourcing has proven to be a valuable term, let me say, in job seeking." Despite this small setback, Linda was able to stay in the company and "work my way up to an information specialist in budgeting" throughout the late 1990s. But, in 1998 the bank merged with a much larger national chain, and, for the first time in her life, Linda was laid off.

Reacting instantly to this loss, Linda followed her "first thought" and went to a staffing company to seek a temporary position, which she hoped would blossom into something bigger. She was "immediately placed within a week," and found a permanent position as an executive assistant to the president in a growing regional corporation that manufactures fire safety products. When the president retired just a year later, Linda was again laid off. Again, reacting quickly, she "did what I had tried before, and it worked well. I went back to the same staffing company—immediately got placed again," this time at a regional branch of a large national life insurance company.

Linda spent the next eleven years there without a promotion, working a series of executive assistant positions to different district and branch managers. During this time, she "had some health issues" causing her to go on unpaid sick leave for four months. "When I came back, the district manager had moved on to greener pastures," she notes, "so it left my position unavailable. I was moved to the receptionist's role, which was fine." The way Linda adds the phrase, "which was fine," belies the neutral attitude she is trying to convey to me. She is just barely able to cover over her disappointment.

Though she does not mention it in our conversation, I later learned that the insurance company Linda was working for was taken over by a global conglomerate headquartered in Paris at the same time that Linda began to experience a more tenuous employment pattern. Throughout 2010, seeking to cut costs, the company began to streamline its lower level support positions, eventually leading to Linda's severance. When I asked her why she thinks she was let go, she explained, "Processes changed. Insurance companies used to send a lot of paper at you. Well, then they slowly declined and put it mostly online. Instead of getting stacks of ten thousand sheets of paper a week, we ended up with maybe one thousand."

Unlike Colleen and Henry, then, Linda does not tell a story of a career that is moving steadily upward. Having been laid off three times and experienced only one major promotion, her trajectory has been steadily horizontal, if not downward, through a series of relatively short-term positions. Still, just like Colleen and Henry, Linda sees her past self as aspiring to a career within a single organization. She always operated with the assumption that a temporal foundation exists (or at least existed at one time) upon which this trajectory was achievable. At times in our conversation Linda sounds like Colleen. She describes her work history as a "career" that kept her "always too busy." She notes that she never wanted to have children because "My life was my career. I worked 60 hours a week. There was only time for my husband and my home." Only by looking back on her past efforts from the present does Linda now see that "I did more than what the company ever expected so that I would have seniority, and it did me no good." Despite having never experienced the markers of the bounded career path, Linda always saw herself as existing within this type of time map—that is, until it was clear that it had always been a bit of a myth.

MOMENTS OF RECKONING

The most distinctive feature of the temporality of unemployment is its eventfulness. Losing one's job is an existential event, with a beginning, middle, and end that can be easily assembled into a dramatic story. As Robin Wagner-Pacifici (2010) has argued, events are "restless." Inherently rhythmic, they are "flows" of causes and effects—first this, then that, then this. Each beat in the rhythm of an events' effect flow provides an opening for meaning making, which social actors struggle over through heated semiotic exchanges (see also Simko 2012). An important mechanism of the restlessness of events is what Wagner-Pacifici (2010:1383) calls the "moment of reckoning"—a "pause" in the effect flow of an event, which precipitates a "realization that the very contours of the social and political world have been transformed." For the job seekers I met, the moment of job loss presented itself precisely as this kind of pause in the flow of daily life, which radically transformed the contours of their worlds. During these moments, respondents were suddenly able to see that the time map they had assumed was intact beneath their feet was in fact in great jeopardy. Long-term, foundational time maps, which typically remain implicit and hidden, were suddenly pushed to the forefront of consciousness.

For some, job loss came seemingly from out of the blue, especially for those who had been working in stable companies that had only recently been destabilized by the 2008 financial collapse. Respondents in these situations found that only in retrospect could they see that things had been heading this direction for some time. Henry's moment of reckoning, for example, could not have felt more abrupt, though he now sees impending signs of it throughout his recent past. Shifting from the longer wavelengths of decades and years, which characterized earlier parts of his narrative, to the shorter wavelengths of months and days, he recalls,

> The day before my birthday—July 19th—I remember it well. I was working at my desk, and I'd gotten up to go out to the restroom, and I was walking down the hall and just happened to glance in our conference room, and I saw our HR manager in there. Then, as I got up even with the door I saw my manager. I knew my number was up.

You knew it then?

I had no clue before.

Really? Absolutely no clue? [Henry nods his head yes] *Wow.*

Matter-of-fact, Friday before that, I was—all of the supervisors and managers were engaged in an employee reduction program. I had to travel to one of my satellite offices up in Linthicum, Maryland and workforce-reduce one of my CSRs. Anyhow, so I walked into the conference room and I said, "I guess you guys aren't here to wish me a happy birthday."

Notice how this radical pause in the flow of his career trajectory spins Henry into a cycle of retrospective-prospective temporal reckoning. Jumping from a recent past—July 19th—to an earlier past—the Friday before that—and back again, he can now see this moment as both unpredictably sudden and tragically predictable. As he continues to describe that day, the pace and rhythm of Henry's narrative slow to a near standstill—the tiniest details take on larger significance, signaling entire worlds of meaning.

July 19th. I mean, you remember the exact date.

I remember the exact time.

What was that meeting like?

Well, I have to tell you, Ben, it was—I mean my manager was pretty emotional. She and I, we really hit it off. [. . .] She always used to commend me for the spirit that I brought to my team. I always had an open door. There was nothing that anyone on my team could never come to me with. I had some pretty challenging situations.

Henry then plunges into a long story about how he went above and beyond the call of duty to rescue a 35 million dollar account that nearly slipped away when the account manager suddenly quit. A heroic tale, Henry heard of the problem on a Friday, jumped in his car on a Sunday, and moved to New Jersey for three months to finish the work and save the contract. Detailing this story spins him into another long tale of when his former boss passed away from cancer leaving only Henry and his current boss to work side-by-side to lead the team through the transition. Finally, returning to the "recent past" of his last day on the job, Henry recalls,

So, when we sat down on July 19th, I mean she was crying.

Yeah. How could she not? Who else was in the room besides her?

The HR manager. Even *she* was crying. [. . .]

How did they break the news to you?

Well, you know my manager started, but then she was pretty emotional, so then the HR manager said, "This was a trip that neither of us wanted to make today." They said, "Unfortunately, you understand what's going on and we've got to cut back even deeper than we had originally thought. Today's your last day."

We talked through and we went through the paperwork and stuff. At the end of that, they said to me, "You know, we normally don't do this because—" and I had witnessed to it the Friday before when I workforce-reduced the CSR. We just had to tell her—we had to get up, escort her out of the room, take her to her desk, let her get her personal things, and she had to walk out the door. They said to me, "You know, we don't think that's right." They said, "Why don't you take some time and—or if you want to, we'll go around and tell the rest of the staff and sales people that are in the office." I said, "You know, I appreciate your offer, but I'll do it myself." I said, "I'm a big boy."

A single detail that occupies no more than a few moments in his life narrative—the sincere regret displayed by his boss and the HR manager—signals an entire complex of meaningful impressions for Henry: his deep respect and warm relationship with his bosses, that this respect was mutual, that he was an admired team leader with remarkable accomplishments. Even more significant is the fact that, just a few days prior, Henry had been in his bosses' shoes. The kindness they show him by breaking protocol and letting him say a proper goodbye to his colleagues further marks this moment. These brief exchanges of emotion, with all their semiotic weight, fix this moment in time as a solid marker in an otherwise fluidly flowing career narrative. It ropes off everything happening before this moment as "before" and everything happening after as "after."

While Henry's moment of reckoning felt sudden, others saw that trouble was brewing long before job loss. Even these bad omens, however, were often explained away or simply endured, leaving respondents still reeling during their moment of reckoning. I met Janice and Cindy several months after they were laid off at the same time from the credentialing department at a managed health care provider. They entered the company when it was a state licensee for the nation's largest healthcare association. Over the course of the next fifteen years, they saw the company through two mergers and two name changes. During the last of these mergers, which occurred in the early 2000s, Janice and Cindy began to see dramatic changes to nearly every aspect of their daily lives in the company. The first signs of change were subtle. Working in different sections of the department at the time, they both got new bosses who resided on opposite coasts. As Cindy puts it, "It became that all of our managers, all of our directors, everybody, they used to be down the hall. You knew everybody. They'd been there forever. They knew their jobs. All of a sudden, my new boss [pause] was in Andover, Mass."

The credentialing department "wasn't doing so well with this new infrastructure," Janice notes, so the department director was replaced with a new director from California. "She was a formidable force," Janice recalls. "She was just—talk about company oriented; everything was for the company." The new director began holding weekly conference calls with the department and making two visits in person a year. "When she came in, it was like a hurricane to clean house. It was like, you're not doing this, you're not doing that. If we spoke up in a staff meeting, she was like—it would always be 'One company, one team. You're not thinking about the company.' Boom, that was it."

The clearest expression of a harder, more company-focused management style came with new performance expectations. "You've got to hit this mark; you've got to hit these numbers," Cindy recalls. "And this was the funny part too: and you've got to hit it with no errors [laughs wryly]. I mean, it got to the point—I did my job, I worked my butt off, but nothing was ever good enough for them at one point." Foreshadowing things to come, she adds, "That's how they managed to phase out credentialing."

As Janice tells me late in our conversation, even by this time "the writing was on the wall. They had been talking about outsourcing for a while even before this." The credentialing department in an affiliated company was outsourced to India just a year prior to Janice and Cindy's layoff. "We worked closely with them," Janice recalls, "so it was like, 'Okay, if they're outsourcing them, we can't be far behind." Worries were increased, then, when the company began a major reconstruction project, which scattered the credentialing department to several temporary offices on different floors. They recall,

Janice: [To Cindy] I don't know what it was like on the third floor, but I was on the fourth floor. It slowly—you saw all of these Indians—contract workers coming in to the office.

Cindy: Yes.

Janice: [. . .] Well, I remember when the renovations were almost finished. They started at the top and worked their way down; it was six stories. They said, 'Oh, sixth floor is all done.' We wanted to . . . see what it was going to look like with all this new stuff, cuz they made the cubes smaller. [. . .] I remember, I went up on the sixth floor and we were walking around. The cubes were all empty but they had the little nameplates out. We started noticing it was like—names that were like 16 feet long.

Cindy: [...] It was just—after a while it became—you know, I hate to sound racist, but the running joke there was that the sixth floor, we started calling it Little India.

Janice: I called it Little Pakistan. On the fourth floor we were calling it Little Pakistan.

It was not too difficult for Janice and Cindy to see what was ahead. New bosses who were no longer just down the hall, unreasonable expectations for work performance, rumors of similar departments being outsourced, and then an influx of IT specialists with strange names who had already staked their claim in a newly renovated office.

Remarkably, the actual day that Janice and Cindy were laid off still came as a surprise to them. As Cindy remembers,

We kind of—you know, you could see what was going on with the outsourcing. At the same time, we had no inkling that day. They called us in to this [meeting] and it was funny. We sat down. Sat next to—I think it was Barbara. She said, "Oh, I bet she's gonna talk to us about how we're up and talking too much or something like that." And I said—the HR person was sitting behind us. I said, "Barbara, something bigger is going down." She goes, "Well, what do you mean?" I said, "Why would HR be here?" I said, "This isn't a, you know, you're slacking off meeting."

As it was for Henry, the meeting during which Janice and Cindy were let go was conducted in such a way as to enhance the surprise. However, unlike Henry's experience, the emotional tone of Janice and Cindy's meeting was far colder. Janice remembers,

I came in that morning and there was actually a Post-It note on my computer from Mary Sue [her boss] saying staff meeting, blah, blah, blah, first floor, nine o' clock. [...] Normally if we had a staff meeting it was in an email when you turned on your computer. I kinda said out loud, "Why did Mary Sue leave me a Post-It note about a staff meeting?" [...] When I got in there and I saw people sitting there but I saw some people *weren't* sitting there, I thought okay, this—but it was still kind of—I wasn't quite sure.

Having sat down with a group of other employees who looked just as confused, Janice and Cindy suddenly realized what was going on when the HR manager walked in and began taking attendance. "Never in fifteen years had anyone ever taken attendance at a morning meeting," Janice recalls.

Next, Mary Sue entered carrying a piece of paper. Walking briskly and sitting down without looking anyone in the eye, she began to read from the paper.

Janice: *[To Cindy]* She sat there with the—

Cindy: Just staring at the paper.

Janice: She just read it. "Due to, you know, profit blah, blah, blah, and it's been decided that—so the credentialing department—and these are the words she used. She said, "As of August 12th," she said, "your jobs are being eliminated and are being outsourced overseas."

Cindy: Uh-huh.

Janice: I just sat there like, "Holy shit. It really happened," you know?

There is a four second pause as Janice and Cindy allow me to take in the weight of this memory. Cindy picks up where Janice left off.

CINDY: She finished her statement, which took all of what, 30 seconds?

JANICE: Oh yeah, just to say HR will review with you, blah, blah, blah, blah, blah. She got up and *walked out the door*. I was in shock [. . .].

CINDY: [. . .] I was pissed at that. I was like, "Excuse me, where is Mary Sue going?" [The HR person] said, "Oh, we find in situations like this it's best to be, you know, to let HR handle the situation." I felt like saying, "Bullshit!" She's afraid to face the people that she's been manager of for so long and tell me, a 56-year-old, middle-aged woman who's divorced—I don't have a second income to help me out. I'm lucky I got to the point I was—she's afraid to tell me, "Guess what, honey, you're on your own." She couldn't bear to face it.

JANICE: Yeah. "Find a job and live your life."

CINDY: Six months later, boy, I'm living the high life.

Despite all the signs that this moment was just on the horizon, Janice and Cindy were not prepared for the temporality with which the moment arrived. And how could they be? Conducted as a kind of sneak attack to mitigate any uncontrollable emotional outbursts, the suddenness and coldness of the meeting fixes a clear before/after point in the narrative flow. As in Henry's case, the smallest details matter: the specific date, the paper in Mary Sue's hand, the way she walked and held her head, the specific configuration of words used to terminate their employment. Each of these performative signals causes entire worlds of meaningful impressions to flow from employer to employee, fixing the moment forever in time as a new center of gravity that will pull their future trajectories into a new orbit.

As these examples illustrate, moments of reckoning are crucial for creating the temporal circumstances in which job seekers' old time maps become visible. These moments arrive with an *intentionally contrived* temporality that makes job loss feel sudden and unexpected to those being let go, even when there is ample evidence of what the company is up to. A more drawn out process, employers' logic implies, might give employees time to foster resentments toward the survivors of the cuts and perhaps organize a response that could get out of management's control. Even in the moment of "reducing" their workforces, then, flexible businesses are guided by a logic of contrived unpredictability that, in the midst of giving them a larger economic advantage through a streamlined workforce, can give them an emotional advantage on unsuspecting employees in the very act of letting people go. There is better and worse timing in the way one lays people off, the logic seems to run, and businesses try to calculate the risks of bad timing to shelter themselves. The percussive temporality of these contrived meetings, however, passes that emotional risk down to the worker.

HYSTERESIS AND STAGNATION

Through moments of reckoning, the link between past and future that workers had forged under the career time map is suddenly cast into a crucible, which rapidly melts that connection, making a once solid temporal structure that grounded a vertical and linear trajectory distort into a new and unrecognizable shape. Following these moments, respondents typically found themselves spiraling out of control emotionally. While this reaction may seem self-evident, a closer look at how and why emotional collapse tends to follow job loss reveals the crucial role played by temporality, more specifically the timescape of "crisis" in which social time seems to come to a stand still. Far from being a simple matter of insecurity, a deeply troubling aspect of job loss is the sudden lurch into a timescape with no rhythmic structure—no schedules, no deadlines, no routines—which triggers deeply felt moral emotions, such as guilt, shame, and anxiety (Garrett-Peters 2009; Jahoda, Lazarsfeld, and Zeisel 1971).

For some, the timescape of crisis felt surprisingly liberating at first. A world without rigid temporal boundaries gave some a rare chance to relax and regroup after many years of busyness. Some took advantage of this freedom by becoming, as one respondent cleverly put it, "funemployed." Linda, for example, recalls that right after being laid off she "became very lazy." When I asked her what she meant by lazy, she replied, "I took some time off, just played around a little. [. . .] Instead of looking for a job, I went line dancing. Instead of looking for a job, I took my girlfriend to Charlotte. Instead of looking for a job, I went shopping. I mean, I just did the things that I had never done before because I was always working." Similarly, Shirley, a 49-year-old laid off graphic designer, at first began to pursue some of her favorite hobbies, such as fishing, photography, and scrapbooking, but found that,

> My frame of mind is not—I look back at things that I did on the side for hobbies, in addition to all the clubs and things I was involved in, and now I sit there and I can't even do it.
>
> *Why? What is it that's keeping you from doing it, do you think?*
>
> Guilt. If you've got time to do this, you've got time to look for work. Work.
>
> *So you feel like that should be the priority?*
>
> Oh yeah. I cannot take the—I think what you're asking is, can I take on a retirement mentality?
>
> *I hadn't thought of it that way. That's interesting.*
>
> No, I can't do that.

The critical moral evaluations that Linda and Shirley apply to their time is typical of those I talked to. While job loss may have at first provided the chance to reconnect with old friends, take trips to interesting places, and reconnect with old hobbies and interests, these activities always take place against the backdrop of the imperative to be busy. Deeply internalized chronological time disciplines produce a background mood of guilt that spoils their attempts to lead a life of leisure without its twin: work.

Other respondents did not pause to relax after their moment of reckoning; they put their noses right back to the grindstone. When Henry returned home on the day he was laid off, he called his brother-in-law to break the news and then immediately went to the unemployment office.

> I signed up for *[laughs nervously]* unemployment compensation. I got hold of the benefits center and started the process with my COBRA and—you know, I'm a pretty—I like structure, I like organization, and I like to have all my ducks in a row. I just began the process that day.
>
> *Really? You started looking for jobs right away?*
>
> Yeah. Some of my friends said to me, "Why don't you take some time?" I said, "You know what? I don't want to take time off." I love to work. I enjoy building

relationships and building teams and building client relationships. Partnering with the sales team—I loved it.

You were just in your element, yeah.

Totally.

Henry's nervous laughter at the mere mention of unemployment benefits signals the deep shame he associates with unemployment. His immediate response to this moral emotion is to deploy the trusty face of Chronos, the benevolent moral guide: seek out a routine, focus all attention on that rhythm, and begin to fill it with as much productivity as possible. Chronological time discipline, while taking place outside the world of work, produces warm emotional memories of the healthy synchronized rhythms from that world—building, partnering, and connecting.

As Henry's example shows, respondents typically approached crisis by relying on a stock of strategies for action that had worked in the past. Because many respondents I talked to had never been jobless for more than a few weeks, however, they often began their job search using strategies that are better suited to a bygone era of corporate capitalism. Linda, for example, went back to the same staffing company she had used twice before. When she arrived with copies of her paper resume, the company informed her "We don't submit resumes mostly. We do it by video." Shocked, she recalls, "I wasn't told about this ahead of time, so when I arrived, I was put in a room with a computer, webcam, and asked to give a sixty second elevator speech." "Elevator speech? That was new terminology to me *[laughs]*." Later that month, calling the company to find out what had become of a particular application, she found out that the company had itself gone out of business. The people who were supposed to be helping her find a job were now losing theirs too. "They didn't even notify me. I got a recording saying to contact their New York office. This was not a good sign *[laughs]*."

Like Linda, other respondents spoke of early experiences when once reliable strategies for action seemed out of step with the times, a condition Pierre Bourdieu (2005) calls "hysteresis." Henry, for example, had the remarkable fortune, just days after being laid off, of finding a job listing that was "right in my sweet spot"—the customer service department of a large trucking company. "My biggest challenge," he notes, "is that I had never applied for a position outside of my company—in thirty-eight years." Scrambling to find help, he contacted a career-counseling firm that gave him advice on phone interviewing. "For the next couple of days, I just engrossed myself in learning about the company." Feeling rushed but prepared for the interview, Henry remembers,

I had positioned myself in front of my kitchen table looking out the window. [The employer] calls and we start talking about the position, and the interview's going actually pretty well. Then, she said to me, "Well, tell me about your trucking experience." I said, "Well, I've never worked for a trucking company before." I said, "I've worked with trucking companies in both of my previous roles. I had extensive relationships with a lot of major carriers—[name of this company] being one—where you scheduled deliveries and tracked shipments and worked with your freight management people and things like that. She said, "Well, it sounds like you really don't have any trucking experience. I'm going to end the interview right now."

Oh my gosh. Just because of that?

I said, "I didn't see that as—it wasn't a requirement on the job description." She said, "Well, I think it's something that you would need to have, so sorry for taking up your time." Click. Then, I'll tell ya, then I was pretty devastated.

Henry's disappointment put him into a tailspin, unable to resume his job search for several weeks. He had learned his first hard lesson about job seeking in the new economy. Because there are so many equally qualified individuals competing for the same positions, hiring managers spend much of their time looking, not for the "best person for the job" but for ways to filter out applicants whose resumes do not fit perfectly within a job description. With this level of competition, applications and interviews can often turn on a single detail. Henry had put all his energy into becoming the "right person," when the hiring manager was looking for the "right resume."

As their job searches continued to return negative results using their existing stock of strategies, respondents described a deeply disturbing temporality of stillness and stagnation. As I heard from many respondents, their initial strategy of applying only to "good jobs" quickly opened up to applying to just about anything. Several respondents who had once worked in white-collar jobs began applying to entry and management positions in the service sector, such as fast food and retail. Colleen, for example, eventually moved back to her hometown in North Carolina and took a part-time job at a local family restaurant to help pay her way through a masters program in family therapy. Having gone from earning six figures in the glamorous media industry to this, she notes, "I feel like in some ways I've reverted to the status of a 12 year old. Right now I'm working part-time as a hostess. [. . .] I remember when I left North Carolina from undergrad, my thought was I am not going to come back there no matter what. So, to come back at this time—I was 37 when I got back here, and I was 17 when I left. I felt like I had failed."

While Colleen describes a kind of metaphorical and existential regression, a few respondents I spoke to experienced such chronic hysteresis that they were literally unable to move. They describe a kind of "protentional death" in which their old stock of strategies proved ineffective to coordinate even the most basic acts of future making. I was introduced to Gregory, for example, through an advertisement on Craigslist and met him at a Starbucks just down the street from his apartment. At the time I talked to him, Gregory was 33 years old and had lost his job as a technician at a commercial medical processing laboratory 16 months ago. After several months of "funemployment" traveling the country's amusement parks and visiting old friends, he entered a difficult period of job seeking that involved only one promising lead, which fell through. Having descended into a deep depression—something he had a history of already—Gregory described a typical day.

So, do you have any kind of a routine right now to your day?

No.

So what does a typical day look like?

Say I get up—I've been sleeping on the couch for a while. So it's kind of, get up from the couch and turn the TV on. I have a set up where I have my PC hooked up to my television, just from the little entertainment center. So I piddle around on that and either go in through amusing blogs or the Internet. I won't even say I answer emails anymore cause that just seems like it's just too much. People want something from me. Just don't wanna deal with it.

Or video games—and I tend to gravitate towards games that take large amounts of time, things that I would set up civilizations. [. . .] To play a game now, could take anywhere between 24 and 200 hours to play one game. So, you know, I'll go to one of those. Depending on finances, at some point, I'll be motivated to go out and get me a Junior Bacon Cheeseburger. Or just make me some rice and just continue on until very late hours—3, 4, 5 in the morning.

That's typically when you—

Fall asleep on the couch. Sort of ironically it's very large power consumption doing this, between the large TV and very powerful computer. You know sitting here saying, "Oh I'm just trying to save money," but then I'm just using massive amounts of money by leaving these things on twenty-four hours a day.

Gregory is perfectly aware of what is going on with him. He is not in a good place psychologically and should be looking for better ways to cope. "I am playing armchair psychiatrist with myself," he notes, "I just say, 'Are you just self-sabotaging yourself?'" Still, he cannot seem to tear himself away from his entertainment system because, at least in part, it provides a comfortable stock of protentional strategies from his past that always used to do the trick.

> It's kinda what I do anyways. Like when I was working. My down time, I mean that's my comfort zone. That is my blankie and teddy bear when I used to do that. I think it's just I sort of—I seek that hypnotism. When you're playing a game or watching television, you sort of get hypnotized. But then now it's just this perpetual state of hypnosis.

Gregory adds that hypnosis, while palliative in the short term, is beginning to have ill effects, particularly on his cognitive abilities. As a lab technician, he had always prided himself in his ability to remember details and make quick decisions—something he had to do while working in the central receiving area of the lab. "I loved the fast pace and constant pressure. [. . .] How many different irons can you have in the fire and not drop them? Everyone hated doing it. I loved it." Now, he explains,

> It's getting a little bit tougher to remember things. Just being able to recall a list of facts even. My job was always very important for me. I just knew all these numbers and everything. They were constantly changing, so I constantly had them in my head. So this was always being rehearsed. I don't rehearse that anymore and so I can only seem to remember very limited things now. [. . .] So that is very frightening because it's always been one of my strengths in life is my ability to retain information. So now that one of the better cards that I've been dealt in life is . . . dwindling in value, it's a little unnerving.

Having been removed from his familiar work timescape, Gregory can no longer "rehearse" the protentional skills that once gave him satisfaction, such as the quick working memory required of a chaotic workflow. Now, he is left only with the counterpart to those skills—his entertainment system—which he once used to unwind from the job. But these old strategies are terribly out of synch with the timescape of joblessness, creating worrying cognitive imbalances. "I'm passive. I am in this hypnotic state. I am receiving entertainment. I'm not actively doing anything."

The only thing saving Gregory from this downward spiral, he explains, is that he still maintains a connection with friends and neighbors. He says,

> I haven't sort of lost touch with schedules and the external world. [. . .] I live in this duplex, so my downstairs neighbor, he works Monday through Friday 4:00 a.m. to noon. So I can always kind of hear the car coming, and I have that in my head as an external reminder. I have a couple of close friends with whom I enjoy

spending time, and I know their schedules. I mean I have one friend—he works in food service, but I just know his schedule. So I just have to know, like, oh it's Thursday he works from 6:00 p.m. to 2:00 a.m. So because of just maintaining relationships, I haven't lost complete context of external schedules.

Through a kind of vicarious scheduling, Gregory is able to build some temporal structure into his day using the rhythms of his friends' schedules as a metronome. Like a Proustian rope from heaven, these patterns pull his mind back into the outside world.

THE DISEMBEDDED JOB SEARCH

As Gregory so clearly demonstrated, joblessness can lead to spatial isolation. This sense of dislocation from the working world is exacerbated by contemporary digital hiring practices. Just like financial professionals and truck drivers, I saw that the way digital technologies are reconfiguring the spatial aspect of job seekers' lives deeply shapes temporality.

Human Resources departments conduct themselves almost entirely online today. Gone are the days when an applicant would go door-to-door "dropping resumes" and talking face-to-face with representatives of the company in a physical place. This transformation is driven by a combination of technology and changes in the job market. During the time of my fieldwork, there was a drastic oversupply of applicants due to widespread unemployment. Before the financial collapse, there were an average of 1.7 job seekers for every vacancy in America. After the collapse that average grew to 6 seekers for every opening (Standing 2011:79). At the same time, hiring departments had themselves been severely downsized in an attempt to control payroll costs. Consequently, respondents were faced with, on the one hand, increased competition from other job seekers, and, on the other hand, understaffed and time-crunched hiring personnel.

To cope with this imbalance, Human Resources departments in many of the country's mid and large size companies have come to rely heavily on software packages designed to streamline some of the tasks in the hiring process that used to be conducted by human beings. This includes, most importantly, reading resumes. Companies typically require applicants to submit a resume through the company's website as well as fill out a series of online forms, many of which are redundant to the resume, which detail the applicant's employment history. Respondents told me this process typically takes between one and two hours per application. As Guy Standing (2011) has observed, precarious employment practices increasingly ask workers to do a lot of unpaid work in order to secure paid work, what he calls "work-for-labor." Job seekers spend countless unpaid hours "working" online doing tasks that make it easier for hiring staff to do their jobs.

Once their information is received, it is processed using hiring software. Most hiring software works by allowing hiring personnel to filter out resumes that do not meet the criteria of an advertised position. The programs scan resumes for keywords and return a ranked list of applicants that best fit the job description based on—and this is a crucial parameter—the *number of times* these keywords appear in his or her resume. More sophisticated programs also note *where* on the resume keywords appear, the assumption being that crucial keywords higher up on the resume will indicate more recent qualifications. With this list in hand, then, the hiring staff only need to read, say, five or six of the best resumes, rather than dozens.

While online-only applications and hiring software may save company resources by reducing the amount of time managers spend looking at resumes, it reconfigures the process of job seeking in ways that can be maddening for applicants. In this way, the emotional cost of intense job market competition is passed down to the job seeker. A phrase used by job seekers to describe online applications in dozens of interviews I conducted was "the black hole." The black hole refers to the way hiring software creates an empty, depersonalized space into which job seekers feebly chuck resumes. The main effect of the black hole is that it reconfigures the temporality of the resume. Keyword filtering encourages applicants to think of the resume not as a gilt representation of a person's past, but as a purely instrumental document engineered to get past a series of digital firewalls that separate the applicant from the hiring manager. Savvier respondents described spending hours reading and rereading job advertisements trying to figure out which keywords the HR department is looking for, and then reengineering their resume each time to feature those words more frequently and as early as possible in the document. I observed respondents share advice with each other on how best to format a resume so that it will "get past the computers." Though I never saw it, rumors circulated that some applicants in the region were lacing their resumes with extra keywords in such a way that they would be detected by the computer's "eyes," which would get them a higher ranking, but not by the hiring manager's eyes—for example, by typing keywords over and over again in white text against a white background.

The black hole also reconfigures the spatial dimension of the application process. Applicants have few ways of communicating with hiring personnel, whom they can never see face to face or speak to voice to voice. This is, of course, by design. More communication between applicants and hiring staff slows down the process by inundating staff with enquiries. Many respondents I talked to described submitting dozens of applications but never hearing anything back, not even an autoreply email to let them know their application had been received. Silence from employers was even more bothersome when respondents noticed that a particular advertisement remained on the job boards well after they had submitted an application, leaving them to wonder if the position is still open or had already been filled but the ad never taken down.

Online job seeking also tends to isolate applicants in a location where they can access the Internet—typically their homes—rather than allowing them to physically travel to an employer's place of business and see it with their own eyes. Raquel, for example, a 55-year-old former small business owner, told me that she is typically on the computer from 8:30 in the morning to 6 or 7 at night. "It became almost an obsession," she says of looking at online job listings. "It's like, I've been on this computer five, six hours sending my resume and doing cover letters and going to every job posting site I could think of. It just is sickening. It was just really like, okay, got to get out of here."

Jennifer, a 26-year-old photographer's assistant, says she has "problems now and then with being stir crazy." She notes,

> I can't stand being in the house all the time. I just like, just got to walk out of there sometimes. [. . .]
>
> *Tell me more about that kind of stir-crazy feeling? Where is that coming from?*
>
> It's the same thing everyday. I have the Internet at my fingertips but there's only so many times you can check the job boards. There's only so many times you can figure out what other ways you can be managing something.

As Raquel and Jennifer point out, the Internet disembeds the job seeking process, making it easier to apply to more jobs in a day than would be possible going door to door. However, it also turns job seeking into an isolating search through placeless space. As Raquel says,

> It's always just send an e-mail to jobs@. It seems like that's the catchall thing for resumes and stuff now—jobs@ something, something, something, and it might be a string of letters. It's not really a name of a company, so you don't know who you're applying to. You're hoping it's not some circus looking for workers [laughs].

Combined with the more existential feelings of stagnation that come with job loss, then, respondents' sense of isolation and dislocation within the black hole of online applications left many feeling as though they could gain no traction or momentum in their lives.

In sum, the wrenching disruption of the career time map caused by job loss affects the temporality of people's daily lives. It creates a timescape of crisis—the inability to coordinate the micro-rhythms of even basic acts of protention. Crisis arises because of a sudden dislocation between the protentional strategies job seekers once relied on to create meaningful action and the present situation of a competitive job market full of companies offering precarious contracts. The strategies that worked in an era when companies were looking for the "right person" rather than the "right resume" and when positions were competed over by two people rather than twenty no longer help to create a sense of forward movement. The stillness can be paralyzing and terrifying. Job seekers' protentional "gaze" becomes more and more short-term oriented. Life becomes more narrowly defined by emotional survival in the present. The big retrospective questions— What happened and why?—and the big prospective questions—Where am I going? How do I get there?—are the last things on their minds. This feeling is only exacerbated by the isolation of online job seeking and digital hiring practices. Crisis, then, does not generate the need for some new grand set of plans, at least not at first, but for something that can get them off the couch and out of an emotional funk. They need something practical.

GAINING MOMENTUM

Having struggled in a kind of "temporal vacuum" for months on end, it takes considerable strength for job seekers to emerge from protentional death and begin to think more long term. Respondents noted that, working ones way back into a state of forward movement is difficult to do on one's own. One is benefited greatly by, as many described it, "getting out there"—generating some kind of forward momentum through interaction with others. The first steps were often taken through mundane acts of synchronization, which created pockets of energizing rhythmic action. Leanne, a 59-year-old former office administrator at an evangelical Christian megachurch, was forced to move her online job search to a nearby public library after her computer gave out. She recalls,

> I feel like it really helped me from getting totally defunct in it all and go to sleep, watch TV, get tired of doing that, still watching TV, and all that.
>
> *Yeah, what is it about that? I mean, just having something as simple as that—you have to go to the library.*

It gets you out. It makes you take your shower, because you're not going to go somewhere looking there smelling nasty. When you take a shower and you get dressed, you actually feel better about yourself, because you're not sitting around in your jammies. [. . .] There's all these little things that you need to do. It's giving you a schedule, and I had no schedule in the beginning until I found out I had to go to the library. Then I started having a schedule. And guess what? I started meeting people.

There you go.

I was out in the sunshine and the smell of the air. Then, it got to the point of I didn't want to go home. I wanted to stay out. It made me feel good. [. . .] And don't go home and make a sandwich, take your sandwich with you. Go sit in the park or go somewhere. Go sit in a parking lot and watch all the people. It's activities and it's life moving. Stuck at home, you don't see any life.

As Leanne makes clear, even basic acts of synchronization with others can help jolt job seekers out of stagnation by placing them in a new timescape that is full of, as she puts it, "life moving." Aside from conducting their job search away from home, respondents reported great success with strategies like cleaning the house to prepare for the arrival of a working spouse, exercising at a gym or public park, or volunteering in a local organization.

Having gained a toehold on some experience of progress, which provides a much-needed mood boost, many respondents emphasized the importance of creating a routine for one's job search in order to sustain that momentum—the more rigid and predictable, the better. Respondents often engaged with the benevolent face of Chronos, recreating the disciplining rhythmic structure of a nine-to-five work schedule. At the time I spoke to Linda, for example, she was recommitted to a program that has her up early and out of the house all day. "Last week I started back in [on a schedule]," she tells me brightly.

I get up at 5:30 a.m., I eat, I do my walking or running or I do my exercise. Monday mornings I hit that computer. 8:30 a.m. every Monday morning I hit that computer. [. . .] I'm looking for jobs. Then, based on the job, I'm rewriting my resume. Rewriting my resume means redoing my LinkedIn, which redoes my Twitter. I'm spending a good six hours a day on the computer, perhaps for one job.

Clocks and schedules help Linda build a familiar timescape—a kind of phantom workday—that allows her to take some tentative steps into a radically unfamiliar future. This is unpaid "work-for-labor," to be sure, but because it mimics the temporality of real paid labor, it feels meaningful.

Having gained some momentum by deploying chronological techniques, job seekers reap renewed energy and can finally face the prospect of looking beyond the immediate future. Their protentional gaze begins to widen again. They can entertain the idea of constructing a new narrative and new grand plan that will provide some sort of medium- or even long-term orientation in social time. In this way, they begin to shift from future making focused on the short-term to future making within longer and longer wavelengths of time.

Employment assistance centers and job transition support groups are important places where many white-collar professionals go to begin constructing these new medium and long-term narratives together (Garrett-Peters 2009; Lane 2011; Sharone 2007; Smith 2001). Career Transition Ministries (CTM) was one of many popular job search support groups that respondents in the Richmond, Virginia area attended regularly. Run by Jim, a 62-year-old financial planner who works for a global insurance conglomerate headquartered in the city, CTM operates under the auspices of a local Catholic church. Having lost his job due to downsizing in the 1990s, Jim personally knows the struggles of job loss. He started CTM in 2008 with a group of his fellow parishioners as a reaction to a number of corporate office closures in the city that left hundreds of white-collar professionals without jobs following the financial collapse. CTM provides a number of free services. The main feature is a series of public talks by career coaches, business executives, HR personnel, headhunters and other consultants working in the burgeoning "change management" industry. CTM also provides one-on-one mentoring and publishes "the binder"—a collection of materials about the contemporary job market—which has advice on virtually every detail of job seeking, from tips on state unemployment benefits, to networking techniques, to examples of how to answer a behavioral interview question.

The church is located in an upper-middle class suburb that is home to many of the largest corporate employers in the city. Driving there, one passes corporate office parks with artificial ponds and fountains surrounding their large (now mostly empty) employee parking lots—symbols of a more prosperous time. Strip malls and planned housing developments connect the office parks to the church. CTM meetings are held in the church's parish hall—a large roundish room with a vaulted ceiling, bell tower at top, and slightly elevated stage area at one end. The room features twelve round tables that seat eight to ten people each. During the winter of 2012, when I attended CTM meetings most frequently, these tables were often completely full. Participants tended to be in their late 40s to early 60s, mostly white, and had a history of steady employment in large corporations. An unspoken norm in the group was "dress for success." Men tended to wear business suits or collared shirts; women in dresses, makeup, and jewelry. Over the course of several months, I learned that many had never been unemployed before and lost their jobs through downsizing, outsourcing, and automation.

Weekly CTM meetings follow a standard structure. Jim begins with a prayer that typically invokes God's help for the participants' successful and "speedy transition." Then he announces how many people CTM has helped "land," as he calls finding employment, often adding that, "Many of them were just like you and were sitting exactly where you are sitting now. And they landed." Jim then asks participants for any good news of progress toward employment. Participants announce a call back, an interview, an offer, and occasionally even a new job, which is met with rounds of applause from the audience. When he sees a lot of new faces in the audience, which happened frequently during my time there, he delivers the same sobering speech about job seeking in the contemporary economy. "There is no more employment for life," Jim says, leaving a dramatic silence in the room. "Everyone will be changing jobs throughout their working lives, probably several times. This is not the last time you will be in this position." So, he explains, "You need to arm yourself" with new skills and techniques.

As the last part of Jim's speech suggests, while CTM advertises itself as a space for developing skills and techniques and a clearinghouse for cutting-edge advice, its real function, I observed, is to motivate through the use of ideological speeches. CTM draws on a highly formalized ideology of positivity, connectedness, and forward movement to construct an emotionally compelling vision of the future, grounding its claims in the burgeoning Positive Psychology movement and the so called "new science of happiness" (Ehrenreich 2009; Wallis 2005). The speakers I saw at CTM meetings included a former headhunter for a Fortune 500 company turned career coach, a networking consultant, a former member of CTM who has become a career coach, an executive coach at one of the nation's largest commercial banks, a sales consultant for a local consulting firm, a life coach and therapist, and two HR managers for large corporations headquartered in the city.

The ideology of positivity, connectedness, and forward movement—and how it connects to a new conception of the future—was presented most clearly by Kathy Kerr, an executive coach at a large commercial bank and member of the International Coaches Federation, the official licensing body for the field of career and life coaching. Kathy matches the demographic of the room. In her mid 50s, graying blond hair, and dressed in a business suit, she begins her talk by telling her own story of job loss. Having been laid off twice, moved her family across the country twice, and worked for three years as an unpaid intern in the HR department of a local university to get to her present position, Kathy knows what her audience is going through. "I've been in your shoes," she says. "I know how hard it is to be out of work." On the positive side, she realizes now that "I didn't really like those first two jobs anyway. I wasn't happy." Even though she had to struggle as a part-time worker with no pay for so many years to get where she is today, her perseverance has paid off. She is now able to "do what I always wanted to do—work with people, help them transition through work problems." With this story, Kathy draws out the contours of a flexible time map— precarious employment that puts the onus on the job seeker to carve out his or her unique path in life.

As Kathy does here, other speakers encouraged participants to see the positive potential in flexible time maps. Bill Goldman, a former headhunter for a Fortune 500 company, put it this way,

> Your next job will only last for three years. The day is gone when you can give your career to your employer. He doesn't want it and he won't take it. So, you need to take control of your career and do it yourself. You can either bumble through life from job to job, or you can make it so that jobs come to you rather than you having to go out and seek jobs.

Using subtle turns of phrase, Bill and other speakers noted that, while it is true that your employer will no longer watch over your career and guarantee its security and predictability, this should be seen as a sign of liberation rather than anxiety. Rather than seeing it as the death of the career, you can see it as no longer having to "give your career away" to someone who will not treasure it the way you do. Echoing mid-20th century critiques (i.e., Whyte 1965), the bounded career is thus defined as a prison; it was a way to trick employees into giving up the one thing that they should have as free individuals: personal responsibility.

Speeches like these signaled to participants that a new time map has emerged—one in which the onus is on the individual worker to become the organizer and director of his or her own customized life trajectory. The key to constructing that trajectory, according to CTM rhetoric, is to simply take hold of the potential for control that is being given to you by job loss. As speakers emphasized, you have to "make the jobs come to you" by constantly "networking"—forming new connections and nourishing established connections with people who might lead you to a new opening. *Even when you are employed*, speakers emphasized, you still need to network. Constant connection ensures that when the moment of job loss arrives, which speakers assumed to be inevitable, the seeds of the next opportunity have already been planted. A good worker in the new economy, then, is by definition a professional job seeker—one who is constantly sowing the seeds for another transition, even when he or she appears to be securely employed.

Speakers were adamant that a positive, energetic, forward-looking psychological orientation is the essential characteristic of the successful professional job seeker.[3] As a career coach, Kathy Kerr explains that her task is to tell job seekers how to cultivate this attitude. Using an overhead projector, Kathy displays a graph of what she calls the "change curve," a popular tool used throughout the change management industry to coach individuals through the "emotional rollercoaster" that comes with work transitions. Kathy notes that "job transition is a series of emotions" and that the graph depicts "the natural course of emotional change for human beings going through a hard transition." Some "go through this change easily," progressing smoothly to a state of hope and exploration, while some get "stuck" in the attitude of anger, resentment, and resistance. Kathy says she judges where clients are on the curve by "the degree of positivity and forward looking attitude in their speech." Speech is an important indicator because "the stories we tell ourselves can limit us." "The negative stories we tell ourselves are usually based on some kind of fear. Fear prevents you from moving forward."

Kathy gives the example of a client she had who lost his job and was angry toward his employer. "He just couldn't seem to get past this anger," she recalls. He was "focused on the past," and could not move forward to a state of hope and exploration. So, Kathy suggested he "write that employer a letter telling him exactly how he feels." Leaving a dramatic pause, she adds, "But *don't mail it.*" The audience laughs. "Bring it back to me for our next session." At the next session, she asked him to read the letter aloud. Then she suggested he take it to a nearby stream, tear it up, and throw it in the water. "This is a pretty extreme technique," she admits, "but this symbolic, behavioral demonstration allowed him to stop looking to the past and move through the change curve." She adds, "When you worry, you're giving your power away."

3. As Ofer Sharone (2014) has documented, the emphasis on positivity and individual agency may be peculiar to American unemployment culture. Comparing American and Israeli job search experiences, Sharone finds that American job seeking advice distinctly emphasizes the "self" rather than the "system" when thinking about pathways and barriers to employment.

As Kathy emphasizes, positive emotions are the only things that truly propel one forward through precarious employment, not because they allow one to better enjoy life, but because they are strategic. As another speaker put it, "You have to project confidence. Even if you're having a bad day, fake it! The attitude you have during your job search affects everything you do. If you are down and negative, it will come across in every interview and every networking opportunity you have." Portions of several CTM meetings were dedicated to techniques for generating a reserve of positive energy that could be drawn upon at any moment. During a talk by Jolene Jenkins, for example, who is a life coach and therapist, participants were asked to place the tip of a plastic straw between their front teeth and hold their mouths in that position while she gave a short talk on the neuroscience of positive thinking. After a few minutes, they were asked to remove the straws. "How do you feel?" Jolene asked. "Can you feel your smile? It's still there, isn't it? You might even feel a little happier. That's because the act of smiling has made your brain think you're happy. Your brain is saying, 'If I'm smiling, I must be happy.'" Jolene explained that numerous "scientific studies" have shown that putting one's body into states associated with positive moods can actually create those feelings. She then distributed a handout entitled "Confidence Boosters," which included twenty-eight techniques for generating a positive mood "from the outside in," that will improve one's job search. For example, "Dress up every day—you never know who you will run into—people you meet/know need to see your 'success persona.'" And "Write emails with only positive words—eliminate 'no' 'can't' 'won't' 'couldn't' 'not' etc." That this handout is titled "confidence" boosters and not "mood" boosters is indicative of the instrumental attitude toward positive feelings being encouraged.

Returning to Kathy Kerr's presentation, to conclude, she emphasizes that everything she has said is "just talk." What is really important is that one becomes "action-oriented" and designs a plan with clear goals that can be worked on day-by-day. Like other speakers, Kathy encourages job seekers to put most of their energy into networking because "people hire people they know and like." However, networking was also discussed as a kind of good in itself, as an activity fitting the positive, outgoing, forward looking professional job seeker (Spillman 2012). The hallmark of a good networker, Kathy emphasized, is one who can give a good "elevator speech"—a ten to thirty second "sales pitch" for oneself as a job candidate that participants are encouraged to have at the ready when they encounter a networking partner. A good elevator speech is one that "conveys energy," "leaves a lasting impression," and, above all, "sells yourself."

At the end of Kathy's talk, the audience was asked to break into small groups, perform their elevator speeches, and rate each other on a 1-10 scale. Evelyn, sitting across from me at a table with six other participants, began her speech so quietly that it was difficult to hear her in the din of the room. After the others politely ask her to speak up, she nervously began her speech by saying, "I used to be a data analyst for the FAA and I'm looking for jobs as a data analyst." She hesitates after this sentence, stops, and says, "I'm sorry. I can't really do this." The group immediately jumps in to support her. One group member gives some advice. "I noticed you started by saying, 'I used to be' and not 'I am an analyst.' You should say 'I *am* an analyst' because the other way is a bit too rearview mirror." Others agree and ask her to try again. She begins her speech again, her voice now slightly trembling. "I am an analyst," she peeps. Becoming more upset, she begins to tear up, much to the group's horror. Others begin to console her and advise her to "write it down and rehearse it in the mirror until you can give it confidently and without thinking about it."

After job seekers have picked themselves up and gotten into a position to be helped, what, according to CTM, does it take to get a job in the flexible economy? A kind of flexible and strategic emotional life. Constant networking combined with a massive reserve of internally generated positive emotions and a well-crafted (but spontaneous sounding) advertisement for one's "brand," ensure that a potential employer will never be encountered at the "wrong time." Like the flexibly employed, the flexibly unemployed are encouraged to be continually emotionally available for the next unpredictable opportunity to work. They must cultivate an emotional culture of good timing, which includes the capacity to recognize opportunities to charm, persuade, and impress and quickly organize one's psyche to deliver those goods when the time is ripe. This form of selfhood is better equipped to take advantage of flexible employment strategies, which operate on the logic that individuals are responsible to recruit employers to "Me Inc.," as one CTM speaker described it, rather than the other way around. The individual is the employer and the employer is actually a consumer of the "skillsets" on offer in the market.

The question that remains, which I take up in the next chapter, is to what degree job seekers accept this image of the self. When they do accept it, how does it help them make sense of the new kinds of risk they are being asked to shoulder?

CONCLUSION

My encounters with white-collar job seekers show that numerical flexibility—one of the core strategies of today's lean companies—can create sudden, jolting disruptions in the way workers make futures.[4] Job loss is a "moment of reckoning" (Wagner-Pacifici 2010), a radical "pause" in the flow of life, which exposes a deep rift between the short-term future—the routine steps one takes to remain securely employed in the short term—and the long-term future—the grand trajectories of employment on offer. For the job seekers I met, this rift was often already an objective reality long before the moment of job loss but remained subjectively hidden to them, making their moment of reckoning seem all the more epiphantic. Like Wile E. Coyote in a Roadrunner cartoon, job loss forced them to look down to see that the surface they thought they had been traveling on had long since disappeared.[5] This is what makes numerical flexibility feel precarious. Though it is often discussed in terms of material insecurity, precariousness is the paralysis that emerges when the fallacies of familiar versions of the future are exposed by something random, unforeseeable, or even unthinkable. This is precariousness in its literal definition as "dependent on chance." The shock of job loss fragments the cultural system that had supported forward social action leaving a sickeningly still and stagnant texture to social time. Job seekers encounter a kind of "protentional death," in which basic synchronization and forward movement are difficult to achieve with a familiar stock of strategies. These experiences not only confirm that the old time map is eroded, but also narrow their temporal gaze to the immediate present. They become hungry for practical solutions to the immediate problem of stagnation.

Job search support groups encourage the white-collar unemployed to fill the temporal vacuum created by job loss with new strategies and plans based on a new time map. But while they advertise these strategies as purely practical, they are in fact deeply ideological. They are not just meant to get people back on track, but also to encourage them to accept and even embrace a flexibilized life for the rest of their lives. They define the career as a paternalistic prison and encourage job seekers to take control of flexible employment practices by cultivating a strategic emotional life. They are encouraged to make themselves emotionally available in order to capitalize on hiring opportunities by become positive, energetic, and savvy networkers.

As I discuss more in the next chapter, the framework of job seeking as future-making helps us understand why, as other scholars have found

4. There may be other "speeds" to time map disruption, which I cannot consider here because of the nature of the data. Would a more gradual temporality of job loss—say through a series of demotions, furloughs, and hours reductions, which ultimately lead to joblessness—still trigger the "protentional death" I see in these data? Or would workers be able to evolve their habits and strategies to the slowly changing situation, making the transition to a flexible time map seem less shocking and disorienting? .
5. Thank you to Allison Pugh for suggesting this provocative metaphor.

(Lane 2011; Pugh 2015; Sharone 2007; Smith 2001), job seekers sometimes initially welcome disruptions to the old regime of secure employment arrangements. They realize that there was actually not much to recommend the bounded career other than its financial security. It had its own problems. When one's protentional gaze has been so brutally truncated, then, the rhetoric of positivity, spontaneity, connectivity, and forward movement can be a welcome medium-term relief. It generates inner wealth in the absence of economic and social systems that can provide outer wealth. The catch, of course, is that workers are now being asked to take on the long-term risks that employers once willingly shouldered. Job seekers must become both the builders and followers of time maps of their own design. When things turn sour again, a failed time map is now synonymous with a failed self (Sharone 2014).

The notion that flexible capitalism has created a fast-paced world full of busy and overworked people has become a common trope (e.g., Menzies 2005; Wajcman 2015). What I hope to have shown in the last three chapters is that in the midst of that welter are pockets of radical stillness that should not be overlooked (Rosa 2009). Today's "underemployed" and unemployed are the most powerful symbols of this ironic slowness. Placing these workers alongside the speed and fluidity of financial professionals and truck drivers, allows us to see that their experiences of social time are all connected by the same temporal structure, which is shaped by an imperative to undergo constant and unpredictable change in search of the moment of profit. Where truck drivers and financial professionals occupy the "peaks" of flexible time, job seekers occupy the "troughs." Trucking and finance involve adapting one's mind and body to the unpredictable swings of attention and energy associated with rapid economic growth; job seeking to the periods when that ballooning system collapses under its own weight and the economy needs people to wait until they are needed again. Where the former shoulder the risks of capitalism's potential for success, the latter shoulder the risks of its potential for crisis. In all three cases, we see the same processes of adaptation to a shift of risk onto the worker, just to different beats in the erratic rhythm of flexible capitalism.

Where white-collar job seekers stand out from the other cases, however, is their encounter with a clearly discernable event through which to have an epiphany of economic change. Truck drivers and financial professionals are so immersed in the challenges of keeping up with their jobs that they do not have the time—that is, the temporality of contemplation—to consider if they are pushing themselves into a risky mental, emotional, or physical situation until it is already too late. Therefore, they often just keep grinding through the day hoping that things will get better or easier. There is no question among job seekers, by contrast, whether or not something is amiss. The existential pause of job loss forces them to contemplate—to slowly widen their truncated protention to a longer wavelength of time and consider life on the level of the time map. Once they do this, they can see that they have been going about things all wrong and begin to engage in a protentional activity that is quite rare among those living in the peaks of flexible capitalism: plan. But it is a specific kind of planning that is oriented almost entirely to the next few discernable beats in the rhythm of one's employment trajectory, after which point things will surely change again and they will again have to reorient. It is a distinctly medium-term form of planning. Job seekers, then, are not "prisoners of the present" (Sennett 2000; Silva 2013) so much as they are prisoners of the middling future. The somewhat disorienting message they receive from this temporality is that in order to be a good worker today, one must plan to change. Workers need to rationally orient themselves to a change imperative so that, when it comes, it is not a shock to the system anymore because life has become a kind of routine chaos.

CHAPTER 6
Moral Order in Flexible Times

We have now seen the kinds of timescapes and time maps on offer to financial professionals, truck drivers, and job seekers by the flexible economy. Now, I would like to explore what conceptions of a good life these workers build upon that temporal scaffolding. What moral dilemmas do they face and how do they make sense of contradictions? Answering these questions requires me to look at both the "thin" and "thick" moral ordering of work. We must look not just at the feelings of artistry or drudgery in the actual tasks of work (a thin conception of work morality), but also consider how repeated exposure to those experiences over a course of months, years, or even decades influences larger questions about the good life in general (a thick conception). As these workers return to their jobs again and again, what possible ways to become who they want to be are afforded to them? How do they connect the rhythms and trajectories of their workplaces to these larger projects of moral development?

In this chapter, I look more closely at the relationship between work time and moral order in each workplace. What does repeated exposure to wild fluctuations between frustrating stretches of desychronization followed by expansive moments of unification mean to truck drivers and financial professionals? How does the transition from an old to a new time map through the crucible of job loss shape job seekers' conceptions of the good life? When I asked respondents to reflect on their work at this level, I observed a perplexing contradiction in their speech. Respondents told me that disrupted workplaces can actually deliver them into surprisingly satisfying experiences of labor that may not have been available to them in more secure and predictable workplaces. The catch, however, is that the imperative of constant change that characterizes these workplaces makes it difficult to see what the proper level of investment should be in the future—of time, of energy, of emotional identification with a role, etc. Things can suddenly change and workers find that they have unexpectedly overinvested themselves in work, pushing themselves into dangerous, anxious, or morally ambiguous territory. When the connection between present and future is always so tenuous, the meaningful edifices workers build to honor their working selves can quickly crumble, thus coming back to haunt them later as sources of suffering. What is meaningful about flexible work, then, is often also what makes it feel unsustainable in the long term.

THE WORK-GAME

As discussed in Chapter 2, in his landmark ethnography of late 20th century factory life *Manufacturing Consent*, Michael Burawoy (1979), drawing on the earlier ethnographic work of Donald Roy (1953, 1959), developed the concept of the "game" to understand how industrial laborers adapted themselves to the productivity demands of the Taylorist factory. Burawoy observed the common game of "making out"—trying to exceed the maximum piece rate on easier factory machines in order to buffer oneself from lower productivity on more difficult machines. He saw that this game transformed the political relationships among employees and between employees and management. As the worker becomes ever more engrossed in and obsessed with his individual productivity, his definition of good work becomes hyper-individualized. This deflects attention away from the ways management is in fact indirectly asking employees to ratchet up the intensity of labor through self-discipline (Clawson and Fantasia 1983). Self-induced work intensifications become a common good that distracts workers from the long-term implications of their actions for the rest of the crew.

Though he does not focus on work time per se, Burawoy's analysis shows that games on the Taylorized shop floor tended to individualize the temporality of each machine. Each worker comes to the machine with a conception of his personal ability to outpace management's predetermined rate. As a result, he begins to focus more on what it takes to "beat the clock" rather than working as intensely as is physically and mentally safe (and economically fair) for himself and the other workers on the floor. What is most important to note about Burawoy's observation, then, is that management can individualize work time by *relaxing direct surveillance and enforcement*—letting workers take more control over the flow of work and thus determine for themselves what it takes to ratchet up productivity. But this freedom is then coupled to new incentive structures that pit worker against worker, thus shifting the locus of intensification from the outside of the workspace to the inside. As time becomes more customized to the individual worker in a game of competition, then, he is afforded opportunities to take ownership of intensification amid heightened risks and thus feel gratified when success is achieved despite the challenges.

As I explore below, Burawoy's analysis of the work-game and the individualization of time remains crucial for understanding the moral order of flexible work (Kojima 2015). Though "making out" had more to do with the routinized temporality of industrial work, which may be becoming rarer today, it directs our attention to the way the customization of time around the individual can encourage workers to embrace more risk without direct coercion (Sharone 2007). The question, then, is what sorts of work-games flexibilized workers create, how those games shape the meaning of good work, and what those conceptions of the good imply for workers' attitudes toward the downward shift of risk that is so characteristic of flexible capitalism.

THE BUZZ OF FINANCE

At first blush, financial professionals appear to be thriving in flexible capitalism. As I discuss in Chapter 3, their timescapes can be stressful and disorienting, but it affords them opportunities not only for unimaginable profit but also for certain kinds of "flow" experiences (Csikszentmihalyi 1990) in the form of work rhythms that can seamlessly merge, producing feelings of unity, togetherness, connectedness, and collective energy (Knorr Cetina 2012; Zaloom 2006, 2012). Timescapes of unification, then, are the sites of work-games for financial workers. They can be deeply meaningful and shape the moral order of their workplaces.

Dealmakers, for example, discussed a kind of glorious, almost heroic aspect to the temporality of their unpredictable, marathon-like work sessions, which made the stress much easier to bear (at least in the short term). Unifications occurred most frequently during the end of a deal cycle, known as a "live deal."[1] Many respondents I talked to were working

1. Respondents contrasted "live deal mode" with "pitches." Pitching involves putting together a "pitch book," which is a formal, polished, and bound set of sales materials given to clients. This book is typically prepared by junior level personnel and used by senior level bankers during sales meetings. Finishing a pitch book often entails rather mind numbing work for junior analysts, such as flipping through hundreds of pages of text and charts to make sure the margins, fonts, and layout are perfectly polished. Pitch books are often not read thoroughly, or even at all, when deals fall through in the early stages, which they typically do.

in powerful Wall Street firms at the epicenter of the financial crisis of 2008. During these hectic months, which saw the collapse of "too-big-to-fail" firms, like Bear Stearns, and the downgrading of gigantic corporations, like General Motors, respondents reported being constantly involved in live deals, sometimes many simultaneously.

Gillian, now 27 years old, worked as a junior analyst at a large asset management firm right out of an Ivy League university and was promoted to associate after the financial collapse. "The weekend we worked on the Bear Stearns collapse," she recalls, "I got to the office Friday. I didn't leave until the middle of Sunday." After telling her I cannot imagine working that many hours straight, she promptly replied,

> But it was awesome! It was so exciting. We were working on something that was on the front page. It was a really big deal. It was really secret. We were ordering food every four hours until like 2 a.m., then you're meeting [again] with coffee. There's actually a picture of me that I have with my—I showed up Sunday morning. [. . .] Everybody went home to take a shower except me, cuz I was the most junior and somebody had to man the phones. My associate came back and took a photo of me asleep with my coat over me with everybody's phone in a circle around me (figure 6.1). [. . .] The stressful times were often the most fun.

Figure 6.1 Gillian catches some sleep midway through the Bear Stearns deal.
Photo provided by the respondent, used with permission.

The "triage" environment of the financial collapse allowed Gillian to string together energizing tasks that ensured her attention would remain consistently entrained with the rhythm of a live deal. This environment is stressful, but the peak experiences it generates can outweigh the stress.

Tom, head of a private equity group in a large investment bank, expressed similar thoughts, this time using an analogy to describe dealmaking that felt more appropriate than his earlier references to military combat.

> Part of it is there's *esprit de corps* that comes from just knowing you've got the whole night. [. . .] You're not the only ones [working late]. It's not uncommon to see a group of people there, certainly at 10 at night, sort of having dinner together, the last one not leaving until 4 or 5 in the morning [. . .]. It's like a college dormitory. [. . .] There is a lot of horsing around and giddiness, but also a sense that you need to get something done because you've got an exam.

Being desynchronized from the normative cycle of Monday to Friday, 9 to 5 actually facilitates the meaningfulness of work during live deals, Gillian and Tom suggest, because an abnormal temporality feels special, exotic, and sometimes even luxurious. This is bestowed, in part, by cultural representations of deal making as "really secret" and worthy of the "front page," but also, more subtly, by forms of lavish expenditure, such as ordering food from restaurants every few hours. The ease with which clock and calendar times are pushed aside, then, depends on the ability to produce unifications during work. The perceived "preciousness" of their time creates more favorable conditions for generating this kind of timescape.

Through the game of peak experiences, financial professionals are readily able to find artistry in their work. As one trader put it, "[Traders are] always operating with these unknowns—a lot of balls in the air flying around. And one of them can pop up at unexpected times. A lot of people . . . hate that uncertainty. I love it. That's a high for me, sort of. That's the buzz." As another trader responded when I asked him what he likes about his job, "I have a different day every day. When I get up in the morning, I have no idea what the market is going to bring." Disruption can be stimulating. Financial workers find the thin moral order of their labor precisely in its speed, uncertainty, and irregularity because it affords them absorbing challenges and transcended peak experiences.

Financialized Time Maps

On the face of it, then, it would seem that financial professionals have it good. Compared to most, they stand at the top of the structures of power and sit at the crest of the waves of financialization that are driving flexible temporalities from above. As Richard Sennett (2000:63) puts it, "The true victors [in the new capitalism] do not suffer from fragmentation. Instead, they are stimulated by working on many different fronts at the same time; it is part of the energy of irreversible change." Things may not be this clear cut, however. Even among financial professionals, work presents certain moral dilemmas, especially on the level of the time map.

Many of the financial professionals I met had anxieties about how their jobs are shaping them as people. When discussing work in this sense, they reflected on the types of long-term trajectories afforded to them. Much like the white-collar job seekers I met, financial professionals were openly exposed to the precarious time maps of flexible capitalism (though with much less financial risk, of course). Many of the bankers, traders, and analysts I met had been downsized in the past, especially following the financial collapse, and generally reported heightened anxiety around the time of yearly evaluations when the least productive workers would get "canned." As one project manager in the bond trading group told me, "You gotta have your rocket skates on. Don't get comfortable." Never assume your job is secure; always be ready to pick up and move. This kind of cutthroat environment fosters a distinct culture of overwork (Galinsky et al. 2004). When competition is so tight and positions so insecure, outward demonstrations of hard work, including the willingness to put in long hours and be ever available to work, become a good in themselves. This may be especially the case in American financial firms (Wharton and Blair-Loy 2001).

Similar to other "time hungry" professions, such as corporate law or medicine, the dominant story of the culture of overwork in finance and how it shapes the possible selves of its workers has focused on women. The high expectations place unequal pressures on women, compared to their male counterparts, because of the many other concerns of home life they are also typically held responsible for (Blair-Loy 2003; Hochschild 1989). It will come as no surprise that I found these tensions and anxieties among the women financial professionals I met. The gendered nature of financial time maps continues to form a major part of the moral order of these workplaces.

Gillian, for example, who just moments before in our conversation had gushed about the euphoria of the Bear Stearns deal, surprised me when she said she has just left her position at the investment bank to pursue a business degree and enter the field of healthcare management, despite having won an extremely competitive promotion. When I asked her why she chose to leave, she said,

It was partly seeing there are almost no women where I work. I was the second woman in my group. I am the only female associate . . . I saw the woman I worked for, who I have a lot of respect for, who's brilliant. She had a baby. She came back. We were working on a very intense hostile transaction. It was tough. She actually drew a line and said, "I have to go home at 6:30. I have to see my son." There was a part of me that said she wasn't available between 6:30 and 8:00 and that meant that I'm home an hour and a half later . . . I wanted her to succeed, but I was kind of, "Okay, that's really annoying." It was really inconvenient. I'm glad she saw her kid, but I realized that I was in an industry that work-life balance is tough because it's not actually how smart you are. A lot of it is how hard you work. And because it's a service business, it's how available you are. Do I really want to be in an industry where I'm valued on how available I am versus my individual contribution?

When Gillian looks around the office, she sees a temporal order that rewards people based on how "available" they are not how "smart" they are. "I was not seeing a future for the sacrifices I was making," she notes. "I was seeing what it did to people who are managing directors, who have really made it, and being like, 'I see that you've made it and I don't like your life.'"

Echoing Gillian, Casey, a 25-year-old MBA student and former M&A analyst, recalls,

For a brief period of time, there was some overlap where I was there at the same time as this woman who did have a couple of children, but she was more senior, so she had managed to make it work for a certain amount of time. She had managed to work out this deal where she didn't travel, which—I'm not sure how she did that. And then she also could work from home on Fridays. So that worked for her. Obviously, she had to get to that level where she had a certain amount of history and credibility and respect, I think, in order for her to get that. But she ended up being let go during a period of layoffs.

Seeing this affected Casey profoundly. She began to think about her own viability in finance because she had always planned to have children. Just like Gillian, Casey ultimately decided to leave investment banking and pursue an MBA in order to move into a non-finance related area of business. "I just felt like life is so short," she muses, "and I did like the high intensity environment, and I liked that I was learning a lot, and I felt like it was interesting on some level, but I just didn't think that was sustainable." Time maps allow the worker to connect effort and reward—to explain why the expenditure of emotional and physical energy today is worth it tomorrow.

Gillian and Casey could not see a time map that created satisfying links between past, present, and future.

More experienced women I talked to who had worked their way into upper level management positions seemed to embody Gillian and Casey's worries. I met Marybeth, CFO of the asset management firm I observed, on a particularly hectic day. She was hunkered down in a temporary office because she works from home three days a week (excluding weekends), and was on the phone chewing out an IT specialist when I walked in. "I needed that file at like six this morning. It's 8:30 now," she yells, "Call me when you get it fixed." Now in her mid 50s, Marybeth tells me that she was a dance major in college but quickly realized, "as much as I love the arts, I don't want to be a waitress the rest of my life." She switched to a business major and found out, to her surprise, that she was good at it. She began in banking right out of college, first as a bank teller, and worked her way up the career ladder into senior management.

Several years ago, she arranged to work only four days a week at the office so she could spend more time with her two children, one of whom has special needs. She has found that these four days rarely make a dent in her to-do list, so she had an office built at home, outfitted with the same extravagant three-monitor setup used throughout the firm. She frequently spends long hours at the office and then works at home during her "long weekends" away. "I'll be at home and I'll log on just to check email and do a few little things, and before I know it, the entire day is gone. One day, my daughter told me, 'Mommy, we're really sick of seeing the back of your head'"—referring to the fact that she is so often buried in her computer screens. Hearing this, Marybeth has attempted to "put some solid boundaries on my screen time. I can log on at six, but that means I have to log off by ten." But this causes other anxieties. She holds up a sheet of paper with a printed list of to-do items on the front and handwritten list of other items on the back. This list is "just totally overwhelming. Some of these things are like a year old right now. It's totally out of control." She says, "It's amazing how fast time goes. If I could get 36-hour days, I would definitely take them and I would still only use four of those hours for sleep."

I ask Marybeth if she feels like the men in the office are having these problems too.[2] She says,

2. Men in Marybeth's office were much less likely to report these problems. I asked many of them in interviews about any troubles they have with balancing work and family life. Men consistently responded that, while they do experience tensions, their wives or full-time nannies prevent these tensions from becoming unsustainable.

It's harder for women with kids because I don't have a wife at home and I don't have a full-time nanny either. I could get a full time nanny if I wanted, but I don't. I want to raise my kids. So, I'm very aware of the fact that I just can't always do everything that I want to do or everything that the men can do. But, you know what? So be it! Just don't pay me as much! [laughs wryly]

Do you feel like you're being penalized because you're a woman who wants to raise her kids?

I can't think about it that way. That may be the case, but I don't have the upper level management view of things enough to know if that is the case. But, like I said, so be it. I'm going to raise my kids. That's why I hate performance reviews, though. I never know what to put. I mean, what am I going to tell them: "Started this thing but never finished it." No! You can't put that! [laughs wryly]

Marybeth is being modest about her performance at work. As CFO of one of the most powerful financial firms in the world, she is now at the top of her game by anyone's standards. Still, she tells me about a state of constant anxiety caused by two desynchronized temporal orders: on the one hand, the rhythms of financial dealmaking, which demand constant availability and a sense of urgency. On the other hand, the rhythms of care, which also demand constant availability and a sense of urgency. From the outside, Marybeth seems to have made this tension work by negotiating a flexible schedule, but on the inside it feels unsustainable. "Anxiety is what I live with all day, every day," she says.

The time maps of finance are deeply gendered. For the women I talked to, this typically means they experienced more acutely than men grinding desynchronizations between the rhythms of dealmaking or markets and the rhythms of care. This pressure contributes to ultimately pushing women out of the profession (Blair-Loy 2010). Indeed, I persistently asked the men in my study about these conflicts, but they rarely discussed the kinds of tensions that women respondents did. When these tensions were discussed, men often explained that they have found tolerable workarounds, like full-time nannies. This story will come as no surprise to most observers, but it bears repeating as it illuminates one of the major moral dilemmas of elite knowledge workplaces.

Phantasmagoric Moral Order

In focusing so closely on the story of the gendered nature of work time and the fraught boundaries between work and home, our picture of elite workplaces has tended to miss how the moral order of knowledge work is shaped by the actual tasks and spaces that make up those jobs. We have not looked closely enough at what elite knowledge workers do at work (Bechky 2006). Aside from the pressures placed on financial professionals because of an uneasy fit between work and non-work life, then, I also noticed that the highly abstracted and disembedded character of the work presents moral dilemmas. These subtle tensions showed themselves when I began to consistently hear a curious turn of phrase among the market workers at the asset management firm I observed. Again and again traders and analysts used phrases like "I would hope," "I would think," and "I would guess" when referring to themselves as having demonstrated expertise and success on the job.

Alex, a 28-year-old analyst, mentioned to me that having a quick and capacious memory is important for his job because analysts are often asked to recall and disseminate very specific numbers about company financials on the spot. Then, in an off handed way, he remarks, "I would like to think I've gotten better at this—that people see I can do a better job at analyzing and disseminating company financials." At first, I thought nothing of Alex's turn of phrase. But then I heard it again just moments later when talking to Allison, another young analyst. Having interviewed her several months earlier when she was just out of the intern program, I asked her to reflect on how things have changed since our last conversation. She says, "The hardest thing for me has been the learning curve." Like Alex, she has had to gain a working knowledge of dozens of companies and then become better at producing that information at a moment's notice. "I would like to think," she says, "that people see how I've gotten better at that."

I then began to hear versions of this turn-of-phrase among traders too. When I asked Trevor, a derivatives trader, how he knows when he is having a good day, he first gave a wry chuckle, as though to say, "How does anyone ever know if they're having a good day?" He then replied,

> For the trader, it is very hard to know day-to-day how you're doing. Maybe I wanted to get something at a certain price and I got it at a better one. That would be good. Or tomorrow, for example, I've got a meeting with a big-time guy. If that meeting goes well, then that would be good. But it's hard to know until further down the line if you're really doing well. I would hope that in the long term, I am doing well.

As I discuss in Chapter 3, the digital trading floor produces a phantasmagoric experience of place, where the reality that matters—massive sums of money—is concealed within the disembedded and abstracted world of representations that provides access to that reality. Financial reality is not given easily; it can only be apprehended by learning to see it as "really real." Market workers' frequent use of the phrase "I would think" in regard to their work performance suggests that this phantasmagoric relationship to the objects of their work may extend to their experience of moral formation as well. Market workers have some idea that they are doing good work, but it is always partially concealed by abstractions. Experiences of excellence must be painstakingly constructed from multiple subtle signals over time. It is only after many of these subtle indications have accrued—a good trade here, a good meeting there—that workers can gain some understanding of themselves as good workers.[3]

Trevor drove this point home in a later conversation when I told him that I had been riding around the country with truck drivers. Not answering any particular question, he mused, "I imagine that truck drivers' work is more ..." he hesitates not wanting to sound rude, then continues, "I don't want to say simple, but it's just—a trucker probably knows when he's done a good job because he got the stuff there on time." He pauses again and then tacks back, "On the other hand, I imagine truckers are limited in what they can possibly do. They can't drive six trucks at once. They can't haul a billion pounds. There are limits for them. I *can* drive six trucks because I have technology and other traders, analysts, and all that." Trevor is pointing to a curious moral dilemma within the phantasmagoric workplace. On the one hand, it is difficult to know if one is becoming excellent because the evidence of expertise lies in abstract accomplishments that must be painstakingly assembled from dozens of indications, like a year's worth of evidence that one has effectively hedged the risk of a client's portfolio. From this perspective, Trevor is actually a little envious of truck drivers because the evidence of their expertise is so immediate and concrete by comparison. On the other hand, Trevor sees that the very abstracting techniques that make expertise difficult to see in his job are precisely what let him

3. Though I am not able to explore this in greater detail, I would suggest that the moral dilemmas of abstracted work are not unique to traders and may be common across the vast expanse of occupations that require working in front of screens all day. As D. A. Wallach (2015) describes in an essay for the *Pacific Standard*, "A strange thing about [computer based] work is that it is difficult to estimate its consequence. Working on an assembly line, it would be quite obvious how many widgets one produced in a day, and the value of those widgets. Building a house, one could look at the progress each week, the rooms framed, the concrete poured, the windows installed. But this relatively new digital work leaves in its immediate wake only fatigued hands and eyes, and a cascade of digital activity that is more difficult to apprehend. And I don't just mean this metaphorically: For all the track-ability of digital activity, there is so much activity that it is hard to track, and even harder to analyze. What are we all doing all day? What is the impact of this work?"

merge with the flow of the market and generate massive profits. Without the abstraction of the financial market, he would be, like a truck driver, limited by physical restrictions on the speed and scale of the exchanges he can possibly make. "That's why you join a big shop like this one," Trevor remarks, "because you can scale things up almost infinitely. I mean there are limits, of course, but they aren't that rigid and clear." The phantasm of the digital deal room conceals evidence of personal excellence precisely in the process of facilitating a feeling of expansiveness that allows the worker to merge his mind with the global flows of the market.

In sum, both the times and spaces of financial work present subtle moral dilemmas. Financial timescapes can be energizing. The "buzz" is exactly what many workers signed on for, so when things are going well this sense of disruption can be gratifying. Chronic exposure, however, can be difficult to square with longer-term commitments to friends and family, especially for women interested in raising children. In addition to the dilemmas of the work-home interface, however, are questions about skill and expertise. It can be difficult to pin down precisely how the working self is developing when the accumulation of skill must be meticulously built from assumptions about how the abstracted world connects to the real world. A sense of increasing excellence, much like the objects of financial exchange itself, must always be reconstructed from abstract achievements like a better price, a good meeting, or a cleverly constructed spreadsheet. At the same time, engaging with this abstracted world is precisely what affords financial workers the peak experiences through which they generate unimaginable profits. A more concrete form of labor would *block* access to the buzz of finance. Contradictions like these make for a fragile moral order because when things begin to go poorly at work, when workers are downsized, or when problems arise at home, the tensions can become unsustainable.

RUNNING HARD

As Trevor so clearly observed, truck drivers have a different relationship than financial professionals to the flexible economy. Objects in a truck driver's world are more concrete, in the sense that they are subject to all the frictions of the real material world. They cannot make a derivative of fifty tons of frozen chicken. At the same time, I noticed an unexpected similarity between financial professionals and truck drivers in terms of their structural relationship to flexible time. Both groups find that their workplaces give them a certain sense of autonomy and control over the labor process, while at the same time taking autonomy and control away by exposing them to cutthroat competition. This contradiction is surprisingly similar to that found by Burawoy (1979) in his analysis of industrial work-games. Financial professionals can basically work when and where they want, but to be successful they must submit themselves to impossibly time-hungry demands, such as wealthy clients and an absorbing screen world, thus never being able to switch off. Their time is *too precious*.

Through new forms of contract labor, many truck drivers are also granted a certain degree of freedom, in this case the freedom to manage many aspects of the labor process without a heavy-handed manager directly overseeing them—a freedom that would be envied by many blue-collar workers. But this is coupled with heightened regulations and surveillance techniques, such as GPS-enabled digital logbooks, that take that control away through remote management. As a result, both types of workers must contend with the contradictions of the "freedom to self-sweat"—the ability to shape the labor process through the cultivation of inner discipline, which ultimately pushes the mind and body to extremes when that freedom is coupled to powerful incentives (Belzer 2000; Fraser 2001).

Where truck drivers differ significantly from financial professionals in this dynamic, however, is that they have been asked to self-sweat in a job that is actually physically dangerous, that is increasingly economically unfavorable for them, and that does not carry the kind of cultural prestige that financial professionals enjoy. Working flexibly is both more risky and less profitable for them. The moral dilemma of truck driving involves reckoning the apparent freedoms of cruising the open road as a "professional driver" with the contradictory messages implied by physical discomfort, surveillance, an impossibly rigid set of time regulations, and the fact that they simply do not make a lot of money by working so hard.

Indignity

As I describe in Chapter 4, truck drivers live syncopated lives, rushing in the off beats of everyone else's daily rhythms in order to deliver goods to American consumers when and where they want them. Despite providing this essential service to the economy, many drivers I spoke to talked of a pervasive sense that the sacrifices they make each day for the job go mostly unrecognized. They perceive that most Americans see them not as the "backbone of the economy," but as "just some dumb trucker" whose job is so simple, so mindless, that anyone could do it. This message comes from a variety of sources but is conveyed most clearly by two parties: the FMCSA and shipping and receiving facilities.

Many drivers find that the inflexibility and one-size-fits all nature of the HOS regulations contradicts their perception of the job as a profession, which is an especially accurate description of those involved in independent contract work. One veteran owner-operator put it this way,

> The thing I resent the most is that the people in the FMCSA treat us all the same. [. . .] I've got . . . over 30 years of driving, close to three and a half million safe miles. But yet I'm treated like I'm a rookie. I know my limits. If I want to drive 11 hours today, I'll drive 11 hours. I know I can lay down 700 miles. Some days, if I want to drive a thousand, I should be able to say, "I can do a thousand miles today." No problem. I know what my limits are and when I'm tired. I guess the point I'm trying to make is: I don't need a babysitter.

Many drivers I met, but especially veteran owner-operators who had experienced the heyday of independent trucking in the 1970s, see the FMCSA as a kind of "big brother" figure. They understand their work to resemble other kinds of professional labor, which requires the trust and autonomy to do the job as one sees fit. One driver noted how other types of professionals who, for example, work in an office are not treated with the same degree of scrutiny over their time as drivers. They can extend their workday to fit whatever task or project needs to be completed. "Take for instance—you're in your office and you need fifteen or twenty extra minutes to finish your day. You call your wife and say, 'I'm going to be fifteen minutes late.' [. . .] That's our workday [too]. You just say, 'Thirty minutes is what I need to get done.' But yet it comes down on us monetarily." This driver notes that, just like knowledge work, truck driving is task-oriented. Success in the job is not marked by completing a shift but by completing a delivery. Yet, unlike knowledge professionals, he points out, drivers seeming freedom to work independently is contradicted by surveillance-enforced shift work regulations. If a driver finds that he needs, say, fourteen-and-a-half hours to make it to his destination, he risks a fine as high as $11,000. As one driver put it, "We have so many people [who] want to squash that thumb down—like big brother or daddy wanting to squash that thumb down on his son in order to make him act straight." He resents being infantilized in this way. "If you take the pressure off, and let us, the professionals do what's right and do what's safe, we're going to do it."

While many drivers I talked to had resentments toward the FMCSA, some just took the HOS for granted as the way things are. Not a single driver I encountered, however, had nice things to say about shippers and receivers. The harsh exchanges drivers have with shipping clerks and dock loaders are a subtle reinforcement of the sense of indignity they feel more generally. The most poignant of these experiences occurs during the frequent long waits that happen without justification at loading facilities. As one driver put it,

> [Shippers] show complete disregard for my time. They don't know what I've been through in the last few days to get the load there—that I've gotten no sleep. So when they say things like, 'We'll call you' and give you a nasty look when you ask how long that might be, I get so pissed.

Especially problematic is an obvious desynchronization between motor carrier firms and shipping facilities that exacerbates drivers' feelings of powerlessness. Clerks and loading dock employees are typically paid by the hour, so there is little incentive for them to work fast and to keep track of the speed of individual loads (Viscelli 2010). Moreover, shipping/receiving employees do not have access to drivers' logbooks, which means, even if they did care about a driver's time, there would be no easy way to coordinate with him. For drivers, of course, each minute spent not moving is potential revenue wasted. Their entire mood can swing because of logbook difficulties. As a result, drivers frequently experience disrespect in the form of aimless waiting because of shipping/receiving employees' lack of knowledge about drivers' limited time. One driver recounted delivering to an upscale supermarket in downtown Chicago this way,

> They force you to sit on a hard bench for four, five hours and wait to unload when you could be out there [in your truck] sleepin'. [. . .] Would you like to sit on a hard bench for four or five hours . . . and watch these people unload you and taking their time doing it? And joking around? "Here's a driver, who cares about him?" [. . .] Anymore, nobody appreciates us, the work we do and the hours we put in out here.

The problem here is structural—two different incentive systems that result in chronic desynchronization—but repeated exposure to that timescape infuses it with moral emotions. As one driver commented, "It wouldn't take much to make waiting better for us. Just common courtesy, like if [shipping clerks] could just give me some kind of estimate—doesn't matter if it's 4 or 10 hours, I don't care—that's still better than, 'We'll call you.'" Drivers understand and accept the many "arrhythmias" of the logistics system; however, that these are continually pushed downstream to the driver without justification feels disrespectful because, more often than not, drivers are held responsible for smoothing over these inefficiencies using their own bodies. What is more, they often do so without compensation. Unlike financial professionals, drivers' jobs can be unprofitable precisely because they have behaved so flexibly.

The Run Hard Ethos

It would seem, then, that truck drivers have it bad. They lie at the bottom of a status hierarchy within a flexible logistics system that externally enforces rigid time discipline. As Sennett (2000:63) notes, the spontaneity and uncertainty that may give those at the top a buzz, "become more self-destructive for those who work lower down in the flexible regime." From this perspective, we might be tempted to assume that truck driving, like a lot of today's flexible shift work, is a "bad job" (Kalleberg 2011). Again, my research suggests a more complex picture when we step back and look at both the drudgery and the artistry of extreme shift work for the self. Despite the indignities of the job, many drivers I talked to remain proud of themselves because the (seemingly) self-directed nature of truck driving affords them experiences of creativity and perseverance. Without question, they must endure unpaid waiting, rigid scheduling, and subtle surveillance, but in the "off beats" of these degrading experiences they get to be, much like an entrepreneur, savvy problem solvers. This was born out by the fact that *both* independent owner-operators and the more rigidly controlled "company drivers" I talked to discussed similar experiences of excellence in their jobs. Both types of drivers constructed moral order around a kind of work-game they call "running hard."

"Running hard" means many things for drivers—a willingness to drive fast, drive far, sleep and shower irregularly, take fewer breaks, take a difficult and low-paying load when no one else will—but adds up to an ethic of rugged perseverance. The run hard ethos allows drivers to construct a conception of themselves as tough, street-smart businessmen who are willing to get the job done even when the risk is high and the reward low. Truck driving can be incredibly stressful and fatiguing, but developing the capacity to run hard through those difficulties can be a source of meaning and pride when everything finally clicks in those perfect moments of unification. Running hard is a work-game that facilitates managements' desire for workers to push themselves harder and harder, even if the resulting financial payoff for drivers is low.

When I asked Paul, a 50-year-old company driver with 15 years behind the wheel, what excites him about the job, he quickly replied,

> A part of me wants to say that I really like the—if it doesn't seem odd—the challenge of it. Because, to me, I take a lotta pride in the fact that I haven't been late

with a load. Not ever. And to be able to sorta do what it takes to, on a day-to-day basis, pick up a load and get it where it needs to be and get it there on time. Takin' into consideration all the issues that we've talked about here today—the drive and the fatigue, the traffic—and still on a daily basis do a good job. I take a great deal of pride in that.

Paul's sense of artistry in his work is connected to the flexible virtue of consistently generating "good timing." The task of delivering freight to a precise time-space coordinate is deceptively difficult. Regardless of an external reward, completing this task with excellence can be intrinsically rewarding. Reveling in the challenge of good timing is one of the signs that a driver has cultivated a professional attitude. As another driver noted, "I actually like the 14-hour rule, in a way, because it makes you plan everything out that much more. It rewards guys who are good at problem solving."

Other drivers constructed dignity around the cognitive demands required to push through long periods of monotonous driving while maintaining awareness of danger and being ready to react quickly. "I feel like I'm a better person inside the truck compared to outside the truck," one driver mused. "I'm more of a conscientious person. I'm aware of my surroundings more. I guess it's almost the same thing when you're a parent. Like when I'm with my daughter, my eight year old. [. . .] I'm not as loose as I normally would be because I gotta be aware of everything around me." The virtues bestowed on them by their refined attentions are made all the more significant because of the clearly discernible dangers of the job. As one driver remarked about his attention,

It's just having that—what's the word I'm looking for? Knowing what other drivers are gonna do before they even do it. It's like you can sense it, you know?

Like intuition or something?

Peripheral vision or whatever they call that. [Turning his head back and forth] You just kind of keep yourself going back and forth noticing everything. Be observant; that's all. I couldn't tell you how many times I've backed out of something cuz I knew something was gonna happen. [My truck is] eighty thousand pounds—you could fucking kill somebody, you know what I mean?

As another driver remarked, "Whenever I'm driving behind a car and I see mom, dad and the kids in there, I imagine that is my family in there. I couldn't live with myself if I killed someone with my truck." Drivers expressed deep respect for and a healthy fear of the responsibility of driving a massive vehicle around the general public. The skills required to conduct themselves safely in this environment—caution, unwavering attention— were a distinct source of pride.

When things are going especially well, some drivers even described a transcendent "flow" state that sounded similar to the unification experiences of live deals and absorbing financial trading. As one driver remarked,

> You try to push yourself . . . and once you get going, then I develop a rhythm and a flow. [. . .] I get in the truck. Boom, four hours until my first stop. There for a half an hour. Okay. Boom, next stop. Five stops in a row and you feel like you can just go on and on and on. [. . .] That's when you get into a rhythm. It's like a quarterback. They're throwing one pass after another. The receiver's catching. He throws an incomplete, but no interceptions; then he throws five touchdowns in a row. [. . .] Once he gets into a rhythm, he's like Johnny Unitis, Joe Namath, 'Slingin' Sammy Baugh, all those great ones that ever played the game. He's got it all rolled up into one—can't touch 'em. Same thing with this job.

Turning a chaotically desynchronized timescape into splendid unification can create emotional highs. By "pushing yourself," this driver suggests, he can creatively transform an environment of dissonant "incompletes" into a harmonious crescendo of completed runs. Much like the factory workers that Roy and Burawoy studied, then, the drivers I met seem to turn the battle with time into a game, which can open up forms of self-expression that are surprisingly satisfying. There are hidden thrills to getting an impossible load in on time, even if it means sacrificing sleep, hygiene, and diet.

Compared to the "buzz" of financial work, however, the highs of running hard are different in one crucial way. Drivers were able to see excellence grow in themselves more easily over time. This seems to be because their work is less abstracted (Crawford 2009; Sennett 2009). The markers of good driving, unlike good financial dealing, easily lend themselves to stark contrasts between achievement and failure. You deliver on time or you are late; you drive safely or you are reckless. A disaster in financial dealing needs a long-winded explanation; nothing needs to be explained when truck drivers fail. Veteran drivers could easily mark the progression of their skills by discussing how many "safe miles" they have driven or how many times they have been late with a load. Truck drivers are anything but trapped in a "bad job." Despite the indignities of their work, they are readily able to discuss excellence and skill development, and are more easily afforded such experiences compared to the financial professionals I talked to.

The Risk of Running Hard

Running hard, as enticing a game as it can be, comes at an extremely high cost. As discussed in Chapter 4, truck drivers are tasked with transmuting two incompatible rhythmic systems—clock time and freight time—using corporal practices of entrainment. Engaging in entrainment essentially means intentionally exposing one's body and psyche to damaging stimuli. Thus, drivers must develop a stimulus shield, which allows in only the right amount and kind of stimulus necessary to protect the sensorium from being overwhelmed, while still allowing them to perform their jobs (Schivelbusch 1979). Engaging in entrainment with the help of a stimulus shield is an effective way to deliver freight. It works. And for some, it even provides enticing flow experiences. Entrainment cannot be sustained for very long, however, before the body simply gives out.[4]

The risk to drivers' bodies was driven home to me when, after having spent several months around truck stops, I became aware that I could identify a truck driver from a distance by his walk. Encased behind the stimulus shield of their trucks, remaining paradoxically motionless in their seats as they careen down the road, drivers begin to develop a hunched posture and a stiffness in their shoulders, necks, and knees that results in an ambling, forward-leaning gate. Their walk hints at other chronic conditions in drivers' bodies that are better observed statistically. Drivers have, for example, higher rates of obesity, diabetes, heart disease, and sleep disorder than virtually any other occupation (Dahl et al. 2009; FMCSA 2006; Sharwood et al. 2012). These "lifestyle risk factors," as studies of driver health call them, are in part a result of routinely exposing the body to certain necessary desynchronizations—such as disrupted eating and sleeping patterns—that are required by flexible shift work and are therefore intentionally let in by the stimulus shield. For truck drivers, then, a distinct challenge to their imaginations is not necessarily the drudgery of labor itself (i.e., it's a "bad job"), but envisioning a sustainable working life of any kind once their bodies give out in their 40s, 50s, or, at best, 60s.

I met Tommy, for example, who is 48 years old and has been driving for over 16 years, at a truck stop in central Virginia. Sitting in the small television room/café attached to the truck stop, I watched Tommy walk— slowly, hunched—from his truck, which was some distance away. Dressed like most drivers in jeans and a baseball cap, as he got closer I noticed that he has a graying, stubbly beard and walks with shoulders that are completely misaligned, like Chaim Soutine's *Le Patissier*, one sitting several inches below the other. Striking up a conversation with him, I find out that

4. As Freud suggests, using his metaphor of the encrusted "vesicle," while the stimulus shield protects drivers' "inner core" from the potentially traumatizing environment that surrounds them, this protection is secured only by sacrificing parts of the "outermost layer" (Freud 1922:31).

Tommy is on an "unintended break," because his dispatcher bungled his delivery time and got him there a full day late. He has now been waiting for four and a half hours (unpaid) to get further instruction on what to do with his late load.

Being indeterminately indisposed, Tommy was happy to sit and chat with me for several hours. Like a lot of drivers I met, when he was younger he found the act of moving a tractor-trailer down the road at high speed exhilarating. Having finished a tour of duty in the first Iraq War, he worked a series of "little jobs,"—roofing, construction, food service—but "never could make anything go." He attempted college for a year on the GI Bill but, he says, "I just couldn't do it." Having no home, no vehicle, and no job, he realized that he could get all three by becoming a truck driver. At first, he loved truck driving because of the speed and independence. "It makes you feel alive. You're just waking up in the morning and it's—and it just seems like all that pressure and everything, it seems like a release. You're doing 100 miles an hour through California in the desert when you're supposed to be doing 55. Just being a rebel. It makes you feel good." Like a lot of drivers, Tommy's initial experience of the freedoms of driving came against the backdrop of the increasingly undesirable employment options that are available to workers without a degree, which not only pay poorly but also typically involve heavy-handed supervision from a boss.

The exhilaration wore off for Tommy, he figures, after about five years of running hard. "I guess I progressively got older and I burnt out on it." I ask him what made him burn out. He replies, "The pressure. [...] I'm under pressure ninety-nine-point-nine when I'm out here driving, and you don't make the appointment, and they charge you for it, or you get a bad mark on your record, and you want to do good, and you're on that timeframe, and under pressure, and . . ." He trails off and pauses. "Sixteen years of it. The first five, I could handle it, and then I think I just got overloaded. [...] Now, I'm just trying to stop and get out of this." Tommy's initial feelings of freedom were slowly outbalanced by the realities of making money in a deregulated market. He had been made free to work himself harder and harder.

As I observed when he walked in, Tommy tells me that a big part of burning out is the toll hard driving has taken on his body. "Right now I could probably . . . walk into a doctor's office and him tell me I could go draw disability because of my shoulders. It's just bone on bone. I ain't got that much longer because of that. I've done all I can do." Unfortunately, like many drivers I talked to, Tommy is finding it difficult to get out of the industry now. During the last decade of running hard, he has accrued a number of speeding violations that make it difficult for him to get anything other than long-haul jobs. "I had a plan. I haven't been an idiot," he says.

"My plan was to get out there and get some experience and drive for two, three years—maybe five. Stay with the same company. Don't get no trash on your record, speeding violations or whatever, stay clean and then go drive local jobs like UPS, FedEX, twenty dollars an hour, lifetime. That was my plan." That plan has been put on hold again and again over the years, though, because he knows no other way of driving than running hard, which inevitably lands him with another violation. All Tommy can hope for, then, is to keep his record clean before his body wears out so that he can clear his license and find another easier type of driving-related work, such as local freight delivery or dump truck driving. "It's coming," he says, trying to sound encouraging. "Something's gonna change. I'm gonna try and find another kind of work for me to do before I'm way too old. I guess I'm already there, but maybe not."

Truck drivers find themselves in a similar moral dilemma to financial professionals, but they must navigate that dilemma without the same financial rewards and with consequences that are far more costly for the body. There are pleasures in the trucking industry that are hard to find in other areas of blue-collar work—independence, skill-development, professionalism, and even peak experiences. But with that dream comes the reality that the margins of success are incredibly tight, requiring drivers to ratchet up the intensity of work year after year in order to stay afloat (Viscelli 2010). Too young and not financially secure enough to retire but too chronically fatigued to keep driving for much longer, drivers eventually come to terms with the fact that running hard, however meaningful it may be in the short term, delivers them into an unsustainable time map.

The financialized and deregulated timescapes examined so far reveal an interesting commonality: flexible capitalism invites both high and low status workers to intensify their own labor by creating enticing "work-games" (Burawoy 1979; Roy 1953). The buzz and expansiveness of financialized timescapes and the rugged challenges of running hard as a truck driver afford workers the chance to build meaningful edifices that honor the self as skillful, experienced, and excellent. But in the process of generating moral meanings, these games also make it difficult for workers to see when they have overinvesting of themselves in risky activity. As their needs, desires, and necessities change over time, then, they risk hitting some sort of hard limit beyond which things become emotionally and physically dire. In the long run, they often find themselves torn between the short-term good offered by doing excellent work and the long-term good of living a sustainable life. They are stretched between two antagonistic conceptions of the good that operate on two different levels of social time. The pursuit of one threatens the pursuit of the other.

As I discuss in Chapter 5, job seekers experience flexible capitalism primarily on the level of time maps rather than timescapes. They must transition from an anachronistic security-oriented conception of the future to a more precarious future through the crucible of job loss. This moment of reckoning, at first, generates a stagnant "protentional death," which job seekers must slowly work their way out of by reconstructing links between short, medium, and long term futures. Job seeking, then, is most certainly hard work; it is just not paid (Sharone 2014; Standing 2011). I found that job seekers' attitudes toward precarious time maps mirrored the work-game dynamic I saw in the other two cases—only now the game took place on the level of the lifecourse (see Sharone 2007; Smith 2001 for a similar finding). Situating the three cases side by side reveals a common connection: flexible capitalism stretches workers between energizing short-term absorptions and unsustainable long-term consequences.

The Energy of Job Seeking

The initial stages of job seeking narrow respondents' protentional vision such that they are looking for any source of motivation to pick them up and get life moving again. For the white-collar job seekers I met, job search support groups like Career Transition Ministries helped provide this lift. It was often not the self-help rhetoric of positivity and individual responsibility that job seekers initially connected with in these spaces, however, but the simple physical and psychological highs generated by the basic protentional acts of job seeking, like networking and resume writing, which they learned how to do there. As Ofer Sharone (2007:405) has observed, "Engaging in the work of job searching, as structured by self-help discourses and practices, temporarily absorbs unemployed job seekers in a highly professionalized work-game." This game involves constructing action plans and schedules, making strategic decisions about resumes and cover letters, networking with new people, and helping others by looking out for job openings. Over time, as this activity generates a kind of stimulating "flow" state, job seekers can finally take a breath and begin to consider larger narratives about the medium- and long-term future as well. Among the job seekers I met, when they went looking around for such narratives, there were very few options out there. In online media, self-help books, and at places like CTM, they were fed a remarkably uniform set of messages about positivity, entrepreneurialism, and risk-attraction that encouraged them to embrace disruption.

Linda, for example, first connected with CTM because it showed her how to network. The energy she gained from networking triggered deeper changes in her self conception. After describing some early successful networking encounters, she notes, "I have learned tremendously. [...] I no longer introduce myself as an introvert. I am becoming a people person." Linda sees this as a positive change. "I am becoming a new person," she smiles. She also notices a downside.

> The con side of that is my friends don't understand. They're seeing somebody they don't know. [...]
>
> *They've noticed a change in you?*
>
> A complete change. I have turned 180 degrees.
>
> *Wow. Tell me more about that. What are they reacting to? How are they reacting?*
>
> [...] My best friend said, 'I don't know who you are anymore and I don't know whether I like you.
>
> *What is she reacting to?*
>
> My outwardness. My ability to say no, my ability to—if there was a discussion and I didn't agree, I walked away. I enter into the discussion now. I have a right to my opinion. I have a right to disagree with you and I'm not—I guess I was always being used. I let myself be used.

By engaging in the simple practice of networking, Linda feels she has unlocked new aspects of her personality—confidence, extroversion—that she did not know she had. This has led to an epiphany that has completely reoriented her outlook on work more generally.

> I think losing my position was the best thing that could have happened to me.
>
> *Really? Because it's given you this, kind of, new perspective?*
>
> I wasn't happy in the [old] position. It was a chair. I've learned the difference between a chair and a career. It's given me the opportunity to expand my horizons and it's allowing me maybe to be the person that I was always meant to be. [...] I can't have what I've known as a career. There may be longevity, but . . .
>
> *When you land that next opportunity, do you think you'll have a different outlook once you've landed there? What will it be like, do you think?*
>
> It won't be 60 hours a week. I will exceed my responsibilities, but not to the point that I've exceeded them before. I will not give my life for any career. *[Two second pause]* I say that, but if I were to start work tomorrow—I would hope that

I've learned enough and I'm familiar enough with what I am now, that I wouldn't go back [to a corporate job]. Would I go back? I mean that's a what-if.

Linda is torn between different ideas of good work, which is reflected in the tentativeness of her speech. She is still in the midst of a conversion to a new way of understanding the relationship between her narrative trajectory and what is possible in the future within the precarious labor market. She has come to see her former self, which naively embraced the myth of the career but settled for a series of dead-end office "chairs," as a pushover, someone who "let" herself be "used." She will never again, she claims, "give herself" to a company. On the other hand, there is more than a hint of doubt here. If hired by another corporation, she "hopes" she has "learned enough" not to overcommit. But that is a big "what-if." The conversion is anything but total.

Linda's hesitancy points to a disorienting moral dilemma created by precarious time maps. From one perspective, practices like numerical flexibility seem to allow white-collar job seekers to fully acknowledge a suspicion that career labor was never all that great anyway. As much as the career may have made the promise of security through seniority, that promise was actually either false or, even when it was true, engendered workaholism. In this way, things like short-term, casual, and temporary work can actually be a chance to transform oneself under one's own power and evolve into a new version of oneself—possibilities that may have been nullified by commitment to a single employer or occupation. This attitude is not simply the blind regurgitation of self-help individualism, but the direct result of the protentional practices on offer to the flexibly unemployed. Networking, making strategic decisions, and continually upgrading oneself for the next job transition can be invigorating because they allow absorption in the immediate work of regenerating links between the short- and long-term futures. They create a flow state. This is a far better situation than wallowing in self-pity, complaining about bad jobs, or getting "stuck" in the past.

As Linda's hesitancy suggests, however, the precise contours of these links and how much emotional investment one should make in them in the long-term are frustratingly difficult to judge. If and when one does get hired again, how does one tell if the effort to get such a fleeting new position will be worth it in, say, three years? What is the appropriate attitude to take toward future job losses now that one knows they are incredibly draining, but also curiously rewarding? The moral work of precarious job seeking, then, involves reassembling the link between short- and long-term futures in such a way that one can honor the hard work of constant job seeking while at the same time maintain emotional stability in the face of constant change. Among the job seekers I met the only compelling and readily available narrative in American culture to carry out this moral work was entrepreneurial individualism.

The Entrepreneurial Attitude

Linda's comment that "losing my position was the best thing that could have happened to me," may seem strange. Like other scholars who have analyzed American unemployment culture, however, I heard that phrase again and again (Lane 2011; Sharone 2014; Smith 2001). Throughout our conversations, respondents wanted me to understand that things are not as bad as they look from the outside—that, in many ways, their moment of reckoning was a blessing. Respondents wanted to see themselves as "entrepreneurs" of a new future rather than "victims" of past injustice because this language helped them navigate the disorienting moral dilemmas of precarious time maps.

Job seekers see becoming an entrepreneur as the only truly viable, morally legitimate alternative to the traditional career time map. By entrepreneur, many I talked to literally meant becoming a small-business owner. But the idea had other meanings. For some, it meant continuing to work in large organizations, but protecting oneself from those precarious places by withdrawing feelings of loyalty and commitment, that is, trying to "lay low," "keep my head down," and "look out for number one." I talked to Marlon, for example, just a few days after interviewing his mother Sheryl, who had recently been let go from her call center job at a large corporate bank after twenty years of faithful service. Following in his mothers' footsteps, Marlon, 26-years old and a recent college graduate, was fired from his position as a personal banker just a few months later. In addition to his own experience of job loss, seeing his mother cast aside, who was one of the bank's star employees, profoundly affected Marlon's view of what it means to be a good worker.

> People feel that the hard work and loyalty that I give to a company is gonna be paid off. I don't think so. Now, am I saying that I'm gonna go work for a company and just screw a company? No. But my mom—man, as kids, anytime it was night and we were home, we didn't even have to ask where my mom was. She was working to 6, 7, 8, 9 at night. She was never home [. . .] The company doesn't care! It's not like, "Oh, well, she works all the time, we can't let her go." [. . .] To me, it's not worth doing all the extra effort and stuff that is above and beyond your job to try to impress people, because, in the long run, it really just doesn't matter. 'Cuz if you're gonna get fired, you're gonna get fired. There's nothing you can really do except for do your job to 100 percent the best of your knowledge.

Notice the tension in Marlon's view of work. On the one hand, he has (grudgingly) embraced a post-loyalty, post-longevity vision of corporate labor. He saw what the expectation of reward for seniority got his mother and vows never to fall into that trap. On the other hand, Marlon cannot bring himself to "screw" a company; one must still put "100 percent" into the job. How these seemingly contradictory attitudes are linked in Marlon's mind was not entirely clear to me until he told me that he and his fiancé have decided to start their own business. "Now, when I work somewhere, I kind of lay low," he explains.

> It's kind of like, you lay low, and you do what you're told, that's the way to progress in business, and actually, because of all that prior experience, it has led to me and my fiancé looking into starting our own business. Before it was—I never even thought of that. I never even thought of doing that, but now it's like—it's kind of like—I'm a *good* person, but that doesn't mean anything. [Employers] don't see it; they don't care about that. They don't care if you're there every day. So, I might as well go out on my own, start my own thing.

For Marlon, cultivating an entrepreneurial attitude toward work means withholding loyalty from an employer, *but not effort*.[5] Hard work still matters for Marlon, not because it promises the reward of higher rank within the time map of a career, but because hard work is the key to eventually exiting the status game altogether, which, in fact, turns out to be a ruse anyway. Much to Marlon's surprise, then, it is only outside the career time map that he can be appreciated as a "good person." Moral order and the career are now opposed in his mind.

For some respondents, becoming an entrepreneur was not just a way to instrumentally protect oneself from insecurity, but also a good in itself. No one I talked to expressed this perspective more forcefully than Colleen, who "left" her high-powered career in network television after feeling forced out by a glass ceiling and an exhausting work schedule. In one way, Colleen is an entrepreneur in the sense that she is back in school to become a child and family therapist and start her own practice. In another way, Colleen is an entrepreneur because of a profound transformation in her self conception. Reflecting on the years she spent climbing the ladder in the cutthroat environment of network television, she says,

> Media attracts people who want to have power, or they want to be seen to have power. And I definitely was attracted to the power aspect. I think this experience

---

5. Though most respondents I talked to saw the need to abandon loyalty in order to protect themselves in the workplace, not all did. Henry, for example, still finds loyalty essential to his self conception. "I still value loyalty," he says. "I always will. Will I be as tolerant of some people's methodologies? Maybe not [laughs]. In my eyes, I couldn't help but be loyal. I just think that adds so much credibility and value to the person."

[of job loss] has put me in a place where I am interested in empowering others, not having power over them.

That sounds like a profound realization for you.

Well, that's what I think God wants me to get.

Do you feel like that's a bit of a silver lining to all this?

[Laughs] It is and it isn't. I just got tired of getting socked and kicked and cut in the back and you're hemorrhaging at the same time. It's like, okay, how do I find the resolve to go on? And for me, Ben, the answer has been going back to being a Christian. It's God. [...] What does God have to say about me? What is the purpose of everything I'm going through? What I got from that was, "Colleen, when you work for Me, when you're under My employ, you have to know not only how to do the most intricate and complicated, but you also have to know how to do the most basic and pedestrian." That's what this is about.

So that message you're getting is—what does that mean for you?

When I look at someone, whether they are my client in the future or someone that I may meet ... I will not—I will be more sensitive to looking at them not just in terms of just their credentials or just their resumé or—looking beyond the fact of, "Oh, you're how old and what are you doing?" There's a story there and there's still a whole person there. [...] I'm a much better woman now than I was when I had a house and I had the media career. I have a greater heart, a great compassion, much more depth of soul than I've had previously.

Colleen's views are complex, tentative, and reflect the rollercoaster ride she has been on for the last five years. One thing is clear: she now aligns the concept of gaining power by pursuing a career with qualities like egotism, shallowness, and conformity. She sees her former career-driven self as one who only wanted to "have power over others," who had no "depth of soul." Now, by contrast, she sees herself pursuing a more authentic entrepreneurial path, which involves "empowering others," treating others as "whole" people instead of "just their resumés," and feeling fulfilled in life even though one's job is "basic and pedestrian." In short, Colleen has developed a rather robust critique of the career time map and its culture of conformity. She has exposed its dark side (Whyte 1965). As much as it provided her with material rewards, predictability, and prestige, it also consumed her, made her into a workaholic and a social climber who would rather dominate than connect.

The entrepreneurial attitude can take a variety of forms but has a common logic. It elevates the creative individuality required to make it in the precarious labor market so that it feels more honorable than the conformity and naivety required to "submit" oneself to a single employer. It is honorable, moreover, precisely because it is so difficult and risky. As Colleen put it,

> Do I love this experience? Absolutely not. [. . .] But I feel confident—ironically maybe to some people—that my future is bright. I have a lot to offer. I have a phenomenal brain. [. . .] The fact that I can step out of the box of what people tell you you're supposed to do and live my life—there are a lot of blessings in spite of what looks like a pathetic circumstance.

Entrepreneurial individualism is a work-game that takes place on the level of the lifecourse. Rather than take the "easy" route of submitting to a mindless pre-planned career path, one can strike out alone and do the creative (unpaid) work of linking the short- and long-term futures oneself. This reveals the strength, resolve, and creativity within oneself—a form of honor that respondents feel they cannot and could never cultivate within the career time map.

Self-sweating the Lifecourse

There is a catch. As I did with Colleen, I would often suggest in interviews with job seekers that perhaps they had found a kind of "silver lining" in their experience of unemployment by awakening to their creativity, adaptability, and entrepreneurial spirit. They never agreed with this suggestion. As Colleen said, "Do I love this experience? Absolutely not." The apparent freedoms of the entrepreneurial self generate new problems in the very act of creating solutions to old problems. These snags in the silver lining emerge slowly through chronic exposure to multiple rounds of employment, job loss, and job seeking, which can take place over the course of years (Sharone 2007). Similar to the other workers I met, job seekers must ultimately figure out how to navigate the dilemmas of over commitment that come from a kind of "self-sweating" that takes place on the level of the lifecourse. This form of self-sweating is related less to intensifying *work tasks*, and more to intensifying the transformation of *the self* based on the shifting needs of today's fickle employers.

This theme was revealed to me most clearly when I reinterviewed respondents. I talked to Linda again a year and a half after our first interview. Since then, she was hired by another corporation, this time a mid-sized corporate bank, and once again let go less than a year later. The company had hired a new CEO and decided to dissolve the department Linda was working in by moving her role tasks online. Unlike our first interview, Linda narrates her story of job loss with a kind of calm detachment that can only come from someone for whom work crises are a normal state of affairs. Linda says she was "ecstatic" after first landing the job. It was a "perfect fit" and paid just two thousand dollars a year less than her previous position. The excitement, however, wore off quickly. She describes an unsettling anxiety that arose immediately upon beginning work and that came from multiple sources. For one, she was taken aback by "how low my self-confidence had gotten" after five months of joblessness. Also, it "was always in the back of my mind that this position may be abolished and I wondered how I would handle that. I found that I was treading very lightly. I was waiting for the other shoe to drop."

In many ways, the circumstances of this layoff were worse than before because Linda's employer warned her three months beforehand that they were making plans to abolish her position. In a curious move, however, they would not let her tell her colleagues of the decision, nor did they give her an exact date of termination. During those three months she was secretly tasked with putting herself out of a job by establishing new online systems that could perform her work when she leaves. Despite her earlier proclamation that she would never again overwork for a company, she found herself putting in the same old 50- and 60-hour workweeks that she had in the past, but now with full knowledge that every hour spent on work was an hour closer to unemployment. "I'd much rather have the immediate layoff or firing or termination or whatever you want to call it," Linda notes, "because it's done, it's over with, and maybe I would have blamed the company more then. But how could I blame the company when they told me for three months what they were doing?" Perhaps the company thought they were doing Linda a favor, but in practice she was left with the feeling that it was now *her* responsibility not to overinvest in her employment contract because the company had given her fair warning. Through a kind of planned unpredictable impermanence the company passed the emotional risk of worrying about commitment onto Linda's shoulders. Her sense of "waiting for the other shoe to drop" was completely confirmed.

What was most perplexing from an interviewer's perspective about Linda's reaction to this situation is her remarkable capacity to forgive, accept, and remain positive. She tells me that she has now covered the wall in her bedroom with positive sayings, such as "Dare to try" and "If you risk nothing, you risk everything." Before dismissing this unrelenting positivity as some sort of "false consciousness," however, I wanted to understand what it does for Linda in the context of navigating insecurity. I commented to her that,

People looking in from the outside would wonder why you aren't angry or more angry.

I'm asked that question all the time. [. . .] It is my belief that my glass is half full; it's not half empty. I didn't do anything wrong. They didn't do anything wrong. It is a business decision. [. . .] It's corporate America. They're trying to do their best. They're in business to make money, especially a large corporation. They're not only reporting to themselves. They've got a board of directors, an executive committee, and they've got stockholders. And the stockholders say I want more money. So they do what they have to do. [. . .] But if it weren't me being let go, somebody else would have been. [The Company] is trying to rebuild itself. They have a new CEO. [. . .] So with a new CEO coming in, "the new broom sweeps clean."

Linda is not angry for a number of reasons. Number one, anger is not strategic. As she tells me later, anger "makes me a lousy interviewer" and less attractive to hiring personnel. More importantly, anger is inappropriate when the choices leading to her termination were impersonal and logical. It was a "business decision" that makes perfect sense within a shareholder value model of corporate governance. On yet another level, Linda is not angry because she no longer pretends that being with a single company for a long time is necessarily a good thing. She tells me,

The number of people I've seen now who were in positions that they were not happy in, but that they didn't know they were not happy in is staggering. They lose their job and then do an assessment and then figure out that they shouldn't have been doing that job for thirty years anyway. And it's those people that are the positive ones.

So, unlike in our first interview, Linda sees herself continuing to pursue positions in, as she calls it, Corporate America. "I look at it positively," she says,

When I get hired again, I will probably go through those same eight weeks [of anxiety] that I went through last time, but I may not be as scared this time. It may not take eight weeks. It may only last four or six weeks. But if they let me go, it's their loss, not mine.

To bear the downward shift of risk that comes with becoming a disruptable worker, Linda has cultivated an emotional life that is defiantly undisruptable. It is an almost aggressive positivity that provides inner emotional stability in the face of a constantly changing work identity. It honors the core self—the real me—without having to get attached to the outer self—a shifting assemblage of skillsets, titles, and roles. Positivity helps connect present and future, inside and outside in an environment where existential disruptions have become all too common.

Toward the end of our interview, Linda finally confides that even though her most recent job was "probably the best gig I've ever had," she was actually beginning to get restless. "I was ready to move on, honestly," she recalls. "Because I was getting bored with what I was doing. So instead of moving on, I moved out. So, now I can start all over again [laughs]. You know, you knock me down; I get back up. I take little steps. And that's life."

Job seeking in the flexible economy reveals many of the same moral dilemmas I saw in the other cases, but stretched over a longer wavelength of social time. They engage in energizing work-games, like networking, that can be remarkably rewarding and even transformative. They fuel a vision of oneself as an independent and savvy go-getter. These work-games, however, also come with responsibilities to transform the self over and over again in accordance with the fickleness of companies' preference for short-term and open-ended contracts. Much like financial professionals and truck drivers who induce themselves to work intensely on job tasks, then, job seekers induce themselves to work intensely on the *self* by remaining upbeat and positive in the face of change.

Entrepreneurial individualism is a perfect ideological match for this challenge. The cost of shouldering such an intensified form of self-transformation, however, is that one's moral world becomes rather fragile. Everything depends on how well one can take the next disruption. If the armor of positivity fails, the honorable edifice one has erected around the self can come quickly crashing down.

CONCLUSION

Seeing the three cases side by side reveals that the cultural scaffolding of flexible time encourages a kind of obsession, not with the present moment as many scholars have argued (Lubbe 2009; Rushkoff 2013; Sennett 2000; Tomlinson 2007), but with the short- and medium-term futures—the temporal zone lying just in front of the social actor in which "good timing" and the "ripeness" of action are most clearly discernable. Workers are not encouraged to be fully invested in the long-term future because such a place is too difficult to see amidst the imperative of change. But neither are workers encouraged to be fully invested in the present moment because their jobs are often about anticipating whatever is a few steps down the line of action—the next few deals, loads, or positions—to get there before one's competition. Their temporal vision, then, tends to be angled toward the short and middle ranges—the existential space where, as Linda put it, one "waits for the other shoe to drop." Living a disruptable life is not "living in the present" (Standing 2011:16). It is living in a kind of middling future that prevents one from being fully engaged in the here-and-now *and* from being fully engaged with a far off goal. This is precisely what makes it a flexible moral order, obsessed as it is with the next few beats in the rhythm of social action that will present the self with near-term strategic advantages.

This temporal scaffolding affords workers the chance to engage in enticing work-games that generate perplexing moral dilemmas for the mind, body, and emotions. The buzz of finance, the ruggedness of running hard, and the positivity of the entrepreneurial attitude offer workers forms of experience that may not have been available to them in older regimes of work and may also address problems associated with that old order, such as boredom and conformity. By making the most of flexible time, however, workers also discover new sources of suffering and confusion that result from being asked to "self-sweat." The apparent freedoms of the disrupted life come packaged with new responsibilities to drive oneself harder and harder, both on the level of the timescape, in which workers discipline themselves to produce more intensely, and on the level of the time map, in which workers discipline the self to go through intense changes. Chronic exposure to self-sweating over the course of years can lead to troubling feelings that things will surely reach a breaking point. The sources of liberation, then, are also the sources of suffering.

An important question that arises from these observations is why respondents find it so difficult to see and critique the institutional and political sources of their economic suffering, which tend to operate on a long-term timescale. Why do they not see that their absorptions in flexible labor will come back to haunt them in the long run, and that this dilemma is in fact a *built in* capacity of work arrangements and labor processes? It is *intentionally* designed into the workplace by economic elites who want to capitalize on workers' ability to shoulder more risk (Kalleberg 2011; Standing 2011). Part of the explanation may be that American moral culture is notably individualistic and depoliticizing. It notoriously celebrates the triumph of the creative individual, often at the expense of seeing how individual actions are embedded in wider structures of power that affect many (Bellah et al. 2007). As Ofer Sharone (2014) observes in his comparative study of American and Israeli job seekers, cultural contexts like Israel that offer more collectivist explanations for economic suffering can more easily account for the systemic dynamics of flexible capitalism and place greater blame on the institutions and elites who built that system, rather than the individual's capacity to cope. Different moral orders can be stretched over the very same temporal scaffolding.

Two additional considerations are important, however. First, flexible capitalism is a structural response to many of the problems of industrial capitalism (Boltanski and Chiapello 2005). At least in theory, it is meant to be an improvement on past economic regimes. Workers may feel this in their everyday lives. Some forms of flexible work can, at least initially, seem to relieve the frustrations of rigid and regularized temporalities by customizing social time around the individual, giving the impression of more autonomy. From this perspective, the hyper-individualizing experiences of work in flexible capitalism can feel like a welcome change (Halpin 2015).

Second, the subjective experience of flexible social time does not easily lend itself to broad structural thinking because of the way it bends one's temporal vision around an immediate individual work trajectory. Flexible timescapes and time maps are often so complex and fragmented that they require the worker to become obsessed with her personal temporality—my tasks, my schedule, my latest gig, my network, my "brand"—just to get by. Working flexibly is intense. When one's energy, attention, and protentional capacity are so maxed out, it is difficult to step back and consider the grander implications of one's actions within longer wavelengths of "system time." It is not just that American workers are individualistic and therefore somehow culturally blind to the politics of flexible capitalism, then, but that the very texture of social time within their workplaces makes it physically and cognitively difficult to think more systemically and politically about the longer term risks they are taking on (Rosa 2009).

In short, flexible time offers workers a kind of Faustian bargain. It can provide new opportunities for making meaning with one hand and new sources of suffering with the other. Given the hyper-individualized cultural narratives and exhaustingly intense work temporalities that surround them, it is often difficult for American workers to see the long-term costs of this bargain until it is too late. They are continually surprised that the personal attributes that give them the capacity to feel enriched by flexible capitalism's risks often come back to haunt them in the long-term in the form of ill health, relationship strain, and anxiety. Adapting one's sense of success, virtue, and honor to a flexible system, then, makes for a moral order that is not only remarkably fragile, but also makes it difficult to come to terms with the longer-term trajectories of suffering associated with the system's capacity to pass risk down to the worker.

CHAPTER 7
Fragmented and Unsustainable

Humans are fundamentally anchored in the past. We simply do not have the same epistemic access to the future as we do the past. As a result, a great deal of our sense of meaning rests on constructing some sort of connection, however fleeting and imperfect, between experience and expectation. As the historian Reinhart Koselleck (1985:270) notes, "The one is not to be had without the other. No expectation without experience, no experience without expectation." What we have come to know from experience, and how that conditions our current behavior deeply shapes what we think will be coming at us from that fuzzy region called the future (Emirbayer and Mische 1998; Mische 2009; Tavory and Eliasoph 2013). This is why Koselleck (1985) refers to experience as a "space" and expectation as a "horizon." The space of experience is that existential realm in which we pivot between past and future, between retrospection and prospection. We gather memories, skills, and habits from the past, turn toward the future with these tools, and cast up prognoses. These prognoses form a horizon over which we expect certain things to come. But, like a geographical horizon, the horizon of expectation changes as we move forward through historical time, as we collect more experiences that either reinforce or change the shape of our anticipations. Experience and expectation are thus separate but necessary ontological orders. One cannot be reduced to the other, but each requires the other to exist.

Flexible capitalism *purposefully* disrupts these basic existential arrangements between experience and expectation. Creating disruptions in or even destroying established links between experience and expectation is precisely what makes the contemporary fast and lean company competitive. "It's not failure that makes us special," notes Sebastian Thrun (2014), the CEO of a successful tech company, "it's our ability to iterate quickly. It's **fast** failure. [. . .] It's launch, fail, learn, re-launch. I have seen this over and over again: whoever minimizes the duration of each iteration wins." When profit hinges so much on seizing opportunities—to have "good timing" in an ever-changing environment—advantages are gained by dismantling what is fixed, by capitalizing on the gaps between experience and expectation that competitors do not see, even if it means launching head long into high risk situations. This is the logic of flexibility: to intentionally strain the links between conventional understanding and prognosis in order to make way for bold innovation. The effect for workers is an environment of disorienting temporal extremes—erratic and discontinuous patterns of movement that feature contradictory imperatives. Hurry in order to wait. Relax as quickly as possible so you can recover. Start planning to change your plans.

American workers' exhaustion seems to be related to the consequences of expanding these conditions for constant disruption to a mass scale and extending them across the entire life course. Deliberately orchestrated tensions between experience and expectation become the rule rather than the exception. Workers begin to cultivate skills, habits, and strategies of action based on past work experiences and then pivot toward the future, taking hints from the time maps in their organizations about where best to aim their energies. It is at this moment, at the moment of spinning toward the future, that things become strained. Just as they begin to pivot, things change again. Their orientation toward the future is continually disrupted by new irregularities, strained by subtle frictions, and even halted by unthinkable crises. They are made to continually go back to the drawing board to come up with new ways of making meaning of the flow and trajectory of work. As a result, the horizon of expectation seems to morph in the very process of looking at it, making it difficult to know what is worth investing in as a worker. What skills, relationships, and identities should a person take on when nothing seems to stick around? Flexible temporalities test the limits of the unification between experience and expectation that, it would seem, is so fundamental to the human condition.

What I hope to have shown is that this anxious and exhausting experience of social time is not necessarily an inevitable consequence of a highly competitive global marketplace, though that is often the rhetoric. It is largely the result of specific choices made by business owners, policy makers, management experts, and other economic elites to reduce their exposure to the risks of doing business by passing those risks on to workers (Boltanski and Chiapello 2005; Cappelli 1999; Standing 2011). Although there have always been many people living with insecurity and unpredictability, the modern disruptable labor force, as Guy Standing (2012:591) notes, is a "contrived structural feature of global capitalism." It is easier to make something as insubstantial as "fast-failure" into a legitimate business model when many of the hazards of pushing things to that limit can be passed down the line.

Flexible temporalities are critical to this shift of risk. The consequences of bad organizational timing are channeled toward workers by disciplining them to be producers of immediacy, fluidity, and abstraction—to be good at propping things up through the intentional failures of improvisational capitalism. A system of shifts that changes on a weekly (or even hourly) basis, a professional culture that encourages total immersion in work regardless of the hours spent, or a hiring philosophy that sees full-time employment as a worrisome "sunk cost," are ways of indirectly asking workers to do the same thing: smooth out the staccato rhythm of production so that businesses can profit. Understandably, people feel exhausted and anxious when they encounter these risks, but because they are often coupled with enticing and energizing freedoms that may be unavailable to them in more traditionally organized workplaces, they may actually embrace disruption, at least initially (Halpin 2015; Smith 2001). In the long run, however, workers find that the imperative to continually ratchet up the intensity of labor is difficult to sustain. Moreover, the often subtle forms of chronic suffering their actions engender are difficult to make sense of given the hyper-individualized narratives of resiliency available to them.

In this chapter, I explore the human costs of this fraught relationship between flexible time and moral order. How can we critique disruption in such a way that it highlights the problems but also respects some of the genuine freedoms and pleasures that some workers experience? What is the way forward? What might a new politics of work time look like that can help today's workers envision and fight for something better?

THE FAUSTIAN BARGAIN OF DISRUPTION

Much of the criticism aimed at work time in flexible capitalism is expressed in the language of time related stress, the anxieties of economic insecurity, and how those problems are unevenly distributed within society, perpetuating and exacerbating many of the forms of inequality that have long existed (Jacobs and Gerson 2004; Kalleberg 2011; Moen and Roehling 2004; Standing 2011).[1] Flexible capitalism is problematic because it uses

1. This perspective falls in line with what Luc Boltanski and Eve Chiapello (2005:37– 38) call a "social critique" of capitalism, which emphasizes the injustices of poverty and inequality as well as the "egoism" and "opportunism" of the economic elite. Its intellectual origin is Marx.

time to prey on the most vulnerable, mainly to the economic benefit of the most privileged. While I am in complete agreement with this view of what is wrong, I would like to critique flexible capitalism from a different angle: as a moral order. Alongside inequality and insecurity lie problems of meaning, identity, aesthetics, and authenticity that have garnered much less attention (though see Sennett 2000, 2006).[2] Flexible temporalities shape moral order in such a way that workers often *willingly* begin to bear a greater responsibility for the risks of doing business at the same time that they feel exhausted and overextended. A crucial aspect of what is wrong with flexible capitalism lies in this tangle of cultural contradictions and how it interacts with the better-recognized problems of inequality and insecurity. If we do not consider this cultural story, I worry that our seemingly straightforward critique of inequality and insecurity is diminished because we overlook the paradoxes of working flexibly that may in fact prevent workers and employers from seeing that there is an inequality and insecurity problem in the first place.

Before I can properly make this critique, however, I first want to simply describe, in a more general way, the relationship between work time and moral order, which I see as the root of the problem. My first premise is that capitalism influences moral order partly because it produces particularly influential forms of social time (Postone 1996). The timescapes and time maps of economic institutions form a "scaffolding" (Lizardo and Strand 2010) for moral world making; they help organize the movement of social groups (Lefebvre 2013), and the way members of social groups see the past and imagine the future together (Zerubavel 2003). Upon this system of rhythms and trajectories we hang narratives that help us discover links between experience and expectation. In this way, timescapes and time maps act as cultural "affordances" (Gibson 1979)—a set of meaningful clues about the kinds of lives that are possible, likely, and perhaps desirable or undesirable. The words scaffolding and afford are key. Work temporalities, like all forms of social time, do not determine one's moral world— they can in theory always be rejected or ignored—but they do tend to offer themselves up as the most readily available raw materials for building narratives about the good life. They give us indications about how life should

2. This line of argumentation is what Boltanski and Chiapello (2005:38) call an "artistic critique" of capitalism. This critique "foregrounds the loss of meaning and, in particular, the loss of the sense of what is beautiful and valuable" because of the way capitalism shapes culture. Unlike the social critique, the artistic critique does not just seek ways of adapting humans to capitalism by re-conceptualizing its structures, but mounts a further criticism of the very moral and even aesthetic foundations of the economic status quo. Its intellectual origin is Weber.

flow—rhythms of activity and repose, sequences of progression, and trajectories of growth and decay. As one of the most dominant institutions of social time, work time affords people many of the patterns of movement and synchronization as well as lines of retrospection and prospection that are central to moral world-making.

The cases I have investigated provide an opportunity to examine in great detail flexible time as a system of affordances for making moral order in a few specific contexts. These cases by no means exhaust the entire range of effects in disrupted workplaces, but they provide some important clues as to how flexible time and moral order can hang together, which will be helpful for examining other cases. As suggested by Richard Sennett (2000), the best word to describe the temporalities I saw is "fragmented" (see also Olick 2007). When workers are held responsible for staffing the kinds of disruptive innovation that keep flexible capitalism alive, they are rarely able to connect each iteration of their working lives into a smooth flow. Work unfolds in staccato bursts. At the macro level of increasingly short-term, disjointed, and uncertain employment, as I saw with white collar job seekers, organizations orient people's expectations to time spans that roughly map on to next quarters' sales report, the next immediate opportunity for profit, or the end of a project cycle. This intense focus on the near- and medium-term futures makes it difficult for workers to be fully engaged in the present moment as well as develop a horizon of expectation that resides far enough in front of oneself to do things like plan. This level of fragmentation, then, has the primary effect of truncating the "reach" (Mische 2009) of one's temporal vision by making the past an unreliable platform for developing anticipations.

But fragmentation may also exist less visibly at a more granular level within jobs that look quite stable and traditional from the outside. Truck driving and financial services, for example, while perhaps more dangerous or stressful than many jobs, offer familiar work experiences such as a professional identity, continuous employment over a span of years, or even a career trajectory within a single organization. But even in these seemingly stable jobs, we see a similarly fragmented quality to work because of disruptions to the very rhythms of labor. Miniature temporalities, such as one's sleep cycle or the patterns of concentration that make up a larger task, are organized into intense and unpredictable bursts that require substantial commitments of attention and energy followed by unpredictable opportunities for rest and recovery. As a result of this more granular fragmentation, workers find themselves in situations where they have unexpectedly overinvested their minds and bodies in the job. Even if workers' time maps are not fragmented, then, the timescapes they encounter may well be. This latter form of disruption is particularly important for understanding the bodily and emotional experiences that are difficult to capture in, for example, a time-use survey but figure highly in people's moral evaluations of work. The overall effect of fragmentation at both the time map and timescape levels, then, is that the past is often not a very reliable indicator of the future, and the present is exhaustingly chaotic. It is often difficult for workers to see that they are overextending themselves or are becoming too committed to risky work until it is already too late.

Given that flexible practices tend to present workers with a fragmented temporal scaffolding, then, what kinds of moral worlds do they build upon that scaffolding? Among the workers I met, work time lends itself to heroic disruption narratives—stories about the working self that embrace the contradictions and ambivalences of a constantly changing and discontinuous life in such a way that the working self can be seen as successful. The "buzz" of finance, "running hard" as a truck driver, and the liberation of an "entrepreneurial" self are attempts to weave some sort of consistent meaning out of constant change. At the level of time maps, these narratives take the tone of embracing instability as an unexpected source of freedom to roam or to recreate oneself time and again, perhaps even explore parts of oneself that lay dormant within older conceptions of the self. At the level of timescapes, fragmentation invites the language of resiliency—a deeply individualistic semiotics of personal responsibility for coping with work intensifications and the "freedom to self-sweat." In highly masculine work cultures, like the trucking and finance industries that I observed, resiliency takes the form of being able to "handle oneself" on the job—to unexpectedly overinvest of one's mind and body through a period of intensification and then turn around with little recovery and do it all over again. Military and triage metaphors abounded. One could imagine, however, a more feminized semiotics that mirrors this language—a language of rugged resiliency about the ability to push oneself at work while still maintaining high expectations of care, connectivity, and domestic perfection (see, e.g., Cooper 2014; Hochschild 2005; Pugh 2015). There are probably many varieties. Fragmented social time affords a culture of individual fearlessness, where the figure of the creative and rugged individual is both a source of pride when things are going well and a source of blame when it turns out that overinvestment leads to health, emotional, and relationship problems. These disruption narratives link stretches of employment and bursts of effort into a roughly unified middle-range future, allowing workers to gain some footing and a sense that "I am going somewhere" and "I am performing well."

The moral order of heroic disruption is both similar to and curiously different from the moral order of vigilance, constancy, and progress to which 19th and 20th century industrial/bureaucratic workplaces lent themselves. In terms of similarities, both moral orders rest on one of the timeless figures of American culture: the rugged and expressive individual. Just as exhausted factory workers and career-weary organization men coped with the moral dilemmas of their era by cultivating a creative and perseverant self, so to do the Americans I talked to find compelling virtue terms in their "first language" of individualism (Bellah et al. 2007). Additionally, just as Burawoy (1979) and Roy (1953, 1959) found in their examinations of industrial labor, I also see that the language of individualism resonates with the embodied practices of flexible labor—the game-like qualities afforded to workers by engaging with the challenges of disrupted time. These work-games invite meaningful absorptions in hard work at the same time that they facilitate the kinds of self-sweating that benefit employers.

From another angle, however, we see that the moral dilemmas of capitalist time may be shifting with the introduction of flexible timescapes and time maps. The dilemmas of boredom, monotony, and conformity that were so prevalent in an earlier regime of work, while not disappeared, are less relevant to the workers I met. They are more concerned with over-engagement in exhausting tasks, unpredictability, and the difficulty of synchronizing with others because time has become so fragmented. Thus, workers are cultivating new conceptions of work discipline—a kind of anxious intrepidness that can make constant change, unpredictability, and going-it-alone a source of heroic pride. They are confronted by the dilemma of permanent impermanence, which can be simultaneously freeing and terrifying. As Boltanski and Chiapello (2005:461) note, "The tension between the requirement of *flexibility* and the need to be someone . . . is a constant source of anxiety. The slogan that sums up the ideal of a successful life as *becoming oneself* . . . is the typical expression of this tension." As they are stretched between the imperative from work to constantly change and the imperative from the self to cultivate some kind of stable identity, they find moral order in the idea of the individual as a kind of "project" or "work in progress." The framework of individualism, then, is remarkably adaptable to a flexible temporal order. It provides a readymade language that workers can use to explain and justify the inherent contradictions of a disrupted life.

Seen within this longer trajectory of transformation in the meanings of capitalist time, the dilemmas I saw among American workers hint at a certain historical irony. As I discuss in Chapter 2, at the beginning of the industrial era, more standardization, regularity, and security were some of laborers' most pressing requests (Dohrn-van Rossum 1996). In some ways, they got their wish in the form of the chronological temporal order. But this transformation only led to a new set of dilemmas. By the middle of the 20th century, less standardization and conformity, more customization and room for expressive individuality become the battle cries of industrial and bureaucratic workers (Chiapello and Fairclough 2002). A more flexible regime, at least rhetorically, is what workers were asking for. Yet the way it has been delivered on the ground has only generated new dilemmas. Each grand shift in workers' attitudes toward capitalist time is in some sense a reaction to dissatisfactions with the previous generation's desires. The mechanism by which capitalist time can turn from a solution to a new source of dilemma is an historical trend that I can only hint at with these data. It seems to be driven, in part, by the fact that the economic elite have always managed to adapt criticisms of the old regime to the existing power structure and thus sow the seeds for new dissatisfactions (Boltanski and Chiapello 2005). What was imagined by the prior generation to be a boon for workers, then, becomes a source of suffering for the next generation as economic elites figure out new ways to turn work time to their benefit. Again, these are rudimentary observations, but they suggest both continuity and change in the relationship between work time and moral order over the last several centuries, which deserves more concerted attention than I can give here.

In summary, an emphasis on the moral dimension of work time reveals that flexible capitalism, in addition to generating inequality and insecurity, invites workers into a kind of Faustian bargain with the working self. This bargain typically takes the following form: give up familiar ideas about security, standardization, and predictability (often fraught with their own problems anyway) in exchange for the potentially liberating (but ultimately just as problematic) opportunity to be more personally responsible for carving out one's own unique path in life. And as with any Faustian bargain, this one comes with fine print that is often only read after the fact. The new freedoms of working flexibly have been attached to new imperatives that require questionable sacrifices, whose ultimate consequences are difficult to see until it is already too late. The major point, then, is that the Faustian bargain at the heart of disruption culture is difficult to critique in comparison to the more familiar problem of inequality in employment security because, at least for some, flexible work can involve freedoms that workers may in fact enjoy, at least in the short term. For some, though certainly not all, these freedoms may balance out the things that must be sacrificed—at least for a time.

How do we go about critiquing this situation while still respecting workers' own subjective perceptions? How do we critique the culture of disruption without simply saying to workers that they are ultimately complicit in their own exploitation through a kind of delusional enjoyment, mystification, or false consciousness (e.g., Halpin 2015)? In the next section, I explore two responses to this question.

DISRUPTION AS CULTURAL STRAIGHTJACKET
AND STRUCTURAL BLINDER

The first problem with the culture of disruption is that it encourages people to lead disruptable lives *for their whole lives.* This applies to both high and low status workers. This was evidenced by one word that all types of workers used repeatedly: unsustainable. This word was often literally stated in interviews, but it also revealed itself more indirectly in respondents' frustrated attempts to build lasting relationships, in their chronic physical pain or emotional exhaustion, and other experiences that left them feeling like things cannot continue without reaching a breaking point. Unsustainability refers to the notion that, in finding creative and resilient ways to negotiate the chaotic temporalities of their workplaces, which sometimes resulted in surprisingly satisfying experiences, respondents eventually came to the realization that there is a hard limit beyond which they will not be able to continue. Whether it was anxiety, illness, or financial insecurity, workers often noted that even if they wanted to continue working in this way, which they sometimes did, they would eventually no longer be able to handle it. I saw this among respondents up and down the class spectrum. Even the most economically fortunate workers discussed notions of good and satisfying work as also fundamentally cannibalistic. Good work often takes the likeness of burning a candle from both ends. The kinds of moral worlds afforded to the workers I met are problematic, then, because they create a kind of cultural straightjacket. They leave little room for envisioning ways of living other than those that can be easily disrupted. It is thus a remarkably one-dimensional image of the good life.

The cultural straightjacket of disruption is especially problematic when we consider how it interacts with the structural inequalities of the flexible economy. Flexible capitalism has an uncanny ability to make the risk always flow downhill and the reward uphill, but the culture of disruption pretends like that fact does not exist. Disruption has radically different implications for high status and low status workers. For high status workers, it means that even when they have found ways to revel in a disrupted life, within this moral order there is no compelling alternative vision if they change their minds as they get older or if their fortunes suddenly change. Many of the economically successful workers I met were not only anxious about things like downsizings, for example, but also about retirements, vacations, and breaks from work. What kind of meaning might lie in a life that has become settled and slow? The culture of disruption has no satisfying answers to this dilemma. Financial professionals are a perfect example. The intrepid bravery of the "buzz" narrative has clearly unsustainable consequences for their mental and physical health that may threaten their long-term viability as workers and tends to wreak havoc on their personal lives. In the event of job loss or retirement, moreover, it has little to say about what the good life might look like. As Vicki Smith (2001:14) says of heroic disruption narratives, "[W]hile workers may have reason to feel challenged and enabled in ways that empower them, such impressions are ultimately held together by a very slender thread ... by their very design collapsible and retractable." Even within the upper echelons of the American workforce, then, even among those who appear to be winners in the new capitalism, there is still a sense of unsustainability. If work can only feel meaningful if it also feels unsustainable, have the winners really won? As Immanuel Wallerstein (2011:40) notes of those who live well in capitalism, "how well, and for how long do those who live well live?" Despite the incredible economic advantages flowing to highly skilled individuals at the top of the class structure, perhaps the physical, emotional, and interpersonal costs may outweigh the benefits even for them (see Cooper 2014; Fraser 2001; Hochschild 2012 for a similar critique). Heroic disruption is ultimately a one-dimensional vision of the good life that cannot come to grips with the cultural contradictions of working flexibly for ones whole life.

It is essential to recognize, however, that working flexibly typically means something different for low status workers because it carries so much more risk, and therefore so too does a commitment to the culture of disruption. Embracing risk is so much riskier for low status workers, yet the culture of disruption is remarkably ignorant of this fact. As I discuss more below, whereas flexibility for privileged workers often means more control, it can often mean the opposite for less privileged workers. But a culture of heroic disruption treats all flexibility as if these structural differences do not exist. This is the second problem with the culture of flexible capitalism. It tends to sideline open and honest conversations about inequality because it treats all kinds flexibility the same. It thus becomes that much easier to justify using *exploitative* flexible practices among those who stand the most to lose.

The increasing preference for independent contract arrangements in the truck driving industry is a perfect example. Managers can sell these arrangements to drivers as a new "opportunity" to become an "entrepreneur" (seemingly a good in itself, because who wouldn't want to become their own boss?), but they can do so without having to justify to drivers the immense risks taken on with this choice and the fact that even "independent" drivers are often subjected to powerful technologies of surveillance (Levy 2015; Viscelli 2010). Low status workers must strike similar Faustian bargains under flexible capitalism as high status workers, but they do not have the same kinds of economic security or meaningful control over the labor process to shield themselves from the most pernicious consequences. The cultural straightjacket of disruption makes it even less likely that these important structural differences will be discussed and appreciated, both by those who benefit from them and by those who do not. We can continue to talk about flexibility as if it is the same thing for, say, a retail sales worker as for a software engineer (more on this below).

The culture of disruption is both a straightjacket and blinder precisely because it facilitates experiences that can be meaningful for both high and low status workers. My critique, then, is not that workers have some kind of false consciousness that endears them to the causes of their troubles— who am I to say what workers should love—but that the picture of good work afforded to them is so monochromatic. It does not reflect diverse conceptions of good work for different stages of the life course and workers in different structural positions, nor does it propose what a *sustainable* and *long term* working life might look like for anyone. The culture of disruption can be meaningful even for those who one might (patronizingly) argue shouldn't like it. But it also leaves many of these same workers wishing there were more options. As I discuss next, what I think workers want is not "anti-disruption," but a more creative cultural imagination that can accommodate a wide variety of conceptions of good work *including but not limited to* disruption.

TOWARD A NEW POLITICS OF WORK TIME

For all its problems, at least the 20th century labor movement had a coherent politics of work time. The clock hour. The schedule. The shift. The work/home binary. The eight-hour day. The forty-hour week. The career. Loyalty. Retirement. These concepts ended up creating all sorts of problems, which Moen and Roehling (2004) rightly call a "mystique," but they also provided a clear language with which to fight. That is what is missing right now. Flexible capitalism has introduced new forms of social time—new timescapes and time maps—but we continue to fight for good work using antiquated 20th century concepts. We need a new politics of work time, with a new language than can help workers articulate their complaints more clearly and make demands.

Defining Flexibilities

In our political discourse about the workplace, we need to do a better job of acknowledging that flexibility means different things—sometimes even the opposite things—in order to demand certain kinds of work time and reject others. On the level of timescapes, it is essential to distinguish between employer-controlled and worker-controlled flexibility. The former includes practices like on-call scheduling and complex shiftwork systems that can deploy workers in myriad patterns. Employer-controlled flexibility tends to be used in low-wage jobs where employers desire to manipulate workers' movements with precision and efficiency (Kalleberg 2003; Kantor 2014). In many cases, these arrangements are essentially a kind of neo-Taylorism (Crowley et al. 2010). Because control is sought in the context of a rapidly changing and unpredictable environment that features an irregular demand for output, these timescapes require ways of surveilling employees other than a simple stopwatch. They use real-time technologies, such as GPS tracking and remote computer activity monitoring, to gain the kinds of precise spatio-temporal control that Taylor also valued (Levy 2015; Sewell 1998). Flexibility among low-wage workers typically achieves efficiency by taking temporal control away from employees. This might create flexibility for employers, but from the workers' perspective it is not particularly flexible (Lambert 2012).

Rather confusingly from a political perspective, flexibility is also used to describe timescapes that give more control to workers. Scholars typically refer to this kind of worker-controlled flexibility, which is most commonly found in both professional salaried labor and casual contract work, as "flexible scheduling" (Sweet et al. 2014). Workers are given control over when and where they work so long as they are getting the results expected of them. This includes techniques like personalized scheduling, working from home, results-only evaluation schemes, as well as a whole host of paid leave arrangements that allow workers to pause their careers for life events. In most cases, this is the best way to manage the increasingly complex rhythms of today's busy working couples and parents (Bianchi, Robinson, and Milkie 2006). As Phyllis Moen (2011:407) and her colleagues note, work arrangements like these by and large promote worker health and productivity at the same time that they "reduce the risk that individual employees will be penalized in later evaluations for working to their own rhythms."

We risk committing a problematic conceptual elision if we fail to distinguish between worker-controlled and employer-controlled flexible timescapes. Take this job advertisement on the website Jobing.com for the large retailer Macys (2015). Entitled "Job: Retail Sales, *Flexible Scheduling Option!*, Part-Time," the ad begins, "This position uses a scheduling plan that allows an associate to participate in the creation of his/her work schedule by managing availability and identifying a preferred work schedule." The position "allows the maximum amount of scheduling flexibility." Toward the end of the advertisement, however, the picture looks very different. In a section titled Qualifications, it lists "Ability to work a flexible schedule, including mornings, evenings, and weekends, and busy events such as the day after Thanksgiving, special Big Event days, and the day after Christmas, based on department and store/company needs." The word flexible has exactly the opposite meaning in this section as it did in the first section. What is an applicant to think? Does flexibility mean personal customization of time or does it mean that when the company says jump, the employee says how high? Working irregularly on one's own terms is a vastly different experience than being kept constantly on call by a fickle manager (Ehrenreich 2001; Williams 2006). The word flexibility can actually conceal this important difference. As in this Macy's advertisement, organizations can righteously claim that they offer employees "flexibility" when what they really mean is a scheduling system that gives workers less than 24-hours notice of their next shift, or cuts them early from a shift because patronage is down, or penalizes them for not having total availability (Lambert 2012). This is not flexibility for the employee, but a kind of micromanaged chaos that prevents them from being able to coordinate their lives. Creating a clear political agenda, then, requires that we make sure people understand that different types of flexibility have different political implications. This will allow workers to fight for the kinds that give them control and resist the kinds that take it away.

Reconsidering Rigidity

A more careful distinction between types of flexibility needs to be accompanied by a reappraisal of the value of rigidity and certain kinds of fixed and standardized temporal rhythms. Creating good workplaces at the level of timescapes is not always as straightforward as giving employees total control over when and where they work. As I saw among financial professionals, and has been suggested by other scholars (Blair-Loy 2009; Heritage 2014), in workplaces with intensely motivated employees that feature high client contact, rapid project cycles with urgent deadlines, and highly portable work, even worker-controlled flexibility may lend itself to overwork. Telling workers they can work when and where they want might mean they end up working all the time because they can no longer meaningfully distinguish between work and non-work time-space.

Investment banks, perhaps unexpectedly, may be leading the way in thinking more creatively about the hidden costs of worker-controlled flexibility. They have begun to experiment with scheduling rigidity. In October 2013, Goldman Sachs banned weekend work for many of its employees, instating so called "protected weekends." The other leading investment firms quickly followed (Griswold 2014). Interviews with young financial professionals in this study and elsewhere (Roose 2014) suggest that this change may have been a direct response to a shrinking number of applications from young elite graduates. This new generation of knowledge professionals, it seems, are simply unwilling to sacrifice so much for an investment banking job. When desirable applicants voted with their feet for a more sustainable workweek, then, these employers listened. Like all innovations, however, we should approach this one with caution. Does the institution of protected weekends protect all employees equally, or simply the one's firms want to invest in long-term? To whom does the work get shunted when new employees are not allowed to work on the weekend?

Among low-status workers, a similar critique of flexibility seems to be emerging that asks us to reconsider the value of rigidity (Kantor 2014; Lambert 2012). The problem for many low-status workers is not necessarily overwork, though this is also a problem for many, but irregularity and unpredictability of hours and wages (Bluestone and Rose 2001; Golden 2015). Truck drivers, while maybe not the classic case of this dilemma, are a good example of how unpredictability can be punishing on the body and psyche, even when relatively few hours were actually spent on work. It can be exhausting to routinely expect a certain number of hours of work, prepare one's body and psyche for that, and then have that expectation shattered by unpredictable events that produce anxious idleness. As Barry Bluestone and Stephen Rose (2001:58) note,

> Many Americans are both overworked and underemployed. Because of growing job instability, workers face a "feast and famine" cycle: They work as much as they can when work is available to compensate for short workweeks, temporary layoffs, or permanent job loss that may follow.

I would add to this list, erratic schedules. It is an encouraging sign, then, that legislators are beginning to think more creatively about how to adapt

low wage work to the seemingly insatiable demand by employers for irregularity and unpredictability. As of this writing, members of the House
Committee on Education and the Workforce, for example, have introduced legislation that "would require companies to pay their employees for
an extra hour if they were summoned to work with less than 24 hours'
notice," and would mandate that workers be given "four hours' pay on days
when employees are sent home after just a few hours" (Greenhouse 2014).
Similar creative thinking, though far less actionable in the current political
environment, surrounds reforms to the Fair Labor Standards Act (FLSA).
Created in the 1930s to establish the minimum wage, it is now a stale relic
of the industrial age. Scholars such as Susan Lambert (2012) have called
for reforms that would encourage a minimum weekly hours requirement,
which could accompany the continued fight for a raise in the minim wage.
Other ideas include eliminating loopholes that allow employers to exempt
many part-time, casual, and contract workers (truck drivers included) from
the FLSA in the first place (Kalleberg 2011). These ideas do not reinstate
predictability or regularity per se, but they do compensate workers for
being willing to lead disruptable lives and therefore honor the fact that
sacrificing predictability and regularity is indeed an exceptional sacrifice,
rather than simply the way things are.

Measuring New Work Times

Even if we refine our understanding of flexibility, better compensate workers for being disrupted, or more smartly deploy rigidity, there remains the
problem that the way many people work today simply does not fit the old
categories we typically use to talk about work time. This is especially problematic when it comes to measuring work time statistically, say through a time
diary, in order to generate criticisms of inequality and insecurity. The work/
home binary, work/leisure binary, and the clock hour—mainstays of statistical research on work time—may not capture some of the new dilemmas that
flexibilized workers are feeling. It therefore becomes difficult to say whether or
not these pressures are unevenly distributed or not (Vallas and Prener 2012).

What we mean to measure with concepts like the work/home binary,
work/leisure binary, and the clock hour is the expenditure of effort toward
sustaining oneself and ones family. The trouble is that many people today
expend energy in order to sustain themselves and others in ways that can
elude these categories. Many people expend energy on work activities while
at home and vice versa, and may rapidly switch back and forth between
these things (Hochschild 1997). Many people expend energy on activities

that look a lot like work, but they do not get paid for it because they are trying to put themselves in a position to be paid in the first place—we call this networking, volunteering, interning, gigging, and the like (Barley and Kunda 2004). And finally, one of the main things people care about when they expend energy to sustain themselves is not how *long* they do it, but how *intensely* they do it. Working two part-time jobs, one in the day and one at night, may still leave a person underemployed in terms of hours and pay, but it is certainly not underemployment in terms of energy expended (Epstein et al. 1998; Greenhouse 2008). The question becomes, then, how can we measure some of these experiences in order to better capture them empirically, look for inequalities, and fight for change? Outlining an exhaustive program to answer this question is beyond the scope of this book but I can point to a couple of areas.

One idea, as discussed by Guy Standing (2013), is to include new measures within existing time diary methods that better capture the things flexibilized workers do in order to get access to some kind of remunerated work in the first place, what he calls "work-for-labor." Work, which I take to mean energy expenditure in order to sustain oneself/others, and labor, which is remunerated work, are not the same thing (Daniels 1987), and become increasingly alienated under conditions of flexibility as employers find ways of moving workers' less profitable activity off the books. The time a person spends networking at a volunteering event on the off chance that he or she will meet someone who provides a promising gig is work; it is just not paid work. Driving several hours in order to wait in front of a hardware store to be selected into a group of casual laborers is work too; it just is not paid work. How many people, which people, how often, and for how long do individuals work in order to get labor in the first place? What percentage of positions feature, as a basic requirement of the job, the (avail)ability to wait until something happens for which the worker will actually get paid? It is perhaps obvious that, as I saw among job seekers, the long-term unemployed do a lot of work in order to get a paying job (networking, interning, and volunteering), but it is much less obvious that truck drivers also do a lot of work-for-labor. They sometimes spend more hours waiting for a paying load than they do actually driving.

With the increasing use of non-standard work arrangements and irregular shift work, my guess is that a significant proportion of workers are doing a lot of work-for-labor today. Are all these people unemployed or underemployed? Not necessarily. Many may be getting consistent *labor* but are not being paid for the *work* they do to get it. Statistics on these issues are currently spotty at best and rarely feature in broad political discussions of labor market policy. This is perhaps why politicians can so easily talk about economic recovery in terms of "numbers of jobs gained" without having to discuss the *quality* of those jobs and all the unremunerated work-for-labor that they might involve. Thinking more creatively about how we measure the "invisible work" behind and within "visible labor" would help workers point to the kinds of problems they are experiencing that are not necessarily related to the well-worn 20th Century complaint of a low hourly wage.

Even the idea of measuring work-for-labor, however, is still constrained by the framework of the clock hour. Yet, as I have highlighted throughout this study, work time can also be thought of in terms of rhythm. An even more radical approach to measuring work time would be to focus on dimensions of time other than duration. An obvious candidate would be synchronization. One of the main problems respondents in this study discussed was the inability to establish a sustainable relationship among all the conflicting temporal rhythms both within their jobs and between their jobs and home lives—problems of desynchronization or, as Lefebvre (2013) calls it, "arrhythmia." Understanding desynchronizations among working people, within families, and within jobs is crucial for understanding the feelings of intensification and exhaustion that are so commonly reported by today's disrupted workers (Blount and Janicik 2002; Morehead 2001). Interestingly, synchronization is rarely considered in quantitative studies of work time, yet it can be relatively easily constructed from time diary data by focusing on *which hours* and in what *sequences* people switch from work to home to leisure activities (Chenu and Robinson 2002; Lesnard 2004, 2008, 2009). Who are the most desynchronized workers in America? What types of employment contracts and scheduling practices tend to exacerbate desynchronization? Would it be possible to design labor legislation that champions the synchronization of couples and families, the synchronization of part-time jobs, or the synchronization of parts of the labor process that do not effectively communicate?

In short, if we want to fight for better workplaces in today's flexible regime, it would be wise to update the language we use to talk about work time so that it captures the kinds of inequalities and moral dilemmas workers face.

A Culture of Sustainability

None of the suggestions above address what I think may be the most intractable problem: disruption is a cultural straightjacket. Even if we find better ways of talking about and measuring the inequalities and insecurities of flexible time, there remains the seemingly incontestable view held by many employers and workers that constant change, restructuring, and erratic movement are the natural order of things rather than the result of specific choices that governments and organizations have made to capitalize on risky forms of value creation. Disruption, it would seem, is simply the way things are.

It would be tempting to counter this monochromatic culture of disruption with a simple anti-disruption message. We see this, for example, in the so called "slowness" movement, which champions unplugging from one's fast-paced lifestyle and reconnecting with stillness, contemplation, mindfulness, and even boredom (Belkin 2009; Darier 1998; Honore 2004; Russell 1935). In a similar vein, others have called for a return to a culture that celebrates durability, predictability, patience, dedication, and loyalty, perhaps drawing on the ancient icon of the craftsman (Crawford 2009; Sennett 2009). These are laudable virtues, but I wonder to what degree they are actually possible for many workers today within the given structures, especially low-status workers. They are also nostalgic in a way that overlooks some of the pleasures and freedoms that speed and disruption can in fact deliver for some people. For some people, even for those who we might say have "bad jobs," disrupted work can be interesting, exciting, and even pleasurable (Halpin 2015). A culture of slow leisure or loyal craftsmanship overlooks these hidden pleasures, and is also probably only attainable in a meaningful way for the most privileged. If we champion these things, I worry that they will simply become coopted by those who are already benefiting from the flexibility regime—the so called "core" employees—and thus still leave the least benefited workers excluded.

I would suggest that the answer to a culture of disruption is not anti-disruption but sustainability.[3] That is the number one thing for which respondents in this study seemed to be searching. The core demand of a culture of sustainability is that work, whether it is well paid or not, whether it is short or long term, whether it is predictable or not, must still leave the worker able to regenerate herself physically, psychologically, and spiritually in the long term. Sustainability is about challenging the insatiability of capitalist time, which looks for ever-stronger means of sucking productivity from each second of the day while finding new ways of moving that time off employers' balance sheets. It is about resisting the way organizational life continually crowds out the wide variety of choices for how to spend the

3. The virtue of sustainability I advocate for here, which I connect to an artistic critique of capitalism, is shared with another important source of capitalist critique—the environmental movement. As Boltanski and Chiapello (2005:472) note, "The revival of the artistic critique notably takes the form of an alliance with the ecological critique, which at present constitutes one of the only positions from which the multiplicity and particularity of beings—human beings, natural beings and, in some versions, artifacts—are assigned an intrinsic value."

limited time one has on this earth. If ending the stranglehold of capitalist time means workers seek loyalty and slowness or just another fleeting gig, so be it; that is their choice. The point is that employment does not take up so much of our energy. Flexible temporalities require workers to become obsessed with work in a way that is simply unsustainable (Keohane 2015). Sustainability can thus incorporate slowness and other more nostalgic virtues, such as loyalty or continuity, but also leaves open the possibility that some forms of speed and disruption are praiseworthy so long as they also respect virtues like rest, recovery, and long-term vision.

We should keep in mind, then, people like Janice and Cindy, the pair of health insurance workers who were outsourced at the same time. They were two of the few respondents I met who were hyper-aware of the social forces restructuring their workplace, felt angry about the way work is being reorganized, and remained resolute in that anger. They felt they had a right to their anger. Sitting in the unrelentingly positive atmosphere of a job search support group, Janice and Cindy could not have felt more out of place. The narratives of heroic disruption that saturate American unemployment culture—upbeat optimism, entrepreneurship, pasted on smiles—felt disingenuous to them and sounded exhausting. But what alternative framework for explaining their economic suffering did they have? On the one hand, individual failure and, on the other, a kind of vague resentment toward "Corporate America." As a form of gleeful protest, then, Janice and Cindy found themselves going to employer information sessions, not to learn about a new "opportunity"—they knew the job on offer would ultimately be a ruse—but to heckle the HR person leading the presentation. "How does your company deal with pressures to outsource?" they would sarcastically lob toward the front of the room. Recalling the HR representative's frustrated red face, Janice giggles, "That was the most fun I've had in months. I guess I'm not moving on the change curve!"

The image is both disheartening and encouraging. Janice and Cindy clearly feel that "moving beyond" their anger means, in some sense, that the way work has been restructured is permissible—an inevitable and ultimately necessary transformation. They are looking for ways to express a counter narrative that is not yet fully formed in their imaginations. In the straightjacket culture of disruption, however, they struggle to find spaces where such a critical and creative sentiment is available and welcome, and instead find themselves directed to spaces where their concerns will inevitably fall on deaf ears. Their experience suggests, then, that workers' critiques of disruption are too often channeled into the most anemic forms of expression. But it also suggests a deep dissatisfaction with the limits of leading a disruptable life that is ripe for a new politics of time.

APPENDIX
Method and Rhythmanalysis

The fieldwork and interviews for this book, which began as a PhD dissertation, were collected more or less simultaneously among the three groups
of workers between 2010 and 2013. Like a lot of first-time ethnographers,
I ran into many challenges, made many mistakes, and generally felt like
I had bitten off more than I could chew. In this appendix, I try to give the
reader some sense of how I collected the data and came to terms with the
many challenges and mistakes that unfolded in the process.

I spent approximately 100 hours observing two debt trading groups in
an asset management firm in New York City, approximately 300 hours
observing four solo long-haul truck drivers who contract for the same
Missouri-based motor carrier firm, and approximately 50 hours participat-
ing in the meetings of Career Transition Ministries (CTM) and observing
a state-funded career counseling facility located in Richmond, Virginia. In
addition to participant-observation, I initially set out to interview at least
20 individuals from each group. Since gender is a major source of variation
in the literature on work time, I also set out to interview an equal number
of men and women. In the end, I interviewed 24 financial professionals (10
women, 14 men), 26 job seekers (13 women, 13 men), and 16 truck drivers (all men). The demographic and occupational details of the samples are
presented in Tables A.1, A.2, and A.3.

I ran into several problems recruiting women truck drivers into the study
and ultimately decided to abandon this plan. There were a number of demographic reasons that explain my difficulty. First, the industry is overwhelm-
ingly male and women tend not to work as solo long-haul drivers. They are
more likely to take up a team driving position with their spouse (Bernard,
Bouck, and Young 2000; Chen et al. 2015). Secondly, women solo drivers
face a number of safety issues at truck stops that force them to keep to
themselves inside the relative security of their trucks. As a man and as a

Table A.1 FINANCIAL PROFESSIONALS

Pseudonym	Age	Gender	Married	Children	Occupation
Brent	31	M	N	N	Analyst
Bill	64	M	Y	na	Trader
John	mid-30s	M	Y	Y	Investment banker
James	mid-30s	M	Y	na	Investment banker
Tom	early-40s	M	Y	Y	Private equity
Kathleen	50s	F	Y	Y	Investment banker
Duncan	27	M	N	N	Private equity
Gillian	27	F	N	N	Investment banker
Alec	33	M	N	N	Aircraft lessor
Mike	25	M	Y	N	Structured finance
Mark	57	M	Y	Y	Private equity
Nick	47	M	Y	Y	Trader
Stephanie	mid-20s	F	N	N	Analyst
Casey	mid-20s	F	N	N	Analyst
Elizabeth	early-30s	F	Y	N	Trader
Katherine	mid-20s	F	N	N	Private equity
Genevieve	mid-20s	F	Y	N	Consultant
Philip	early-40s	M	Y	Y	Fund manager
Rick	mid-40s	M	Y	Y	Trader
Steve	early-30s	M	Y	Y	Trader
Marybeth	early-50s	F	Y	Y	Fund managing director
Cynthia	late-20s	F	Y	Y	Trader
Chuck	mid-40s	M	Y	Y	Trader
Allison	mid-20s	F	N	N	Analyst
Don	late-40s	M	Y	Y	Trader
Trevor	mid-30s	M	Y	na	Trader

person who wanted to respect the security of women drivers, I did not feel comfortable approaching them in their trucks (which are their homes as well as their workplaces) to solicit interviews. It is important that future research document the temporal lives of women truck drivers as they likely face work and family pressures that are different from men. Given my subject position as a male-identified ethnographer, and given the fact that I was collecting ethnographic data in two other sites, it ended up being beyond the scope of this project to thoroughly study women drivers.

I also stopped short of interviewing twenty truck drivers. I found that, after sixteen interviews, I was beginning to hit a saturation point and was not finding new evidence that dramatically contradicted my existing knowledge (Small 2009). I also found an additional (and in some ways

Table A.2 TRUCK DRIVERS

Pseudonym	Age	Gender	Married	Children	Type of driver
Mohsen	45	M	Y	Y	Owner operator
Willy	51	M	N	Y	Lease operator
Tommy	48	M	N	Y	Company
Dax	37	M	Y	Y	Company
J.L.	58	M	Y	Y	Owner operator
Rick	na	M	Y	N	Owner operator
Luis	58	M	Y	Y	Company
Jeff	32	M	N	N	Lease operator
Carl	45	M	N	na	Company
Alvaro	55	M	Y	Y	Owner operator
Paul	50	M	Y	Y	Owner operator
Randy	57	M	Y	Y	Company
Matthew	42	M	N	Y	Company
Walter	45	M	N	Y	Company
Kevin	27	M	N	N	Lease operator
Brian	early-40s	M	Y	Y	Dispatcher

better) source of data on the fatigue debate in US trucking. This came in the form of hours of video footage from four "listening sessions" conducted by the Federal Motor Carrier Safety Administration (FMCSA), which I transcribed and analyzed. (The videos were made publically available on the FMCSA's website in 2011 but were removed in 2012.) These listening sessions took place in 2010 and 2011 as the FMCSA debated revisions to the Hours of Service (HOS) regulations. Drivers, managers, owners, and union representatives sat in front of the FMCSA panel or called in via telephone to ask questions and give statements about the proposed changes to the HOS. These data allowed me to observe drivers and regulators talk face-to-face about work time issues. They deeply enriched my understanding of the interview data because I was able to see one driver after another explain how they work with (and against) the HOS rules to the very people who have drawn them up.

GETTING IN

Recruiting interview participants and gaining entry to each of the ethnographic field sites was full of challenges and pleasant surprises. Financial professionals are often so busy that they have difficulty setting aside even

Table A.3 JOB SEEKERS

Pseudonym	Age	Gender	Married/Children	Education	Previous occupation
Bryan	28	M	N/N	BA	Medical researcher
Crystal	33	F	N/Y	BA	Marketer
Raquel	55	F	N/Y	HS	Non-profit admin
Jennifer	26	F	N/N	BA	Photographer
Sandra	37	F	N/Y	BA	Stock clerk
Ana	29	F	N/Y	HS	Business owner
Gregory	33	M	N/N	Some college	Lab tech.
Sheryl	40s	F	Y/Y	Some college	Call center worker
Matt	20s	M	N/N	BA	Food service
Marlon	26	M	Y/Y	BA	Personal banker
Ramone	27	M	N/N	HS	Handyman
Michael	47	M	N/Y	HS	Musician
Shirley	49	F	N/Y	HS	Graphic designer
Leanne	59	F	N/Y	Some college	Office admin
Colleen	40	F	N/N	BA	TV news producer
Victoria	50	F	na/Y	na	Data entry clerk
Everett	23	M	N/N	BA	Call center worker
Jeff	59	M	N/Y	HS	Outside sales
Linda	61	F	Y/N	BA	Executive asst
Jeb	50s	M	Y/Y	BA	Operations mgr
Henry	58	M	Y/N	HS	Cust service mgr
Andy	50	M	Y/Y	BA	Operations mgr
Jerry	54	M	N/N	BA	Claims mgr
Janice	50s	F	N/Y	BA	Credentialer
Cindy	56	F	N/Y	BA	Credentialer
Mark	57	M	Y/N	BA	Data processer

a half hour for a conversation, let alone a conversation with a complete stranger. To get around this problem, I began by meeting ex-traders and analysts at Darden Business School at the University of Virginia and used their network of contacts to meet active financial professionals located in various places in the United States. Respondents often told me they only agreed to the interview because their friend said I was a "good guy" and that the project seemed "interesting."

Given their time constraints and physical distance, I used Skype and Facetime to conduct nine of these interviews. This is not something I would normally have done, as I think physical co-presence is important for in-depth interviewing, but I reasoned that this population would be more comfortable with a digitally remote conversation than most, and that it might be the only way to meet them face-to-face because of their busy-ness. To me, Skype and Facetime interviews felt remarkably similar to co-present interviewing, and I ultimately concluded that, at least for this type of population, they are a good (though not ideal) substitute.

Gaining access to the asset management firm I studied was the most try-ing aspect of this project. I spent approximately a year looking for a finan-cial professional who would agree to let me shadow them or their work team. After spending upwards of an hour talking to one financial profes-sional after another, sometimes about deeply personal things, none would allow me to actually come to their workplace. The resistance to my requests was, not surprisingly, often couched in terms of busyness. Many said they simply didn't have "enough time" or had "too much on" to look after me as well. But I always suspected deeper reservations. The years between 2010 and 2012 were not particularly good for financial professionals' image. They were painted in the media as the villains of the Great Recession, so respondents may have been worried that I was interested in writing an exposé about Wall Street greed.

Like a lot of ethnographers studying busy professionals, friendship ties proved essential for getting past these basic trust issues (for example Down 2015; Zaloom 2006). I was finally granted access in 2012 to one of Wall Street's most powerful bond trading groups by Philip, the project manager, who was a close relative of a graduate school colleague. After a memorably frantic phone call with Philip as he sped around his Connecticut neighbor-hood in his new sports car, he arranged for me to shadow him in his office. I spent many hours in Philip's office, making contact with the two groups of traders he managed during frequent team meetings and then observing the team members directly on subsequent visits. As I discuss below, how-ever, this group had its own trust issues to navigate.

Once I was finally "in" at the asset management firm, I was then con-fronted with the problem of what to observe. Having no formal role in the organization and a limited education in finance, I quickly learned to take on the role of an "intern," often telling traders to "talk to me like you would an intern" when they asked what I was interested in. This gave me some recognizable role in the organization and invited traders to talk about their work in the simplest terms possible. In addition to attending team meetings, I spent most of my time literally watching over bond traders' shoulders, asking them about different aspects of their screens, and getting them to narrate in real-time the kinds of decisions they were mulling over in their heads. At first, I was worried that I would be unable to gain access to what I thought would be mostly silent, solo, computer-oriented work, but I found that traders were readily able to talk about the minute details of their screen worlds. Also, because of the open-plan and team-based nature of the digital trading floor, there was quite a lot of conversation among traders to observe.

I had serious concerns that I would be unable to recruit truck drivers to do in-depth interviews. What was I going to do, walk around truck stops and knock on doors? That would be like going door to door in a neighborhood asking people to let me into their living room for a long chat. My initial fears were fairly accurate. I drove dozens of miles to various truck stops in the hope of finding some drivers "hanging out" whom I could approach for an interview, but each truck stop was just like the last: dozens of parked trucks lining a huge concrete slab, each with the blackout curtains pulled tight. If drivers were up and about, they were in a hurry to get fuel, coffee, or a quick bite before hitting the road again. After some searching, I finally found a truck stop down the street from a Walmart Supercenter with a small attached restaurant that also had a television area and offered free wireless Internet access (the last of these being a rarity in truck stops). The combination of food, TV, and free wifi seemed to pull drivers out of their "homes" and into the open better than any other place I had found. I even noticed some drivers (gasp!) talking to each other there. Also, because of Walmart's notorious ability to strand drivers during shipping/receiving delays, I was able to find drivers who had nothing to do but wait (not an uncommon problem, I would later learn). In this space, then, I was able to (awkwardly) approach drivers and ask for an interview. During my conversations, other drivers would often eavesdrop and occasionally interject or even ask if they could talk to me next, which led to other interviews. Eleven of the fifteen interviews were conducted in this location, the other four in various locations encountered while riding with drivers.

The motor carrier firm I observed is one of the larger players in the industry and is known for its lease-purchase program. It was also discussed in the interviews I conducted, in online trucker chat rooms, and in blogs as being a more advanced company in terms of technology and the quality of its equipment. If I was going to understand how the trucking industry is changing, I reasoned, this company would surely highlight the trends. I was not disappointed in what I found. The company had, for example, rolled out Electronic On Board Recorders across their fleets well in advance of the FMCSA's recommendations to make them mandatory.

Gaining access to the firm was surprisingly straightforward. I contacted the safety coordinator. After one conversation over email and telephone he agreed to put me in touch with a dispatch operator who manages loads for a group of approximately thirty owner-operators, many of whom were doing a lease-purchase deal. Through this manager, I was put in contact with several drivers who were interested in becoming driver trainers. They wanted to see what it would be like to ride with an inexperienced passenger who is learning on the job. Management, then, never forced drivers to participate in the study, something I was intent to avoid, and I always gave drivers several opportunities to say no during the early moments of my "ride-alongs." Drivers told me they saw my research as an opportunity to try out the role of trainer before they committed, which meant that my presence (and inability to help out with the work in any meaningful way) was less of a burden.

I initially recruited job seekers by posting an advertisement to the popular free online classified service Craigslist. I offered participants $50 for a one- to two-hour interview, drawing on funds from a National Science Foundation Doctoral Dissertation Improvement Grant (#000581760). I received dozens of replies within hours of posting the advertisement. I strategically selected prospective participants by filtering out those who had lost their jobs prior to 2007 in order to capture the effect of the financial collapse, which was still pummeling the US economy at that time, and because I knew I would want to follow these participants for a year or more in order to observe their progress.

I heard about Career Transition Ministries through some of my early interviews with white-collar job seekers. I contacted Jim, the founder/organizer, who granted me permission to study the group. During the first meeting I attended, I made an open announcement about the nature of the study and continually made the reasons behind my participation in the group known to the people I met there. I was also uniquely positioned to meaningfully participate in this group because, as a soon-to-be PhD, I was applying for jobs on the academic job market. During CTM meetings that required active engagement, such as reviewing resumes or crafting elevator speeches, I would participate just like the rest. CTM members gave me advice on how to "sell" my research to people who have no experience with sociology and how to keep a positive attitude in the tough academic job market.

"MIKE COMES IN AT ELEVEN"

Ethnographers are commonly taught to "establish and maintain trust" or "rapport" in their field sites because it allows them to become part of participants' taken-for-granted world, thus inviting observations of (all postmodern correctives about objectivity acknowledged) the least contrived version of social life possible. "We have no reason to trust the ethnography produced by someone with whom respondents remained suspicious and distant," notes Karen O'Reilly (2009:175) in her manual for ethnographers. One of the signs that an ethnographer has not established trust is by how visible he is to participants. When participants are comfortable with your presence, they begin to forget you are there and you can more easily get on with the business of observation.

I felt like I gained this kind of trust and relative invisibility with truck drivers and job seekers, but not with bond traders. This was a concern for me, given what I had been taught. I found that some of my most "visible" moments, however, also yielded some crucial information. In retrospect, the lack of trust among traders offered up its own important data (see Briggs 1971; Duneier 1999 for a similar insight). Here is a telling example from my fieldnotes.

11:05a: Mike returns from a meeting. I'm sitting in his chair, so I give it back to him and grab another one from the row in front of us. I'm now sitting between Mike and CH as they both work.

CH and the other guys give Mike crap for coming in so late [traders usually start work at 7am]. Mike explains that he isn't just getting to work (which they know, but are just trying to get a rise out of him). He has been at a meeting all morning.

[. . .]

11:15a: Mike is moving really fast. He keeps clicking around saying, "This is craaaayzeeee . . ." Fingers flying across the keys. But I get the sense that he is doing this as a kind of performance for me and those around him. He gets interrupted by two young analysts who have a question for him.

[. . .]

11:40a: There is a pause in which both Mike and CH aren't busy. CH starts kidding with Mike. He is looking through a stack of papers and reports on his desk, "What is this shit? Mike, why is all your shit on my side?" He starts throwing the stuff in the trash and Mike begins to protest. "What are you doing? I still need to read that?" He reaches in the trashcan and pulls out a now crumpled article. Mike looks at me and says, "Put this in your book, are you seeing this? Are you picking up on how I'm the better trader here? Make sure you get that in there." CH now looks actually a little angry. There's a small pause. Mike and CH lock eyes. Mike seems to notice that CH is actually a little pissed off. Mike: "Are you serious right now?" Then another trader from across the aisle stands up and looks at me, "Do you see this? We spend more time with each other than our wives, so sometimes it can get a little tense."

This sparks a very lighthearted moment. Mike turns back to his desk and starts making all kinds of boisterous noises as he clicks around on his computer. He keeps spinning around to yell at D and CH about different companies. It's clear that he is trying to make himself look like he's working really hard (both for me and for CH). CH takes the bait and says, "Are you trying to make it look like you're doing more work to make us forget that you came in at 11?" Mike protests, "Hey I've only been here for 40 minutes and I've already done more work than you. Look at this" [points to his trade logbook]. CH looks at me, "Are you getting this?" CH asks again, "Seriously, are you just trying to make yourself look good right now?" Mike stands up again in protest and says, looking at me, "Yeah that's it. Hey Ben I'm getting a whole chapter right? You're dedicating an entire chapter to this. Call it 'Mike Comes in at Eleven.'" This gets huge laughs from everyone within earshot. Mike starts talking like he's on *Seinfeld*, "This is gold Jerry! Gold! I'm killing right now." Again, huge laughs from everyone on the floor.

Now I am completely the center of attention. People are saying things like, "Yeah, are we all gonna get a chapter in your book?" "What kind of book is this anyway?" "Hey wait a second how do I know you're really a graduate student? Can I see some ID?" "Yeah, is this guy from the SEC or what? "Just coming to 'hang out' with you guys, right?" Huge laughs all around the floor.

I was uncomfortable with this exchange at the time, but in retrospect it revealed a lot about the work culture of this group of traders. Despite all the claims that their work schedules are leisurely compared to other types of financial professionals (e.g., deal-oriented workers), these encounters revealed to me that there is clearly a cultural pressure to work hard and to demonstrate that through ones relationship to work time. In these interactions, I became part of an exchange about overwork and busyness as a badge of honor (as well as about why these traders might be suspicious of my presence.) It gave me insight into the fact that, though these traders can basically come and go as they please, they are actually under significant *informal* pressure to overwork. This was not information they would share with me in interviews and I never saw them talk to each other about it, but it was forced into the open in these interactions *because* of my "outsider" presence in the room. I was being used as a kind of go-between for these workers to communicate with each other about an unspoken-but-everybody-knows-it overwork norm. In short, while I certainly agree that trust and invisibility are important in fieldwork, there is still much to be learned from moments of suspicion and visibility.

BECOMING A RHYTHMANALYST

The longer I spent in the three field sites, the more I saw rhythm (as opposed to hours or minutes) as the most important concept animating peoples' experience of time. As I went around searching for places in the academic literature where rhythm is given a central place, I inevitably happened upon Henri Lefebvre's visionary (and cryptic) collection of essays *Rhythmanalysis*, and a small group of scholars who are trying to theorize rhythm in everyday life (for example Edensor 2010). But none of these sources, including Lefebvre, actually gave any hints about the best methodological techniques to empirically capture social rhythms for analysis. The best thing I could find was a single passage from Lefebvre in which, with broad brushstrokes, he paints an abstract portrait of how to study social rhythms by paying particular attention to bodies.

> The rhythmanalyst ... will be attentive, but not only to the words or pieces of information, the confessions and confidences of a partner or client. He will listen to the world, and above all to what are disdainfully called noises ... and finally he will listen to silences. [...] He listens—and first to his body; he learns rhythm from it, in order consequently to appreciate external rhythms. His body serves him as a metronome. [...] The rhythmanalyst will not be obliged to *jump* from the inside to the outside of observed *bodies*; he should come to listen to them *as a whole* and unify them by taking his own rhythms as a reference: by integrating the outside with the inside and vice versa. (Lefebvre 2013:29–30)

In his typically abstruse style, Lefebvre sketches the figure of what he calls the "rhythmanalyst"—a kind of professional observer or scientist of rhythms. Note especially that Lefebvre points to the body (both the analyst's and the subject's) as the leading indicator of and instrument for capturing social rhythms empirically. Using this quote as inspiration, I began to experiment in the field with different ways to capture my and others' body rhythms empirically. Many of these experiments failed. For example, while studying truck drivers, I tried breaking the work down into categories of rhythmic processes (traffic, weather, attention, hunger, deadlines, etc.) and then, at regular intervals, rate them on a one-to-five scale in terms of intensity. Placing the ratings in a spreadsheet, my hope was that I would be able to empirically observe what Lefebvre calls "eurhythmias" (synchronizations) and "arrhythmias" (desynchronizations). I still think the idea was a good one, but it was difficult to pull off in practice. What differentiates a traffic rhythm of four from a two? And it began to distract me from taking in other valuable information about the scene.

The technique for capturing rhythms that worked best, then, was to keep meticulous notes about the exact clock times during which things occurred. This is perhaps ironic. In all my attempts to get away from talking about time in terms of clock hours, it was precisely this abstract conception of time that made it easiest to document non-clock time. Clock time provided an easy to reference, standardized language in which to understand how non-clock time rhythms flowed over the course of a day. Here is an example from my fieldnotes of what that looked like practically. This snippet is from the day after the "long night" with Alvaro (see pp. 103–108) in which he had trouble finding parking and had to drive tired through the night.

10:45a: We're rolling. I ask Alvaro how he slept. He says it was okay but at 8am he woke up and "my body was ready to run" but he wanted to get a bit more sleep in so "I just turned over and forced myself to go back to sleep" until 10. But, he says this means he is not as rested as he would like to be and this will limit how much he can drive today. Alvaro says that because he is not fully rested right now, "Now I am working with my body." He's going to "let my body tell me how hard to push today." "Now I'm working against my body." Last night, "My eyes were burning and that tells me that I had pushed myself way beyond my limit; and I hate doing that."

1:23p: Pit stop at a Pilot near Memphis. This is where we wanted to be by last night. Now it's already afternoon on the second day of this load and we're just getting here. We're supposed to be in VA by tomorrow at 8am. It will never happen. We're behind big time.

2:00: Not much happening here . . .

4:00p: Pit stop at a Petro somewhere outside Nashville. Alvaro decides to take a shower while I chill in the truck. Alvaro returns from showering and he is limping. He fell coming out of the shower when he slipped on the floor and managed to half catch himself, but he tweaked his knee. He says, "Luckily this is a light load," which means he won't have to do a lot of shifting. "As long as I get it in gear, I'll be fine." He pops some ibuprofen.

5:30p: We're rolling out. As soon as we get on the highway, we almost get cut off by a box truck coming from the left lane into our lane. A minivan is parked on the shoulder there at exactly the same spot that we almost get cut off. Alvaro reacts with lightening quick reflexes and honks the air horn just in time to warn the box truck from coming all the way over and pushing us into the shoulder, and thus into the parked van. The box truck swerves dangerously back into his lane avoiding the incident. Alvaro curses out loud. "This is exactly the kind of thing that stresses me out," he tells me. "Now my stress level has gone 'whoosh.' Then I start thinking about what could have happened and it just tears me up."

[Marginal note: I'm starting to feel good again after the horror of last night has passed. I think it's because I'm back in eurythmia. I'll be able to eat dinner tonight when I want to because we've gotten back in control over the pacing of this load. We're going to run our hours out completely today, so we'll be stopping at a more normal time, like 7 or 8. The interesting sensation for me right now is feeling hunger for dinner come on and knowing I'll be able to eat soon. Eurythmia here means knowing I can hit that food button on the "downbeat" of my digestive cycle.]

7:45p: We pull into a Days Inn that advertises truck parking on its billboard on the Interstate. I will be able to sleep in a real bed tonight! I offer Alvaro to pay for a hotel room for him too. He declines. "I kinda like sleeping in my own bed, you know." We agree to meet back up at 6 tomorrow morning.

A few things are important to point out here. First, the clock times I record are not at evenly spaced intervals—a "homogenous, empty time" (Benjamin 1974). They are meant only to reflect the "downbeats" of major events that happened during the day. This does not mean that nothing happened between these times, but simply nothing *significant* enough to move the rhythm of the day along. I also occasionally "listened to silences," as Lefebvre puts it. During particularly long stretches of unremarkable driving, I would note things like, "not much going on here. Just driving." I used clock times, then, as a handy notation system to track the rhythms of the day, rather than as objective measurements of time. Second, as in the example here, I often used marginal notes to reflect on my own body state and its cycles. Though I don't do it in this example, I would often check to see if my body state matched that of the drivers. If I was feeling like a meal or sleep break was coming at the wrong time, I would often ask the driver if they were experiencing that as well, in order to make sure it wasn't just me. As Lefebvre suggests, for the rhythmanalyst "his body serves him as a metronome." This might help to make sense of another curiosity in the field note above: I use "our" rather than "his" when referring to Alvaro's logbook hours. In earlier parts of my field notes, however, I do use "his" rather than "our." This was unintentional and not something I noticed until reading over the field notes much later. My guess is that this convention unconsciously evolved over the course of the fieldwork as I became committed to the role of rhythmanalyst, and thus became more synchronized with drivers' body rhythms, taking them on as my own.

Rhythmanalysis, in the end, is not radically different from traditional "thick description" ethnography (Geertz 1973). It involves paying attention to the minute details of the social scene "over the shoulder" of those who are living it. But it does add something to the ethnographer's toolkit by encouraging greater attention to his or her own body as a kind of sensor pointing to data that respondents might not think to talk about unless the ethnographer asks. In this sense, I think of rhythmanalysis as an extremely corporal or embodied type of ethnography. It requires the ethnographer to become aware of how his or her body rhythms interact with the rhythms of the social scene and use this information to ask respondents in situ, informed questions about their daily lives. As a method, rhythmanalysis is embodied thick description.

REFERENCES

AASHTO. 2007. *America's Freight Challenge*. Washington, DC: American Association of State Highway and Transportation Officials. Retrieved March 20, 2013 (www.transportation1.org/tif3report/).

Abbott, Andrew. 2001. *Time Matters: On Theory and Method*. Chicago: University of Chicago Press.

Ackroyd, Stephen, and Sharon Bolton. 1999. "It Is Not Taylorism: Mechanisms of Work Intensification in the Provision of Gynaecological Services in a NHS Hospital." *Work, Employment and Society* 13(2):369–87.

Adam, Barbara. 1990. *Time and Social Theory*. New York: Polity Press.

Adam, Barbara. 1998. *Timescapes of Modernity: The Environment and Invisible Hazards*. New York: Routledge.

Ancona, Deborah G., and Chee Chong. 1996. "Entrainment: Pace, Cycle, and Rhythm in Organizational Behavior." *Research in Organizational Behavior* (18):251–84.

Ancona, Deborah G., Gerardo A. Okhuysen, and Leslie A. Perlow. 2001. "Taking Time to Integrate Temporal Research." *The Academy of Management Review* 25(4):512–29.

Ancona, Deborah, and Mary J. Waller. 2007. "The Dance of Entrainment: Temporally Navigating Across Multiple Pacers." Pp. 115–46 in *Workplace Temporalities*, vol. 17, *Research in the Sociology of Work*. New York: Elsevier.

Arthur, Michael B., and Denise M. Rousseau. 1996. *The Boundaryless Career: A New Employment Concept for a New Organizational Era*. New York: Oxford University Press.

Barbalet, J. M. 1999. "Boredom and Social Meaning." *British Journal of Sociology* 50(4): 631–46.

Barley, Stephen R., and Gideon Kunda. 2001. "Bringing Work Back In." *Organization Science* 12(1):76–95.

Barley, Stephen R., and Gideon Kunda. 2004. *Gurus, Hired Guns, and Warm Bodies: Itinerant Experts in a Knowledge Economy*. Princeton, NJ: Princeton University Press.

Bauman, Zygmunt. 2000. *Liquid Modernity*. Malden, MA: Blackwell.

Bechky, Beth A. 2006. "Talking About Machines, Thick Description, and Knowledge Work." *Organization Studies* 27(12):1757–68.

Becker, Penny Edgell, and Phyllis Moen. 1999. "Scaling Back: Dual-Earner Couples Work-Family Strategies." *Journal of Marriage and the Family* 61:995–1007.

Belkin, Lisa. 2009. "What Is Slow-Parenting?—Motherlode Blog—NYTimes.com." Retrieved (http://parenting.blogs.nytimes.com/2009/04/08/what-is-slow-parenting/).

Bellah, Robert N., Richard Madsen, William M. Sullivan, Ann Swidler, and Steven M. Tipton. 2007. *Habits of the Heart: Individualism and Commitment in American Life*. Berkeley, CA: University of California Press.

Bell, Daniel. 1976. *The Cultural Contradictions of Capitalism*. New York: Basic Books.

Belman, Dale L., and Kristen A. Monaco. 2001. "The Effects of Deregulation, De-Unionization, Technology, and Human Capital on the Work and Work Lives of Truck Drivers." *Industrial and Labor Relations Review* 54(2A):502–24.

Belzer, Michael H. 2000. *Sweatshops on Wheels: Winners and Losers in Trucking Deregulation*. New York: Oxford University Press.

Bendix, Reinhard. 1962. *Max Weber*. Garden City: Anchor.

Benjamin, Walter. 1974. "On the Concept of History." in *Gesammelten Schriften*, vol. 1. Frankfurt am Main: Suhrkamp Verlag.

Bernard, Tracey M., Linda H. Bouck, and Wendy S. Young. 2000. *Stress Factors Experienced by Female Commercial Drivers in the Transportation Industry*. American Society of Safety Engineers.

Bernstein, Peter L. 2005. *Capital Ideas: The Improbable Origins of Modern Wall Street*. Hoboken, NJ: John Wiley and Sons.

Bianchi, Suzanne M., John P. Robinson, and Melissa A. Milkie. 2006. *Changing Rhythms of American Family Life*. New York: Russell Sage Foundation.

Blair-Loy, Mary. 2003. *Competing Devotions: Career and Family Among Women Executives*. Cambridge, MA: Harvard University Press.

Blair-Loy, Mary. 2004. "Work Devotion and Work Time." Pp. 282–316 in *Fighting For Time: Shifting Boundaries of Work and Social Life*, edited by C. F. Epstein and A. L. Kalleberg. New York: Russell Sage Foundation.

Blair-Loy, Mary. 2009. "Work Without End? Scheduling Flexibility and Work-to-Family Conflict among Stockbrokers." *Work and Occupations* 36(4):279–317.

Blair-Loy, Mary. 2010. "Moral Dimensions of the Work-Family Nexus." Pp. 439–53 in *Handbook of the Sociology of Morality*, edited by S. Hitlin and S. Vaisey. New York: Springer.

Blount, Sally, and Gregory A. Janicik. 2002. "Getting and Staying In-Pace: The 'In-Synch' Preference and Its Implications for Work Groups." Pp. 235–66 in *Toward Phenomenology of Groups and Group Membership*, vol. 4, *Research on Managing Groups and Teams*, edited by H. Sondak. New York: Elsevier Science.

Bluestone, Barry, and Stephen Rose. 2001. "Overworked and Underemployed: Unraveling an Economic Enigma." *The American Prospect* 31:58–69.

Boltanski, Luc, and Eve Chiapello. 2005. *The New Spirit of Capitalism*. New York: Verso.

Boltanski, Luc, and Laurent Thevenot. 2006. *On Justification: Economies of Worth*. Princeton, NJ: Princeton University Press.

Bourdieu, Pierre. 2005. "Outline of the Theory of Practice: Structures and the Habitus." Pp. 174–94 in *Practicing History: New Directions in Historical Writing After the Linguistic Turn*, edited by G. M. Spiegal. New York: Routledge.

Braverman, Harry. 1974. *Labor and Monopoly Capital*. New York: Monthly Review Press.

Briggs, Jean L. 1971. *Never in Anger: Portrait of an Eskimo Family*. Cambridge, MA: Harvard University Press.

Buenza, Daniel, and David Stark. 2005. "How to Recognize Opportunities: Heterarchical Search in a Trading Room." Pp. 84–101 in *The Sociology of Financial Markets*, edited by K. Knorr Cetina and A. Preda. New York: Oxford University Press.

Burawoy, Michael. 1979. *Manufacturing Consent: Changes in the Labor Process Under Monopoly Capitalism*. Chicago: University of Chicago Press.

Calhoun, Craig. 2013. "From the Current Crisis to Possible Futures." Pp. 9–42 in *Business as Usual: The Roots of the Global Financial Meltdown*, vol. 1, *Possible Futures*. New York: Social Science Research Council and New York University Press.

Cappelli, Peter. 1995. "Rethinking Employment." *British Journal of Industrial Relations* 33(4):563–602.

Cappelli, Peter. 1999. *The New Deal at Work: Managing the Market-Driven Workforce.* Boston: Harvard Business School Press.

Chen, Guang X. et al. 2015. *Vital Signs: Seat Belt Use among Long-Haul Truck Drivers— United States, 2010.* Centers for Disease Control.

Chenu, Alain, and John P. Robinson. 2002. "Synchronicity in the Work Schedules of Working Couples." *Monthly Labor Review* 125:55–63.

Chiapello, Eve, and Norman Fairclough. 2002. "Understanding the New Management Ideology: A Transdisciplinary Contribution from Critical Discourse Analysis and New Sociology of Capitalism." *Discourse and Society* 13(2):185–208.

Chisholm, Carey D., Amanda M. Dornfeld, David R. Nelson, and William H. Cordell. 2001. "Work Interrupted: A Comparison of Workplace Interruptions in Emergency Departments and Primary Care Offices." *Annals of Emergency Medicine* 38(2): 146–51.

Christensen, Clayton M. 1997. *The Innovator's Dilemma: When New Technologies Cause Great Firms to Fail.* Boston, MA: Harvard Business School Press.

Ciscel, David H., and Barbara Ellen Smith. 2005. "The Impact of Supply Chain Management on Labor Standards: The Transition to Incessant Work." *Journal of Economic Issues* 39(2):429–37.

Clarkberg, Marin, and Phyllis Moen. 2001. "Understanding the Time Squeeze: Married Couples' Preferred and Actual Work-Hour Strategies." *American Behavioral Scientist* 44(7):1115–36.

Clawson, Dan, and Richard Fantasia. 1983. "Beyond Burawoy: The Dialectics of Conflict and Consent on the Shop Floor." *Theory and Society* 12(5):671–80.

Cohen, Adam Max. 2009. *Technology and the Early Modern Self.* New York: Palgrave MacMillan.

Cole, Arthur H. 1942. "Entrepreneurship as an Area of Research." *The Journal of Economic History* 2(S1):118–26.

Collins, Orvis F., and David G. Moore. 1964. *The Enterprising Man.* East Lansing, MI: Michigan State University Press.

Collins, Randall. 2004. *Interaction Ritual Chains.* Princeton, NJ: Princeton University Press.

Collins, Randall. 2008. "Rituals of Solidarity and Security in the Wake of Terrorist Attack." *American Sociological Review* 22(1):53–87.

Collins, Randall. 2012. "C-Escalation and D-Escalation: A Theory of the Time-Dynamics of Conflict." *American Sociological Review* 77(1):1–20.

Conerly, Bill. 2014. "The Death of Strategic Planning: Why?" *Forbes Online*, March 24. Retrieved October 3, 2014 (http://www.forbes.com/sites/billconerly/2014/03/24/the-death-of-strategic-planning-why/).

Conti, Robert F., and Malcolm Warner. 1994. "Taylorism, Teams and Technology in 'Reengineering' Work-Organization." *New Technology, Work and Employment* 9(2):93–102.

Cooper, Marianne. 2014. *Cut Adrift: Families in Insecure Times.* Berkeley: University of California Press.

Couper, Fiona J., Melissa Pemberton, Anjanette Jarvis, Marty Hughes, and Barry K. Logan. 2002. "Prevalence of Drug Use in Commercial Tractor-Trailer Drivers." *Journal of Forensic Science* 47(3):562–67.

Crawford, Matthew B. 2009. *Shop Class as Soulcraft: An Inquiry Into the Value of Work.* New York: Penguin Press.

Crowley, Martha. 2012. "Control and Dignity in Professional, Manual and Service-Sector Employment." *Organizational Studies* 33(1):1383–1406.

Crowley, Martha, Daniel Tope, Lindsey Joyce Chamberlain, and Randy Hodson. 2010. "Neo-Taylorism at Work: Occupational Change in the Post-Fordist Era." *Social Problems* 57(3):421–47.

Csikszentmihalyi, Mihaly. 1990. *Flow: The Psychology of Optimal Experience*. New York: Harper and Row.

Dahl, Soren, et al. 2009. "Hospitalization for Lifestyle Related Diseases in Long Haul Drivers Compared to Other Truck Drivers and the Working Population at Large." *Work* 33(3):345–53.

Dames, Nicholas. 2003. "Trollope and the Career: Vocational Trajectories and the Management of Ambition." *Victorian Studies* 45(2):247–78.

Daniels, Arlene Kaplan. 1987. "Invisible Work." *Social Problems* 34(5):403–15.

Darier, Eric. 1998. "Time to Be Lazy: Work, the Environment and Modern Subjectivities." *Time & Society* 7(2):193–208.

DeGloma, Thomas. 2010. "Awakenings: Autobiography, Memory, and the Social Logic of Personal Discovery." *Sociological Forum* 25(3):519–40.

De Vries, Jan. 2008. *The Industrious Revolution: Consumer Behavior and the Household Economy, 1650 to the Present*. New York: Cambridge University Press.

Dewey, John. 1934. *Art as Experience*. New York: Putnam.

Dimaggio, Paul. 1997. "Culture and Cognition." *Annual Review of Sociology* 23:263–87.

Dohrn-van Rossum, Gerhard. 1996. *History of the Hour: Clocks and Modern Temporal Orders*. Chicago: University of Chicago Press.

Down, Simon. 2015. "Narratives of Enterprise Revisited: Methodological Appendices in Ethnographic Books." *Journal of Organizational Ethnography* 4(1):28–43.

Dror, Itiel E., and Stevan Harnad, eds. 2008. *Cognition Distributed: How Cognitive Technology Extends Our Minds*. Amsterdam: John Benjamins Publishing.

Dubin, Robert. 1958. *The World of Work: Industrial Society and Human Relations*. Englewood Cliffs, NJ: Prentice-Hall, Inc.

Dubinskas, Frank A. 1988. *Making Time: Ethnographies of High-Technology Organizations*. Philadelphia, PA: Temple University Press.

Duneier, Mitchell. 1999. *Sidewalk*. New York: Farrar, Straus, and Giroux.

Durkheim, Emile. 1995. *The Elementary Forms of Religious Life*. New York: Free Press.

Edensor, Tim. 2010. *Geographies of Rhythm: Nature, Place, Mobilities, and Bodies*. Burlington, VT: Ashgate.

Edson, Cyrus. 1892. "Do We Live Too Fast?" *North American Review* 154(3):281–86.

Ehrenreich, Barbara. 2001. *Nickel and Dimed: On (Not) Getting By in America*. New York: Henry Holt & Company.

Ehrenreich, Barbara. 2009. *Bright-Sided: How Positive Thinking Is Underminding America*. New York: Metropolitan Books.

Elias, Norbert. 1994. *Time: An Essay*. Cambridge, MA: Blackwell.

Elsby, Michael W., Bart Hobijn, and Aysegul Sahin. 2010. *The Labor Market in the Great Recession*. Cambridge, MA: The National Bureau of Economic Research.

Emirbayer, Mustafa, and Ann Mische. 1998. "What Is Agency?" *American Journal of Sociology* 103(4):962–1023.

Engels, Frederick. 1969. *The Condition of the Working Class in England*. New York: Granada.

Epstein, Cynthia Fuchs, Carroll Seron, Bonnie Oglensky, and Robert Saute. 1998. *The Part-Time Paradox: Time Norms, Professional Life, Family and Gender*. New York: Routledge.

Evans-Pritchard, E. E. 1939. "Nuer Time-Reckoning." *Africa: Journal of the International African Institute* 12(2):189–216.

Fine, Gary Alan. 1996. *Kitchens: The Culture of Restaurant Work*. Berkeley, CA: University of California Press.

Flaherty, Michael. 2010. *The Textures of Time: Agency and Temporal Experience*. Philadelphia, PA: Temple University Press.

FMCSA. 2003. "49 CFR Parts 385, 390, and 395 Hours of Service of Drivers; Driver Rest and Sleep for Safe Operations; Final Rule." *Federal Register* 68(81): 22456–517.

FMCSA. 2006. *Licit Schedule II Drug Use and Commercial Motor Vehicle Driver Safety (Comprehensive Review)*. Washington, DC: Federal Motor Carrier Safety Administration.

FMCSA. 2013. *Hours of Service*. Federal Motor Carrier Safety Administration. Retrieved October 31, 2014 (http://www.fmcsa.dot.gov/regulations/hours-of-service).

Foster, John Bellamy. 2007. "The Financialization of Capitalism." *Monthly Review* 58(11):1–12.

Foucault, Michel. 1995. *Discipline and Punish: The Birth of the Prison*. New York: Vintage.

Franklin, Benjamin. 1910. *Autobiography of Benjamin Franklin*. New York: Macmillan. Retrieved (http://catalog.hathitrust.org/Record/100487295).

Fraser, Jill Andresky. 2001. *White Collar Sweatshops: The Deterioration of Work and Its Rewards in Corporate America*. New York: Norton.

French, Shaun, Andrew Leyshon, and Thomas Wainwright. 2011. "Financializing Space, Spacing Financialization." *Progress in Human Geography* 35:798–819.

Freud, Sigmund. 1922. *Beyond the Pleasure Principle*. London: The International Psycho-Analytical Press.

Galinsky, Ellen, et al. 2004. *Overwork in America: When the Way We Work Becomes Too Much*. New York: Families and Work Institute.

Garrett-Peters, Raymond. 2009. "'If I Don't Have to Work Anymore, Who Am I?': Job Loss and Collaborative Self-Concept Repair." *Journal of Contemporary Ethnography* 38(5):547–83.

Geertz, Clifford. 1973. *The Interpretation of Cultures: Selected Essays*. New York: Basic Books.

Gell, Alfred. 2001. *The Anthropology of Time: Cultural Constructions of Temporal Maps and Images*. New York: Berg.

Gibson, David R. 2011. "Avoiding Catastrophe: The Interactional Production of Possibility during the Cuban Missile Crisis." *American Journal of Sociology* 117(2): 361–419.

Gibson, James J. 1979. *The Ecological Approach to Visual Perception*. Boston: Houghton Mifflin.

Giddens, Anthony. 1986. *The Constitution of Society: Outline of the Theory of Structuration*. Berkeley, CA: University of California Press.

Giddens, Anthony. 1990. *The Consequences of Modernity*. Stanford, CA: Stanford University Press.

Giddens, Anthony. 1991. *Modernity and Self-Identity: Self and Society in the Late Modern Age*. Stanford, CA: Stanford University Press.

Giddens, Anthony. 1995. *A Contemporary Critique of Historical Materialism*. 2nd ed. Stanford, CA: Stanford University Press.

Gilbreth, Frank B., and Lillian M. Gilbreth. 1916. "The Three Position Plan of Promotion." *Annals of the American Academy of Political and Social Science* 65:289–96.

Glaber, Rodolfus. 1989. *The Five Books of the Histories*. Oxford: Clarendon Press.

Glennie, Paul, and Nigel Thrift. 1996. "Reworking E.P. Thomson's 'Time, Work Discipline, and Industrial Capitalism'." *Time and Society* 5(3):275–99.

Glennie, Paul, and Nigel Thrift. 2009. *Shaping the Day: A History of Timekeeping in England and Wales 1300-1800*. New York: Oxford University Press.

Goffman, Erving. 1977. "The Arrangement between the Sexes." *Theory and Society* 4(5):301–31.

Golden, Lonnie. 2015. *Irregular Work Scheduling and Its Consequences*. Washington, DC: Economic Policy Institute.

Gornick, Janet C., and Alexandra Heron. 2006. "The Regulation of Working Time as Work-Family Reconciliation Policy: Comparing Europe, Japan, and the United States." *Journal of Comparative Policy Analysis* 8(12):149–66.

Greenhouse, Steven. 2008. *The Big Squeeze: Tough Times for the American Worker*. New York: Alfred A. Knopf.

Greenhouse, Steven. 2014. "A Push to Give Steadier Shifts to Part-Timers." *The New York Times*, July 16. Retrieved (http://www.nytimes.com/2014/07/16/business/a-push-to-give-steadier-shifts-to-part-timers.html).

Griswold, Alison. 2014. "The Lost Weekends: How Are Enforced Saturdays Off Working Out for Young Bankers?" *Slate*, July 29. Retrieved November 28, 2014 (http://www.slate.com/articles/business/moneybox/2014/07/goldman_sachs_protected_weekends_young_bankers_want_money_not_time.html).

Halpin, Brian W. 2015. "Subject to Change without Notice: Mock Schedules and Flexible Employment in the United States." *Social Problems* 62:419–38.

Hamilton, Richard F., and James D. Wright. 1986. *State of the Masses: Sources of Discontent, Change and Stability*. New York: Aldine.

Hamilton, Shane. 2009. "The Populist Appeal of Deregulation: Independent Truckers and the Politics of Free Enterprise, 1935–1980." *Enterprise and Society* 10(1): 137–77.

Harvey, David. 1991. *The Condition of Postmodernity: An Enquiry into the Origins of Cultural Change*. New York: Wiley-Blackwell.

Heritage, Stuart. 2014. "Flexible Working Hours Are the Dream ... but Not If You Can't Switch off." *The Guardian*, July 1. Retrieved November 28, 2014 (http://www.theguardian.com/commentisfree/2014/jul/01/flexible-working-hours-dream-switch-off?CMP=fb_gu).

Hirst, Paul, and J. Zeitlin. 1991. "Flexible Specialization Versus Post-Fordism: Theory, Evidence and Policy Implications." *Economy and Society* 20(1):1–56.

Hitlin, Steven, and Stephen Vaisey. 2013. "The New Sociology of Morality." *Annual Review of Sociology* 39:51–68.

Hochschild, Arlie Russell. 1989. *The Second Shift*. New York: Avon Books.

Hochschild, Arlie Russell. 1997. *The Time Bind: When Work Becomes Home and Home Becomes Work*. New York: Henry Holt & Company.

Hochschild, Arlie Russell. 2003. *The Managed Heart: The Commercialization of Human Feeling*. Berkeley, CA: University of California Press.

Hochschild, Arlie Russell. 2005. "On the Edge of the Time Bind: Time and Market Culture." *Social Research* 72(2):339–54.

Hochschild, Arlie Russell. 2012. *The Outsourced Self: Intimate Life in Market Times*. New York: Metropolitan Books.

Hodson, Randy. 2001. *Dignity at Work*. New York: Cambridge University Press.

Ho, Karen. 2009. "Disciplining Investment Bankers, Disciplining the Economy: Wall Street's Institutional Culture of Crisis and the Downsizing of 'Corporate America.'" *American Anthropologist* 111:177–89.

Honore, Carl. 2004. *In Praise of Slowness: How a Worldwide Movement Is Challenging the Cult of Speed*. New York: Harper.

Hornaday, John A. and Charles S. Bunker. 1970. "The Nature of the Entrepreneur." *Personnel Psychology* 23:47–54.

Hubert, Henri. 1999. *Essay on Time: A Brief Study of the Representation of Time in Religion and Magic*. London: Durkheim Press Ltd.

Huggett, Frank E. 1973. *Factory Life and Work: A Documentary Inquiry*. London: Harrap.

Hunt, Edward H. 1981. *British Labour History, 1815–1914*. London: Weidenfeld and Nicolson.

Hutton, Will, and Anthony Giddens. 2000. *On the Edge: Living with Global Capitalism*. New York: Verso.

Innis, Harold A. 1951. *The Bias of Communication*. Toronto: University of Toronto Press.

Jacobs, Jerry A., and Kathleen Gerson. 1998. "Who Are the Overworked Americans?" *Review of Social Economy* 56(4):442–59.

Jacobs, Jerry A. and Kathleen Gerson. 2001. "Overworked Individuals or Overworked Families? Explaining Trends in Work, Leisure, and Family Time." *Work and Occupations* 28(1):40–63.

Jacobs, Jerry A., and Kathleen Gerson. 2004. *The Time Divide: Work, Family, and Gender Inequality*. Cambridge, MA: Harvard University Press.

Jahoda, Marie, Paul F. Lazarsfeld, and Hans Zeisel. 1971. *Marienthal: The Sociography of an Unemployed Community*. New Brunswick, NJ: Transaction Publishers.

Jamieson, Dave. 2015. "The Life and Death of an Amazon Warehouse Temp: What Teh Future of Low-Wage Work Really Looks Like." *The Huffington Post*. Retrieved November 3, 2015 (http://highline.huffingtonpost.com/articles/en/life-and-death-amazon-temp/).

Jennings, Daniel R., ed. 2003. "The Rule of Pachomius, Part 1." Retrieved September 29, 2010 (http://www.seanmultimedia.com/Pie_Pachomius_Rule_1.html).

Jones, Campbell. 2014. "Finance, University, Revolt." *Argos Aotearoa* 1(1):44–51.

Kalleberg, Arne L. 2003. "Flexible Firms and Labor Market Segmentation: Effects of Workplace Restructuring on Jobs and Workers." *Work and Occupations* 30(2): 154–75.

Kalleberg, Arne L. 2009. "Precarious Work, Insecure Workers: Employment Relations in Transition." *American Sociological Review* 74:1–22.

Kalleberg, Arne L. 2011. *Good Jobs, Bad Jobs: The Rise of Polarized and Precarious Employment Systems in the United States, 1970s to 2000s*. New York: Russell Sage Foundation.

Kantor, Jodi. 2014. "Working Anything but 9 to 5: Scheduling Technology Leaves Low-Income Parents With Hours of Chaos." *The New York Times*, August 13. Retrieved November 28, 2014 (http://www.nytimes.com/interactive/2014/08/13/us/starbucks-workers-scheduling-hours.html).

Katz, Jack. 1999. *How Emotions Work*. Chicago: University of Chicago Press.

Keeshin, John Lewis. 1983. *No Fears, Hidden Tears: A Memoir of Four Score Years*. Chicago, IL: Castle-Pierce Press.

Keohane, Joe. 2015. "In Praise of Meaningless Work: Mindfulness Mantras Are the Latest Tool of Corporate Control." *New Republic*, March 2. Retrieved (http://www.newrepublic.com/article/121171/praise-meaningless-work).

Knorr Cetina, Karin. 2007. "Economic Sociology and the Sociology of Finance: Four Distinctions, Two Developments, One Field?" *Economic Sociology: The European Electronic Newsletter* 8(3):4–10.

Knorr Cetina, Karin. 2012. "What Is a Financial Market? Global Markets as Micro-institutional and Post-Traditional Social Forms." Pp. 115–33 in *The Oxford Handbook of the Sociology of Finance*, edited by K. Knorr Cetina and A. Preda. New York: Oxford University Press.

Knowles, Dom David. 1949. *The Monastic Order in England*. Cambridge: Cambridge University Press.

Kojima, Shinji. 2015. "Why Do Temp Workers Work as Hard as They Do?: The Commitment and Suffering of Factory Temp Workers in Japan." *The Sociological Quarterly* 56:355–85.

Koselleck, Reinhart. 1985. *Futures Past: On the Semantics of Historical Time*. Cambridge, MA: MIT Press.

Koselleck, Reinhart. 2002. *The Practice of Conceptual History: Timing History, Spacing Concepts*. Stanford, CA: Stanford University Press.

Krippner, Greta R. 2005. "The Financialization of the American Economy." *Socio-Economic Review* 3:173–208.

Krippner, Greta R. 2011. *Capitalizing on Crisis: The Political Origins of the Rise of Finance*. Cambridge, MA: Harvard University Press.

Kunda, Gideon. 1992. *Engineering Culture: Control and Commitment in a High-Tech Corporation*. Philadelphia, PA: Temple University Press.

Kurzman, Charles. 2004. *The Unthinkable Revolution in Iran*. Cambridge, MA: Harvard University Press.

Lambert, Susan J. 2012. "When Flexibility Hurts." *The New York Times*, September 20. Retrieved (http://www.nytimes.com/2012/09/20/opinion/low-paid-women-want-predictable-hours-and-steady-pay.html).

Lamont, Michele. 2000. *The Dignity of Working Men: Morality and the Boundaries of Race, Class, and Immigration*. Cambridge, MA: Harvard University Press.

Landes, David S. 1983. *A Revolution in Time: Clocks and the Making of the Modern World*. Cambridge, MA: Belknap Press of Harvard University Press.

Lane, Carrie. 2011. *A Company of One: Insecurity, Independence, and the New World of White-Collar Unemployment*. Ithaca, NY: Cornell University Press.

Langer, Susanne K. 1953. *Feeling and Form*. London: Routledge and Kegan Paul.

Lasch, Christopher. 1979. *The Culture of Narcissism: American Life in an Age of Diminishing Expectations*. New York: W. W. Norton & Company.

Lecuyer, Christophe. 2006. *Making Silicon Valley: Innovation and Growth of High Tech, 1930-1970*. Cambridge, MA: MIT Press.

Lee, Heejin, and Jonathan Liebenau. 2002. "A New Time Discipline: Managing Virtual Work Environments." Pp. 126–39 in *Making Time: Time and Management in Modern Organizations*, edited by R. Whipp, B. Adam, and I. Sabelis. Oxford: Oxford University Press.

Lefebvre, Henri. 2004. *Rhythmanalysis: Space, Time, and Everyday Life*. New York: Continuum.

Lefebvre, Henri. 2013. *Rhythmanalysis: Space, Time and Everyday Life*. New York: Bloomsbury Academic.

Le Goff, Jacques. 1980. *Time, Work, and Culture in the Middle Ages*. Chicago: University of Chicago Press.

Lepore, Jill. 2014. "The Disruption Machine: What the Gospel of Innovation Gets Wrong." *The New Yorker*, June 23.

Lesnard, Laurent. 2004. "Schedules as Sequences: A New Method to Analyze the Use of Time Based on Collective Rhythm With an Application to the Work Arrangements of French Dual-Earner Couples." *Electronic International Journal of Time Use Research* 1:371–78.

Lesnard, Laurent. 2008. "Off-Scheduling within Dual-Earner Couples: An Unequal and Negative Externality for Family Time." *American Journal of Sociology* 114(2):447–90.

Lesnard, Laurent. 2009. *The Dislocated Family*. Paris: PUF.

Levy, Karen E. 2015. "The Contexts of Control: Information, Power, and Truck-Driving Work." *The Information Society* 31:160–74.

Leyshon, Andrew, and Nigel Thrift. 1997. *Money-Space: Geographies of Monetary Transformation*. London: Routledge.

Linder, Steffan. 1970. *The Harried Leisure Class*. New York: Columbia University Press.

Lizardo, Omar, and Michael Strand. 2010. "Skills, Toolkits, Contexts and Institutions: Clarifying the Relationship Between Different Approaches to Cognition in Cultural Sociology." *Poetics* 38:204–27.

Lomba, Cedric. 2005. "Beyond the Debate over 'Post'-vs 'Neo'-Taylorism." *International Sociology* 20(1):71–91.

Lubbe, Hermann. 2009. "The Contraction of the Present." Pp. 159–78 in *High-Speed Society: Social Acceleration, Power, and Modernity*. University Park, PA: The Pennsylvania State University Press.

Lukacs, Georg. 1971. *History and Class Consciousness: Studies in Marxist Dialectics*. London: The Merlin Press.

Luker, Kristin. 2008. *Salsa Dancing into the Social Sciences: Research in an Age of Info-Glut*. Cambridge, MA: Harvard University Press.

Macys. 2015. "Retail Sales, *Flexible Scheduling Option!*, Part-Time: Phoenix, AZ, Macy's Paradise Valley Job." *Jobing.com*. Retrieved September 5, 2015 (http://phoenix.jobing.com/retail-sales-flexible-scheduling-option-part-time-phoenix-az-macy-s-paradise-valley/job/5528376).

Martin, Randy. 2002. *Financialization of Daily Life*. Philadelphia, PA: Temple University Press.

Marx, Karl. 1993. *Grundrisse: Foundations of the Critique of Political Economy*. New York: Penguin Classics.

Marx, Karl. 2011. *Capital, Volume One: A Critique of Political Economy*. Mineola, NY: Dover Publications.

McGuire, Joseph W. 1960. "Bankers, Books, and Businessmen." *Harvard Business Review* 38(4):67–74.

McTaggart, J. M. E. 1993. "The Unreality of Time." Pp. 23–34 in *The Philosophy of Time*, edited by L. P. Robin and M. Murray. Oxford: Oxford University Press.

Menzies, Heather. 2005. *No Time: Stress and the Crisis of Modern Life*. Vancouver, BC: Douglas & McIntyre Ltd.

Mische, Ann. 2009. "Projects and Possibilities: Researching Futures in Action." *Sociological Forum* 24(3):694–704.

Mische, Ann. 2014. "Measuring Futures in Action: Projective Grammars in the Rio+20 Debates." *Theory and Society* 43:437–64.

Moen, Phyllis. 2005. "Beyond the Career Mystique: 'Time In, 'Time Out,' and 'Second Acts.'" *Sociological Forum* 20(2):189–208.

Moen, Phyllis, Erin L. Kelly, Eric Tranby, and Qinlei Huang. 2011. "Changing Work, Changing Health: Can Real Work-Time Flexibility Promote Health Behaviors and Well-Being?" *Journal of Health and Social Behavior* 52(4):404–29.

Moen, Phyllis, and Patricia Roehling. 2004. *The Career Mystique: Cracks in the American Dream*. New York: Rowman and Littlefield.

Monaco, Kristen, and Steffen Habermalz. 2011. *Wage Inequality of U.S. Truck Drivers*. Bonn, Germany: Institute for the Study of Labor. Retrieved March 18, 2013 (http://ideas.repec.org/p/iza/izadps/dp5444.html).

Morehead, Alison. 2001. "Synchronizing Time for Work and Family: Preliminary Insights from Qualitative Research with Mothers." *Journal of Sociology* 37(4):355–69.

Mumford, Lewis. 1963. *Technics and Civilization*. New York: Harbinger.

Needham, Joseph, Wang Ling, and Derek J. de Solla Price. 1960. *Heavenly Clockwork: The Great Astronomical Clocks of Medieval China*. London: Cambridge University Press.

Odih, Pamela. 1999. "Gendered Time in the Age of Deconstruction." *Time and Society* 8(1):9–38.

OED. 2012. "Busy, Adj." *Oxford English Dictionary*. Retrieved May 2, 2012 (http://www.oed.com).

Ohio Bureau of Labor Statistics. 1878. *Second Annual Report*. Columbus, OH: Ohio Bureau of Labor Statistics. Retrieved July 29, 2014 (http://catalog.hathitrust.org/Record/000535603).

Olick, Jeffrey K. 2007. "Collective Memory and Chronic Differentiation." *Humanities Research Group Working Papers* 14:1–30.

O'Reilly, Karen. 2009. *Key Concepts in Ethnography*. London: SAGE.

Osterman, Paul. 1999. *Securing Prosperity: The American Labor Market, How It Is Changing and What We Can Do About It*. Princeton, NJ: Princeton University Press.

Pache, Gilles. 2007. "Slowness Logistics: Towards a New Time Orientation?" *Time and Society* 16(2/3):311–32.

Packard, Vance. 1962. *The Pyramid Climbers*. London: Longmans, Green and Co Ltd.

Pearson, Andrall E. 1966. "Sales Power through Planned Careers." *Harvard Business Review* 44(1):105–16.

Polanyi, Karl. 1944. *The Great Transformation*. New York: Farrar and Rinehart, Inc.

Postone, Moishe. 1996. *Time, Labor, and Social Domination: A Reinterpretation of Marx's Critical Theory*. New York: Cambridge University Press.

Preda, Alex. 2009. *Framing Finance: The Boundaries of Markets and Modern Capitalism*. Chicago: University of Chicago Press.

Presser, Harriet B. 2003. *Working in a 24/7 Economy: Challenges for American Families*. New York: Russell Sage Foundation.

Pugh, Allison J. 2015. *The Tumbleweed Society: Working and Caring in an Age of Uncertainty*. New York: Oxford University Press.

Quinones, Ricardo J. 1972. *The Renaissance Discovery of Time*. Cambridge, MA: Harvard University Press.

Rabinbach, Anson. 1990. *The Human Motor: Energy, Fatigue, and the Origins of Modernity*. New York: Basic Books.

Reynolds, Jeremy, and Lydia Aletraris. 2006. "Pursuing Preferences: The Creation and Resolution of Work Hour Mismatches." *American Sociological Review* 71(4):618–38.

Riesman, David. 1967. *The Lonely Crowd: A Study of the Changing American Character*. New Haven, CT: Yale University Press.

Robinson, John P. and Geoffrey Godbey. 1997. *Time for Life: The Surprising Ways Americans Use Their Time*. University Park, PA: The Pennsylvania State University Press.

Rodgers, Daniel T. 1979. *The Work Ethic in Industrial America, 1850–1920*. Chicago: University of Chicago Press.

Roose, Kevin. 2014. *Young Money: Inside the Hidden World of Wall Street's Post-Crash Recruits*. New York: Grand Central Publishing.

Rosa, Hartmut. 2009. "Social Acceleration: Ethical and Political Consequences of a Desynchronized High-Speed Society." Pp. 77–112 in *High-Speed Society: Social Acceleration, Power, and Modernity*. University Park, PA: The Pennsylvania State University Press.

Rosa, Hartmut, and William E. Scheuerman. 2009. *High-Speed Society: Social Acceleration, Power, and Modernity*. University Park, PA: The Pennsylvania State University Press.

Roy, Donald F. 1953. "Work Satisfaction and Social Reward in Quota Achievement: An Analysis of Piecework Incentive." *American Sociological Review* 18(5):507–14.

Roy, Donald F. 1959. "'Banana Time': Job Satisfaction and Informal Interaction." *Human Organization* 18:158–68.

Rushkoff, Douglas. 2013. *Present Shock: When Everything Happens Now*. New York: Current Hardcover.

Russell, Bertrand. 1935. *In Praise of Idleness and Other Essays*. New York: Allen & Unwin.

Sabelis, Ida, Lorraine Nencel, David Knights, and Pam Odih. 2008. "Questioning the Construction of 'Balance': A Time Perspective on Gender and Organization." *Gender, Work and Organization* 15(5):423–29.

Sassen, Saskia. 2001. *The Global City*. Princeton, NJ: Princeton University Press.

Schivelbusch, Wolfgang. 1979. *The Railway Journey: Trains and Travel in the 19th Century*. New York: Urizen Books.

Schor, Juliet B. 1993. *The Overworked American: The Unexpected Decline of Leisure*. New York: Basic Books.

Schor, Juliet B. 2000. "Working Hours and Time Pressure: The Controversy about Trends in Time Use." Pp. 70–80 in *Working Time: International Trends, Theory, and Policy Perspectives*, edited by L. Golden and D. M. Figart. New York: Routledge.

Schumpeter, Joseph A. 1954. *Capitalism, Socialism, and Democracy*. London: Unwin University Books.

Segre, Sandro. 2000. "A Weberian Theory of Time." *Time and Society* 9(2/3):147–70.

Sennett, Richard. 2000. *The Corrosion of Character: The Personal Consequences of the New Capitalism*. New York: W. W. Norton & Company.

Sennett, Richard. 2006. *The Culture of the New Capitalism*. New Haven, CT: Yale University Press.

Sennett, Richard. 2009. *The Craftsman*. New Haven, CT: Yale University Press.

Sewell, Graham. 1998. "The Discipline of Teams: The Control of Team-Based Industrial Work through Electronic and Peer Surveillance." *Administrative Science Quarterly* 43(2):397–428.

Sewell, Graham, and B. Wilkinson. 1992. "'Someone to Watch over Me': Surveillance, Discipline, and the Just-In-Time Labour Process." *Sociology* 26(2):271–89.

Sharone, Ofer. 2007. "Constructing Unemployed Job Seekers as Professional Workers: The Depoliticizing Work-Game of Job Searching." *Qualitative Sociology* 30:403–16.

Sharone, Ofer. 2014. *Flawed System/Flawed Self: Job Searching and Unemployment Experiences*. Chicago, IL: University of Chicago Press.

Sharwood, Lisa N., et al. 2012. "Assessing Sleepiness and Sleep Disorders in Australian Long-Distance Commercial Vehicle Drivers: Self-Report Versus an 'At Home' Monitoring Device." *Sleep* 35(4):469–75.

Silva, Jennifer M. 2013. *Coming Up Short: Working-Class Adulthood in an Age of Uncertainty*. New York: Oxford University Press.

Simko, Christina. 2012. "Rhetorics of Suffering: September 11 Commemorations as Theodicy." *American Sociological Review* 77(6):880–902.

Slocombe, Thomas E., and Allen C. Bluedorn. 1999. "Organizational Behavior Implications of the Congruence between Preferred Polychronicity and Experienced Work-Unit Polychronicity." *Journal of Organizational Behavior* 20(1):75–99.

Small, Mario Luis. 2009. "'How Many Cases Do I Need?' On Science and the Logic of Case Selection in Field-Based Research." *Ethnography* 10(1):5–38.

Smith, Christian. 2003. *Moral, Believing Animals: Human Personhood and Culture*. New York: Oxford University Press.

Smith, Mark M. 1997. *Mastered by the Clock: Time, Slavery, and Freedom in the American South*. Chapel Hill, NC: University of North Carolina Press.

Smith, Merritt Roe. 1980. *Harpers Ferry Armory and the New Technology*. Ithaca, NY: Cornell University Press.

Smith, Vicki. 2001. *Crossing the Great Divide: Worker Risk and Opportunity in the New Economy*. Ithaca, NY: Cornell University Press.

Snyder, Benjamin H. 2013. "From Vigilance to Busyness: A Neo-Weberian Approach to Clock Time." *Sociological Theory* 31(3):243–66.

Sorokin, Pitirim A., and Robert K. Merton. 1937. "Social Time: A Methodological and Functional Analysis." *American Journal of Sociology* 42(5):615–29.

Southerton, Dale, and Mark Tomlinson. 2005. "'Pressed for Time'—the Differential Impacts of a 'Time Squeeze.'" *Sociological Review* 53(2):215–39.

Spillman, Lyn. 2012. *Solidarity in Strategy: Making Business Meaningful in American Trade Associations*. Chicago, IL: University of Chicago Press.

Stalk, George, and Thomas M. Hout. 1990. *Competing Against Time: How Time-Based Competition Is Reshaping Global Markets*. New York: Free Press.

Standifer, Rhetta, and Allen C. Bluedorn. 2006. "Alliance Management Teams and Entrainment: Sharing Temporal Mental Models." *Human Relations* 59(7):903–27.

Standing, Guy. 2011. *The Precariat: The New Dangerous Class*. London: Bloomsbury Academic.

Standing, Guy. 2012. "The Precariat: From Denizens to Citizens?" *Polity* 44(4):588–608.

Standing, Guy. 2013. "Tertiary Time: The Precariat's Dilemma." *Public Culture* 25(1): 5–27.

Stets, Jan E., and Peter J. Burke. 2005. "A Sociological Approach to Self and Identity." Pp. 128–52 in *The Handbook of Self and Identity*, edited by M. R. Leary and J. P. Tangney. New York: Guilford Press.

Strand, Michael, and Omar Lizardo. 2015. "Beyond World Images: Belief as Embodied Action in the World." *Sociological Theory* 33(1):44–70.

Summers-Effler, Erika. 2010. *Laughing Saints and Righteous Heroes: Emotional Rhythms in Social Movement Groups*. Chicago: University of Chicago Press.

Sweet, Stephen, Marcie Pitt-Catsouphes, Elyssa Besen, and Lonnie Golden. 2014. "Explaining Organizational Variation in Flexible Work Arrangements: Why the Pattern and Scale of Availability Matter." *Community, Work and Family* 17(2): 115–41.

Swidler, Ann. 2001. "What Anchors Cultural Practices?" Pp. 74–92 in *The Practice Turn in Contemporary Theory*, edited by K. Knorr Cetina and E. Von Savigny. New York: Routledge.

Tavory, Iddo, and Nina Eliasoph. 2013. "Coordinating Futures: Toward a Theory of Anticipation." *American Journal of Sociology* 118(4):908–42.

Tavory, Iddo, and Daniel Winchester. 2012. "Experiential Careers: The Routinization and De-Routinization of Religious Life." *Theory and Society* 41:351–73.

Taylor, Frederick Winslow. 1911. *Shop Management*. New York: Harper and Brothers Publishers.

Taylor, Frederick Winslow. 1939. *The Principles of Scientific Management*. New York: Harper and Row.

Thatcher, Sherry M,. and Xiumei Zhu. 2006. "Changing Identities in a Changing Workplace: Identification, Identity Enactment, Self-Verification, and Telecommuting." *Academy of Management Review* 31(4):1076–88.

Thompson, E. P. 1967. "Time, Work-Discipline, and Industrial Capitalism." *Past and Present* 38:56–97.

Thrift, Nigel. 1988. "Vivos Voco: Ringing the Changes in the Historical Geography of Time Consciousness." Pp. 53–94 in *The Rhythms of Society, Reports of the Institute of Community Studies*, edited by M. Young and T. Schuller. New York: Routledge.

Thrun, Sebastian. 2014. "The Art of Fast Failure." *LinkedIn Pulse*. Retrieved September 18, 2014 (https://www.linkedin.com/pulse/article/20140913214142-260012998-the-art-of-fast-failure).

Time. 2009. "The Future of Work." *Time Magazine*, May 25.

Tomlinson, John. 2007. *The Culture of Speed: The Coming of Immediacy*. London: SAGE.

Ure, Andrew. 1835. *The Philosophy of Manufactures; Or, An Exposition of the Scientific, Moral, and Commercial Economy of the Factory System of Great Britain*. London: Charles Knight.

Vallas, Steven, and Christopher Prener. 2012. "Dualism, Job Polarization, and the Social Construction of Precarious Work." *Work and Occupations* 39(4):331–53.

Veblen, Thorstein. 1994. *The Theory of the Leisure Class*. New York: Dover Publications.

Vidal, Matt. 2011. "Reworking Postfordism: Labor Process Versus Employment Relations." *Sociology Compass* 5(4):273–86.

Viscelli, Stephen R. 2010. "Buying It: Class, Culture, and the Making of Owner-Operators in Long-Haul Trucking." Doctoral Dissertation, Indiana University, Bloomington, IN.

Wagner-Pacifici, Robin. 1994. *Discourse and Destruction: The City of Philadelphia versus MOVE*. Chicago: University of Chicago Press.

Wagner-Pacifici, Robin. 2010. "Theorizing the Restlessness of Events." *The American Journal of Sociology* 115(5):1351–86.

Wajcman, Judy. 2015. *Pressed for Time: The Acceleration of Life in Digital Capitalism*. Chicago, IL: University of Chicago Press.

Wallach, D. A. 2015. "The Future of Work: In a World Full of Information, Many Gaps." *Pacific Standard*, November 5. Retrieved (http://www.psmag.com/business-economics/the-future-of-work-in-a-world-full-of-information-many-gaps).

Wallerstein, Immanuel. 2011. *Historical Capitalism*. Brooklyn, NY: Verso.

Wallis, Claudia. 2005. "The New Science of Happiness." *Time Magazine*, January 9. Retrieved May 16, 2013 (http://www.time.com/time/magazine/article/0,9171,1015832,00.html).

Waterman, Robert H., Judith A. Waterman, and Betsy A. Collard. 1994. "Toward a Career-Resilient Workforce." *Harvard Business Review* (July-August):87–95.

Weber, Max. 1946. *From Max Weber: Essays in Sociology*. New York: Oxford University Press.

Weber, Max. 2011. *The Protestant Ethic and the Spirit of Capitalism: The Revised 1920 Edition*. New York: Oxford University Press.

Weick, Karl E. 1995. *Sensemaking in Organizations*. New York: Sage.

Wenzel, Siegfried. 1967. *The Sin of Sloth: Acedia in Medieval Thought and Literature*. Chapel Hill, NC: University of North Carolina Press.

Wharton, Amy S., and Mary Blair-Loy. 2001. "The 'Overtime Culture' in a Global Corporation: A Cross-National Study of Finance Professionals' Interest in Working Part Time." *Work and Occupations* 29(1):32–63.

Whipp, Richard, Barbara Adam, and Ida Sabelis, eds. 2002. *Making Time: Time and Management in Modern Organizations*. Oxford: Oxford University Press.

Whyte, William H. 1965. *The Organization Man*. New York: Penguin.

Williams, Christine L. 2006. *Inside Toyland: Working, Shopping, and Social Inequality*. Berkeley, CA: University of California Press.

Williams, Joan. 2000. *Unbending Gender: Why Family and Work Conflict and What to Do About It*. Oxford: Oxford University Press.

Willis, Paul. 1981. *Learning to Labor: How Working Class Kids Get Working Class Jobs*. New York: Columbia University Press.

Wolfe, Alan. 1989. *Whose Keeper? Social Science and Moral Obligation*. Berkeley, CA: University of California Press.

Wren, Daniel A. 1987. *The Evolution of Management Thought*. New York: John Wiley and Sons.

Young, Michael K. 1988. *The Metronomic Society: Natural Rhythms and Human Timetables*. Cambridge, MA: Harvard University Press.

Young, Michael, and Tom Schuller. 1988. "Towards Chronosociology." in *The Rhythms of Society, Reports of the Institute of Community Studies*, edited by M. Young and T. Schuller. New York: Routledge.

Zaloom, Caitlin. 2006. *Out of the Pits: Traders and Technology from Chicago to London*. Chicago: University of Chicago Press.

Zaloom, Caitlin. 2012. "Traders and Market Morality." Pp. 169–86 in *The Oxford Handbook of the Sociology of Finance*, edited by K. Knorr Cetina and A. Preda. New York: Oxford University Press.

Zerubavel, Eviatar. 1979. *Patterns of Time in Hospital Life: A Sociological Perspective*. Chicago, IL: University of Chicago Press.

Zerubavel, Eviatar. 1980. "The Benedictine Ethic and the Spirit of Modern Scheduling: On Schedules and Social Organization." *Sociological Inquiry* 50(2):157–69.

Zerubavel, Eviatar. 1981. *Hidden Rhythms: Schedules and Calendars in Social Life*. Berkeley, CA: University of California Press.

Zerubavel, Eviatar. 2003. *Time Maps: Collective Memory and the Social Shape of the Past*. Chicago, IL: University of Chicago Press.

Zuboff, Shoshana. 1989. *In the Age of the Smart Machine: The Future of Work and Power*. New York: Basic Books.

INDEX

absorption. *See* flow

abstraction, 71
  and financial trading, 71–73,
    83–87, 173
  and truck driving, 119–123
  See also screens, digital

acedia, 32

Adam, Barbara, 13, 29n1

affordance, 200

Alberti, Leon Battista, 35, 35n10

Ancona, Deborah, 102

arrhythmia, 14n6, 15, 178, 213. *See also*
  timescape: of desynchronization

attention, 61–62, 67, 79

autonomy. *See* time, work: control over

balance, work-family, 49, 171n2

bargain, Faustian, 36, 46, 53, 196,
  199–205

bells, church, 33

Benedict of Nursia, 31. *See also*
  monasticism

Bloomberg Professional Service, 74–75

body
  and financial work, 78, 80–81, 81n7
  and truck driving, 103, 107–108,
    182–184

Bolles, Richard, 50

Boltanski, Luc and Eve Chiapello, 199n1,
  200n2, 203, 214n3

boundaries, temporal, 10

Burawoy, Michael, 165–166

busyness, 35, 35n11, 162

buzz, 86–87, 166–168

Cappelli, Peter, 49

care, 171n2, 172

career, 43, 130
  boundaryless, 50
  and discontent with conformity,
    46–48, 190
  disruption of, 49–50
  history of, 43–48
  lockstep, 133
  as myth or mystique, 46, 137–138, 187, 190
  and time discipline, 44
  as time map, 44–45
  and up-or-out norm, 44

Christiansen, Clayton, 8, 50

Chronos, 2. *See also* time, chronological

clock, mechanical. *See* time, clock

coaches, career and life, 156

Collision Mitigation System, 109

conflict, work-family, 49, 66,
  169–172, 171n2

core-periphery of organizations, 6, 214

craftsmanship, 214

Csikszentmihalyi, Mihaly, 80n6

deal room, 73–78, 173

deregulation, 56, 92, 93–97

derivatives, 83

deskilling, 41

disembedding, 68–69
  and dispatch operations in truck
    driving, 119–123
  and financial trading, 69–71, 173
  and job seeking, 150–153
  See also technology

dispatchers, 119–123

disruption, 8, 199, 202–203
  of chronological time, 48–51
  as cultural straightjacket, 205–206,
    213–214

disruption (*Cont.*)
  and demographic changes in the
    workforce, 47–48
  and projectivity, 133
  as structural blinder, 206–207

Edson, Cyrus, 25, 28
Electronic On Board Recorder, 96,
  120–133, 176
emotion
  and financial trading, 86–87
  and job seeking, 140, 144–150, 160,
    192–193
  and truck driving, 100, 116, 181
  and work-games, 42
entrainment, 102–103, 114–115, 168
entrepreneurialism, 47, 48n19, 50,
  188–191
eurythmia, 14n6, 52. *See also*
  timescape: of synchronization

factories, 38
Fair Labor Standards Act, 211
Fairchild Semiconductor, 50
fatigue, 100–102. *See also* sleep
Federal Motor Carrier Safety
  Administration (FMCSA), 97–99
finance, quantitative, 56
financial collapse. *See* Great Recession
financial professionals
  and analysts, 72, 80n6
  as dealmakers, 57
  and density of time, 67, 82
  and diversity of timescapes, 56–57
  and feeling "on," 58, 66–67
  and flexible work schedules, 58, 64
  and junior investment bankers, 59–60
  and liquidity of time, 78–82
  as market workers, 57, 64–87
  and metaphors, 61, 63, 67, 70,
    76, 84
  and new temporal languages,
    60–64, 84
  and pitching versus live deals, 166n1
  and preciousness of time, 61–62,
    89, 168
  and reality of money, 83–87
  and urgency of time, 61, 66–67
  and work intensification, 63
financialization, 22, 55–56, 68

flexibility
  and capitalism, 4–9, 198–206
  employer-controlled versus
    worker-controlled, 208–209
  of employment contracts, 95
  functional, 128n1
  and the logistics system, 94–95
  numerical, 128–129, 128n1, 161, 187
  of work objects and processes,
    7–8, 79, 89
flow, 60, 67, 79–80, 80n6, 166,
  181, 185. *See also* timescape: of
  unification
Foucault, Michel, 39
fragmentation of social time, 201–202
Franklin, Benjamin, 25–28
Freud, Sigmund, 108, 108n7, 182n4
future
  long term, 78, 133
  and meaning-making, 131–133, 201
  middle term, 132, 194–195
  short term, 78, 132, 153, 194
  See also projectivity

gender, 48–49, 68, 169–172
Giddens, Anthony, 68, 82
Gilbreth, Frank and Lillian, 43n18
Glaber, Rodulfus, 32n7
globalization, 69
Great Recession, 20, 130

Hawthorne experiments, 44
Highway Motor Carrier Act of
  1935, 93n2
Hochschild, Arlie, 20n9, 107n6
horarium, 32, 32n4
horizon of expectation, 197
hour. *See* time, clock
Hours of Service regulations
  restructuring of, 97–99
  truck driver experience of,
    99–102, 177
  See also neo-Taylorism

individualism, 47, 195, 203
The Innovator's Dilemma
  (Christiansen), 8, 50
Intel Corporation, 50
intensification, 36, 202
Internet, 49, 70, 104, 152, 222